People Skills

by Casey Hawley

A member of Penguin Group (USA) Inc.

This book is dedicated to two women with unsurpassed people skills, Frances Anne and Frances Jean Pastore. Although their wonderful ways with both the mighty and the fallen are God-given, watching them has been the best tutorial I could have ever hoped for. They are role models for me as they transform the lives of the needy, affluent, deserving, and undeserving.

ALPHA BOOKS

Published by Penguin Group (USA) Inc.

Penguin Group (USA) Inc., 375 Hudson Street, New York, New York 10014, USA • Penguin Group (Canada), 90 Eglinton Avenue East, Suite 700, Toronto, Ontario M4P 2Y3, Canada (a division of Pearson Penguin Canada Inc.) • Penguin Books Ltd., 80 Strand, London WC2R 0RL, England • Penguin Ireland, 25 St. Stephen's Green, Dublin 2, Ireland (a division of Penguin Books Ltd.) • Penguin Group (Australia), 250 Camberwell Road, Camberwell, Victoria 3124, Australia (a division of Pearson Australia Group Pty. Ltd.) • Penguin Books India Pvt. Ltd., 11 Community Centre, Panchsheel Park, New Delhi—110 017, India • Penguin Group (NZ), 67 Apollo Drive, Rosedale, North Shore, Auckland 1311, New Zealand (a division of Pearson New Zealand Ltd.) • Penguin Books (South Africa) (Pty.) Ltd., 24 Sturdee Avenue, Rosebank, Johannesburg 2196, South Africa • Penguin Books Ltd., Registered Offices: 80 Strand, London WC2R 0RL, England

International Standard Book Number: 978-1-61564-642-5
Library of Congress Catalog Card Number: 2014938385

16 15 14 8 7 6 5 4 3 2 1

Interpretation of the printing code: The rightmost number of the first series of numbers is the year of the book's printing; the rightmost number of the second series of numbers is the number of the book's printing. For example, a printing code of 14-1 shows that the first printing occurred in 2014.

Printed in the United States of America

Publisher: *Mike Sanders*
Executive Managing Editor: *Billy Fields*
Executive Acquisitions Editor: *Lori Cates Hand*
Development Editor: *Michael Thomas*
Senior Production Editor: *Janette Lynn*
Cover Designer: *Laura Merriman*
Book Designer: *William Thomas*
Indexer: *Tonya Heard*
Layout: *Ayanna Lacey*
Proofreader: *Tricia Liebig*

Contents

Appendiexes

Introduction

Would you like to know the secrets of making a great first impression, attracting the right people into your life, and building lifetime friendships that are rewarding and enjoyable? *Idiot's Guides: People Skills* takes you from the most basic one-on-one exchange of communication to the ability to handle large groups of people with ease. You will learn to appreciate the personality styles of the varied people you meet and, more importantly, learn to adapt your style to theirs so you build better, more durable relationships.

The study of people skills is perhaps the most beneficial study you will ever undertake because every day offers opportunities to use these new relationship skills. And every person you encounter, whether challenging or charming, offers you the opportunity to learn something from them and to benefit from having known them. Expanding your circle of friends can bring you more joy and more support for the other areas of your life.

Whether you're trying to build a relationship with someone close to you or trying to make new connections, this book guides you through all the skills and steps required. You will learn the how-to's and the don't do's that have been gathered from stories of real relationships as well as the best research on developing people skills.

How This Book Is Organized

Part 1, All You Need to Know About Communication Basics, helps you conceptualize what takes place when one person decides to connect with another. The process of sending and receiving messages is fascinating, and this part tells you how to do it well. If you want to become a brilliant conversationalist, this part tells you exactly how it is done. You will learn how to meet people as well as introduce them, thereby increasing your network of friends and acquaintances. And you will learn how to develop the most valued ability of all, the ability to listen skillfully and thoughtfully.

The exchange of communication and meaningful connections is not limited to just words. In **Part 2, The Number-One Communication Skill: Nonverbal Communication,** you will learn how to develop chemistry through nonverbal communication. Because most of a person's first impression of you is based on nonverbal communication, this part gives detailed information and instruction on how to come across with the right balance of compassion and power.

Of course, not all people you encounter will be enjoyable companions and friends. No matter how delightful you are, there will always be a few people who are difficult no matter the circumstances or the people they are dealing with. With that in mind, **Part 3, Handling Routine Conflict, Difficult People, and Awkward Situations,** shows you how to tread lightly but effectively through the choppy waters churned up by difficult people. You will not only learn how to to avoid conflict when possible but how to deal with it effectively when it inevitably arises. The concept of assertiveness is fully explored so you will know not only when to be assertive but how.

Part 3 also addresses common situations that we all find difficult. You will learn the best way to deliver an effective apology, to break sad or disappointing news, to leave a situation, to offer constructive criticism, or to ask for what you need. These situations are not easy for most people, but this part gives you concrete steps for navigating through each situation successfully.

The first three parts strengthen your ability to engage with people and to connect in a way that makes people want to know you better. When you're ready to take that relationship and build it into a strong, long-lasting relationship, **Part 4, Building Strong, Rewarding Relationships,** will give you the stepping stones to more rewarding relationships that last. You will learn to take an acquaintanceship to a friendship and to maintain that friendship once it is established. Forming strong relationships is one of the primary goals of developing your people skills, and this part will show you how to keep those friendships you have made. Of course, building and acquiring relationships is an investment, but the payback is rich and enduring. You will also learn how to be persuasive when needed, how to give clear information, and how to collaborate.

Part 5, Dealing with Differences in Communication, explores the exciting possibilities of having many different types of relationships. We live in a multicultural world, and learning the best way to invite people of different backgrounds into your life will help you get the most out of your neighborhood, your job, and your community. And it is not just cultural differences that can enhance your life. Learning to draw the best from people of all generations around you is also important. This part details how to go about that. Finally, identifying what is unique about you and leveraging that to its fullest is addressed in this part. You have gifts that comprise who you are, and fully understanding and developing these gifts will build your confidence and enrich your life greatly.

Part 6, Speaking to Groups, shows you how to speak to small or large groups. You will learn exactly what to do if someone suddenly turns to you and says, "Will you say a few words?" And you will learn to be equally poised if you are asked to make a presentation to a group about your favorite charity or topic or work project. This is an opportunity to connect with many people at once, so you don't want to overlook these skills.

In the appendixes, you will find a glossary, a four-week plan for improving your people skills, and a list of additional resources in case you want to continue to study the limitless possibilities of expanding your people skills.

Enjoy this dynamic approach to making new connections, lasting friendships, and profitable acquaintances through developing outstanding people skills.

Extras

Throughout the book, you will see three kinds of sidebars that give you more information about people skills.

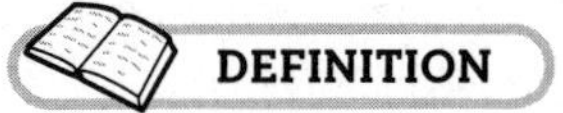

DEFINITION

These sidebars define key words and concepts from the text.

COMMUNICATION TIP

These sidebars are full of tips and reminders that make the lessons in the chapters more memorable and easy to understand.

HOLD THAT THOUGHT

These sidebars provide warnings that will help you anticipate communication breakdowns or conflicts before they happen or remedy them after they occur.

Acknowledgments

Although I appreciate the formal education that contributed to my career in communication, I learned the really valuable lessons on people skills from models and mentors. I have been blessed to have some wonderful guides in my life. The following women are part of the legion it took to teach me and shape me so I can pass their lessons on to others: Belinda Stone, Connie Musselman, Anne Hayes, Joyce Johnson, Janice Blalock, Frances Pastore, Angela Mitchell, Rosa Lauren Ramsey, and Carolyn Caswell.

Trademarks

PART

1

All You Need to Know About Communication Basics

Most of us want three things from the people we meet: to be understood, respected, and liked. Part 1 helps you understand the communication processes that lead to another person's perception of you.

Chapter 1 shows you how to be aware of your conversation partner and communicate so he understands and accepts you more readily. A critical skill in dealing effectively with people, listening, is the topic of Chapter 2. You will learn to be responsive and to show empathy. Every neighbor, employer, and friend desires to have a good listener to connect with, and you will learn exactly what it takes to be a memorable listener. Chapter 3 teaches you to be a great conversationalist. You will learn the five signs of great conversationalists and other communication secrets. Finally, Chapter 4 gives you all you need to know about how to meet people and make an excellent first impression.

Part 1 is the launching pad for all people skills, and you will learn new things about yourself in this part as you read each chapter. You will also learn to take the natural gifts and tendencies you have and adapt them so that your people skills grow, broaden, and serve you well.

CHAPTER

1

What Happens in Great Communication?

Do you know someone who seems to fit in and connect with people no matter the situation? What is their secret? What gives the fortunate few charisma, influence, and pleasure in the company of others?

If you want to be effective with all kinds of people, you must first take a long look at what happens when any two people communicate. This chapter will give you a high-level view of the communication process.

In This Chapter

- The two sides of give-and-take communication
- Improving understanding and increasing your likeability factor
- What people want to know about you
- Rewards and payback for great communication skills

Communication: A Two-Way Street

Every conversation is composed of a sender and a receiver. The two switch roles from time to time as people spend time as both a sender and a receiver. The words play a small role in determining how the receiver will feel about the sender of the communication and how the sender will feel about the receiver at the end of the exchange. Many dynamics go on that determine how successful the conversation will be, including gestures and facial expressions.

COMMUNICATION TIP

Being a great communicator is about looking for ways to make connections through fully engaging with people, relating to their feelings and experiences, and finding conversation bits to offer that interest them. In the end, the most valuable skill of all is listening.

Ensuring That Your Receiver Understands and Likes You

When you send communication to a receiver, your spoken words are only part of your message. Many factors make up your total message. Everything from your last conversation with the receiver to prejudices he brings from his early life form a filter through which your message passes. As your receiver listens, he is adding his own meanings and slant to your message.

The following figure provides an overview of some of the dynamics going on during any exchange between sender and receiver. Prior events, prejudices, and conversations affect what your receiver thinks of you and how he perceives your message. Does the receiver know information about the sender that colors how he feels about the sender and his message? Before the first words are spoken, the receiver may have established a filter that may prejudice what he hears either in favor of you or against you. If you have ever had a difference of opinion with the receiver about where to have dinner, for example, he will be more sensitive to what you say about a dinner choice this time.

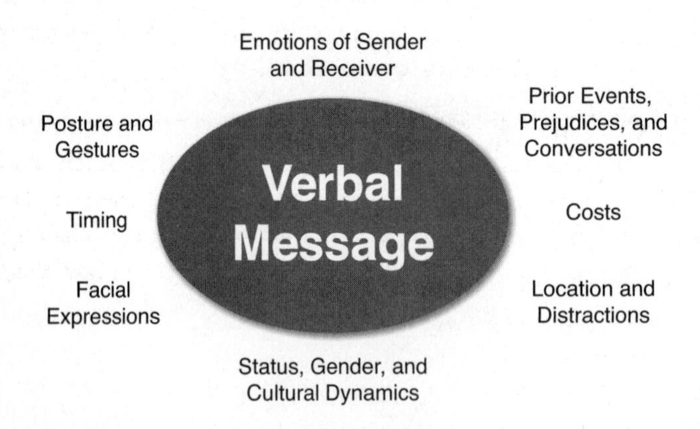

The verbal message is surrounded by many nonverbal messages.

Even the way you stand or slouch or gesture as you speak will affect your message. The receiver reads meaning into your posture, movement, and facial expressions. Do you as a speaker look unconfident and negative or warm and friendly? Are your hands too animated or too stiff and still? These factors can inspire confidence or distrust in your receiver.

COMMUNICATION TIP

Timing is everything. Think about the timing of your important conversations. Has the conversation come at a very bad time for the receiver? Is the timing inconsiderate or is it perfect?

Another possible factor is cost. Is money involved? Some receivers are receptive to an idea as long as it doesn't cost them anything. What may be a small amount of money to you may annoy or discourage the receiver. And money can also be misleading if it is an incentive for the wrong reasons. If your receiver thinks you as the sender are only being nice because you have an underlying financial motive, your credibility becomes suspect. When trust is damaged, so is the relationship.

Don't underestimate the influence of culture and status when two people communicate. Does one person "outrank" the other in an organization? That dynamic may affect the freedom to express differing opinions candidly or to advance a friendship. You also have to consider the culture that the sender comes from, as well as the culture of the receiver. Every organization and community represents a culture with unspoken rules. Are both the sender and receiver aware of, respectful of, and comfortable with the cultural dynamics?

One factor you can never ignore in communication dynamics is gender. Though you do not want to stereotype, being sensitive to possible gender biases on the part of your partner, as well as any biases you may have, is wise. For example, is one partner being more deferential because of his training to treat women with elevated respect? Although gender is not as strong a factor today as it once was, watching for clues to your partner's gender biases—and being aware of your own—will help you plan your words and actions more effectively.

Finally, consider the location of the conversation. Are there distracting noises or activities going on? Is the location on one person's "turf," making that person more comfortable or giving him a perceived advantage? Is the location so formal that one partner is less comfortable than the other? A young person who is considered a wonderful conversationalist may clam up and barely respond if you take him to a ritzy restaurant. Consider the surroundings and how they could be affecting your partner.

Evan's Story

The following story illustrates all of these factors at work when the context of a situation caused a young man to misread some critical communication clues, which led to erroneous perceptions.

A friend of mine took her adolescent son to a reception for students who were being considered for a prestigious scholarship to an elite prep school. Evan had a brilliant mind, but his greatest asset was his effervescent personality. Even at 12, he was a skilled conversationalist, and adults and peers alike enjoyed talking to him. Nothing rattled him, and his natural confidence made him poised beyond his years. The party was to be held at the home of a wealthy real estate mogul, and both mother and son were looking forward to the evening and seeing what opportunities might await.

On the evening of the party, the streetlights happened to be out along the street where they were told to park. This made finding the house difficult since there were no numbers on the houses. The address led Evan and his mother to a small house with a bumpy brick path in front. As they were walking up the path, my friend, who was by now agitated because they were late, said to herself, "This doesn't look right." She was puzzled that the home of one of the city's wealthiest real estate tycoons would be a small, disheveled brick house on a dark street with untrimmed shrubs out front. Even as she rang the bell, she wondered if she was at the wrong location.

They were greeted warmly, however, and alums and students did their best to make the two feel welcome. Everyone was eagerly trying to get to know Evan, as his test scores and the buzz about his leadership and communication skills had been exciting. But as adults and fellow students asked him about his interests and accomplishments, Evan gave monosyllabic answers and never really engaged in a conversation. After a time, people gave up and moved on to more receptive candidates. What was worse, Evan's tone was hostile and his facial expression was full of disdain. Finally, his mother took him aside and said, "What's wrong? These people are doing their best to be nice to you and I've never seen you treat people so rudely."

Evan said, "But you said they didn't look right. I thought there was something wrong with these people and that I needed to be careful since they're strangers."

Suddenly, my friend realized that the last words she had said to her son as he walked through the door were negative ones. She had meant the location didn't look right based on her expectations. He thought she meant they were entering a sketchy situation and should be on guard.

She had completely colored his perception of lovely people, and no matter how gracious their conversation was, Evan viewed them as untrustworthy. He walked in with a barrier against them that did not come down until his mother corrected his perception.

They also found out that the reception was being held in what had been a caretaker's cottage that was now used for informal events. The prep school had felt that adolescent boys might be more comfortable in an informal setting. The caretaker's cottage was on the back of the property. The elegant home, which took up most of the block, fronted on another street.

After clearing up these misconceptions and feeling his mother's approval of the alums, Evan instantly became the life of the party and won over the most influential people in the crowd.

Evan's communication was affected by perceptions, location, and his mother's remarks. These and other factors can completely change how positively a sender communicates. And receivers are simultaneously coloring everything they hear because of the same factors. The verbal message can be completely distorted or enhanced because of all the dynamics in play while a conversation takes place.

Taking the time to face your prejudices and other factors before entering a conversation will help you make the conversation a success. Preparing for conversations takes just a bit of thought and maybe some adjustments in order for you to make a real connection with people and to be understood rather than misunderstood.

COMMUNICATION TIP

Bill Clinton, acknowledged as a gifted conversationalist, is known for anticipating any negative factors in a communication and working to reduce his receiver's concerns and prejudices.

The Three Questions Every Person Wants to Know About You

When you start to talk with someone, that person is subconsciously asking three questions about you:

- Do I like you?
- Are you smart?
- Can I trust you?

You want the answer to each of the preceding questions to be an enthusiastic "Yes!" The following section explore each of these questions and give you the strategies to help you get the positive response you want.

"Do I Like You?"

The first question, "Do I like you?," is a matter of chemistry, but chemistry is something you can influence. Most "chemistry" is determined by nonverbal communication, which I will address in Part 2. Six of the key factors in chemistry, also known as likeability, are courtesy, openness, flexibility, authenticity, balanced assertiveness, and tactfulness.

Being courteous doesn't mean you have perfect Emily Post–approved manners; it means you consider how your actions and comments will affect others. Will your actions make your partner enjoy the conversation more or less? Would your partner prefer you to go first or last in the conversation or activity? Would he like you to talk more or less? What could you do to enhance the situation for others?

The second likeability factor, openness, means being open to getting to know unusual or unique people, perhaps unlike anyone you have known before. You are open to participating in conversations you might not have chosen, going to events that are outside your usual routine, and trying new foods or sports you've never tried. Flexibility is a character trait of people with extraordinary people skills. Being flexible means you can adapt to diverse people and opportunities, which opens you up to a wider range of experiences and new friends.

COMMUNICATION TIP

The flexibility factor gives you the ability to connect with neighbors, co-workers, and peers in an enjoyable way that makes people want to be around you more. They will not feel the pressure to conform to your expectations because they know you will meet them more than halfway.

When you have a mental list of your likes and dislikes and try to live by that list, you may unintentionally shut people out. Experimenting by tossing aside that list and trying to enjoy a few hours of activities or places an acquaintance likes may lead you to enjoy something you never dreamed you could. And even if it winds up not being for you, the relationship points you earn may turn an acquaintance into a friend.

Being flexible and open to the suggestions of others says to them, "I may not have chosen this activity, but I'm choosing to be with you. If you enjoy this activity, I'm willing to give it a try in order to spend some time with you." People love to share their hobbies, favorite places, and interests with others. Most people enjoy the role of teaching a novice the ins and outs of a game or a tradition or an art. Be generous and allow others to teach you; in the role of the student, you will be very popular since so many people want to teach rather than learn. Learners are in high demand. Being a lifelong learner means you never run out of new things to learn or teachers who will want to share their knowledge with you.

You also need to develop the right balance between assertiveness and passiveness. You should be assertive enough to express an interest in other people and in engaging them in going out and getting to know them better. There are times, however, that you need to be more passive and not come on too strong with certain people, or, if you feel you have been too assertive, to hang back a bit until balance is regained. Be quiet and wait; adjust to the pace your acquaintance wants as you both see what kind of relationship will unfold.

Tactfulness is the fifth key likeability factor. Don Gabor, a former FBI agent who trains security professionals, offers this advice for being TACTFUL:

T = Think before you speak.

A = Apologize quickly when you blunder.

C = Converse, don't compete.

T = Time your comments.

F = Focus on behavior, not on personality.

U = Uncover hidden feelings.

L = Listen for feedback.

COMMUNICATION TIP

Many of the ways we can be tactful and increase our likeability we learned as young children, such as minding our manners, thinking before we speak, and letting others go first.

The final factor in likeability is authenticity. Being yourself, being real and sincere, is necessary to create long-lasting relationships. Although we all want to be our "best self" when we meet someone, we should still be our *real* self. Being honest creates a comfortable rapport in which you will be consistent in what you say. Even though you may accommodate your friend by attending a tattoo convention when you don't like tattoos yourself, you can be honest and say that though you find the culture fascinating, tattoos are not for you.

Your quirky sense of humor, the fact that you collect 45-rpm records, or your love of body-surfing are all part of what make you fascinating. Not everyone will connect with these things, but the people who do will like you all the more because of them. If everyone had the same interests, the world would be plain vanilla. Show the world your fudge ripple and your sprinkles. They are not for everyone, but they will draw many who will become fans of all the things about you that bring variety to their lives.

Finally, whoever you are, be consistent. Be the same person with the yard crew that you are with the most prominent person you know. Have you ever noticed that some people actually change the way they enunciate when they talk to someone of higher status? Similarly, their voices may become more melodious when talking to someone they want to impress. They may, on the other hand, be unusually sharp with a store clerk whom they see as existing only to serve them. Each person has something of value to offer and is deserving of equal respect. You may be surprised at the wisdom and far-flung interests of that yard man.

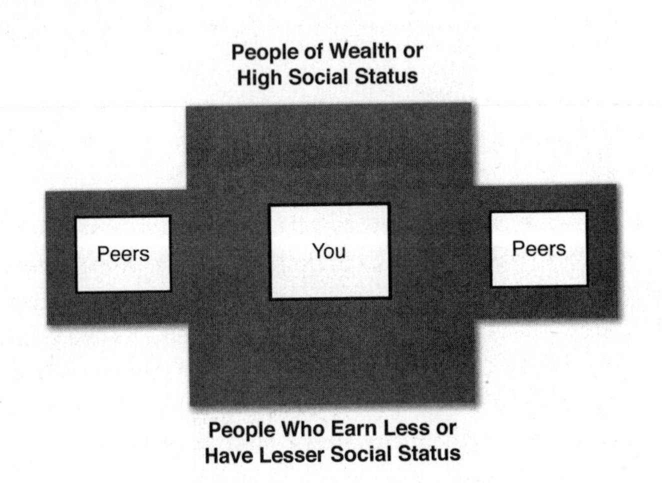

Do you alter your manner of speaking and choice of subject matter based on a person's status?

HOLD THAT THOUGHT

People who have achieved wealth and social status seem to have radar for people who are being flattering just to gain access to their inner circle.

Being genuinely interested in people brings a reward all its own. Interested = interesting!

"Are You Smart?"

The difference between smart and not so smart is in the eye of the beholder. First impressions are important when people are sizing you up and deciding whether they consider you smart enough to listen to and perhaps get to know a bit better.

The first thing you say to someone and the last thing you say are the most critical parts of a conversation. Your opening remarks, especially, can sound pretty dumb if they are inappropriate for your audience. Observe the person you're trying to connect with and try to adjust your comments to his lifestyle, interests, and personality. This courtesy of taking your conversation partner's preferences and comfort level into consideration is not dishonest; it is just good manners.

Opening remarks should never be controversial, even if you're trying to be memorable. Start out light and don't overwhelm people with your 50,000-watt personality immediately. Avoid personal comments as well. Give the other person an opening to do more of the talking up front so you can size them up.

"Smart" can mean something different to each person. We all have known people who were "book-smart" but had little common sense. Smart doesn't necessarily mean educated or brainy. Some "street smart" people are charismatic and are welcomed into the circles of the wealthy and highly educated. But most people don't want to hang out with people who aren't smart on some level. If a stockpile of intellectual information is important to you, you will be drawn to people who invested in educating themselves either formally or informally.

There is nothing wrong with enjoying the company of people who value knowledge, but you do need to offer something of intellectual value in return. You may not be able to achieve quickly the large body of knowledge they possess, but you can find an area that interests people and read deeply in that area. You can continue to update your knowledge of that subject so you can offer interesting conversation. If your friends like art, you can learn about art history or choose a few painters from different eras and become well-versed on them. If your friends are computer whizzes, make a habit of reading C-Net for breaking news in that area.

Often what people want most in a friend is someone who thinks as they do. So if your friends are conservative and you aren't, be sure you consider the choices you make with your words and time. An ill-considered act or comment may be a "dumb" move in their eyes.

HOLD THAT THOUGHT

There is nothing wrong with finding models you admire and learning from them; just be sure you don't compromise any of your values.

If, instead, you feel you need to develop more relationships with a fun-loving crowd who will help you loosen up a bit, they may think other types of things are dumb. They may think that sitting around talking about art is just about the dumbest thing they can think of to do.

So the key is to prepare yourself to be a good conversationalist for the people you will be with. Read articles online and current books that will enable you to contribute to the conversations and not just observe. Attend an occasional seminar or lecture at a local university. Continually freshen your intellectual stores to stay interesting. Have you ever had a friend who told the same stories year after year? Don't be that guy!

"Can I Trust You?"

Trust is vital to any relationship. People who brag, exaggerate, or misrepresent themselves alienate the very people they're trying to impress. The adage of underpromise and overdeliver works very well in relationships. It is fine to underwhelm someone at first and then exceed their expectations. If you overwhelm them in an effort to impress, their disappointment may be hard to overcome. It's better to let someone gradually get to know how great you are than to tell him how great you are up front. You run the risk of not living up to your own press, and making a comeback from that disappointment is difficult.

It works better to turn the spotlight on the other person at first. Allow others to peel back your layers gradually and discover all your wonderful qualities and accomplishments for themselves. Adults prefer to discover for themselves rather than be told.

Consider this scenario. You walk into a car dealership in the first stages of considering buying a car. The sales professional comes up and starts telling you one great feature after another about the car. "This car got the *Car & Driver* award for quality. The mileage is much better than our competitors' cars. It has a bumper-to-bumper three-year warranty. It's on sale right now and you can get a rebate. It's available in ten colors." How do you feel? Think you might back up a bit? Most people want to investigate for themselves, whether browsing cars or meeting someone. Be comfortable enough to let that happen and don't try too hard.

The Payoff for Learning Great Communication Skills

The rewards for learning great communication skills are many. Of course, the companionship and camaraderie are wonderful. But there are tangible rewards as well. Today, great communication skills top the list of what employers look for in almost every job. It isn't the best number cruncher who makes partner in the accounting firm; it's the accountant who's good with people and can communicate good news and bad news. Opportunities for everything, including getting into the best schools and getting into the best organizations, increase if you develop strong communication skills.

Investing in developing these skills will make you an attractive candidate in the social arena, as well as in your career or avocation. Chapter 2 will be the first in a series of chapters that will show you step by step how to acquire the kind of communication skills that people relate to and find attractive.

The Least You Need to Know

- Your partner's opinion of you is influenced by factors such as prior events, prejudices, gender, social status, timing, cultural dynamics, surroundings, and facial expressions.
- The six key factors in likeability are courtesy, openness, flexibility, authenticity, balanced assertiveness, and tactfulness.
- The first and last remarks in a conversation are the most influential.
- Three questions every person asks about you are "Do I like you?," "Are you smart?," and "Can I trust you?"
- Build trust in a new relationship by underpromising and overdelivering.
- Let others discover how great you are. Adults like to learn for themselves instead of being told.

CHAPTER

2

How to Be a Great Listener

Many people work a lifetime to perfect their conversation skills, when, in reality, the skill that makes people feel you're a great conversationalist is listening. Great listening skills are so powerful that they make you memorable. You will be sought after as a person others want to have conversations with because listening skills are so rare. Everyone wants to talk; few have the wisdom or the skills to listen. This chapter teaches you to be a truly great listener. Listening is one of the most valuable skills you can develop if you want to be effective in dealing with people and forming enjoyable and productive relationships.

In This Chapter

- Making people feel "listened to"
- Strategies for powerful listening
- Steps to becoming a better listener
- How to respond when people speak to you
- Extreme listening skills: empathy statements

The Importance of Listening

You may feel that you're a good listener, but are you sure that you demonstrate the skills that make a person "feel listened to"? You may wait patiently while others talk and even hear all they say, but is there outward evidence of your listening that makes others walk away and think, "She's one of the best listeners I've ever talked to"?

Few people achieve this level of expertise in listening. It's a skill that will draw people to you and make them find value in being with you.

COMMUNICATION TIP

Listening skills are effective game-changers with people of any age—from teenagers to octogenarians!

Why Listen?

Imagine that I asked your neighbors, co-workers, friends, and acquaintances to name the best listeners they've ever encountered. What if your name showed up on everyone's list? How would that affect your friendships and your relationships with your customers, boss, co-workers, and others?

People may or may not like the person who talks a lot; everyone likes and values the person who listens a lot and who responds in a way that says, "I listened." Consider how extraordinary listening skills can help you with these key people:

Family and friends. Long-term relationships are hard to maintain through the years, and listening more and talking less is the most effective strategy to avoid breaks in these relationships. Friendships deepen and become more valuable when you make a commitment to listen actively to others. You will become the go-to friend if you're quick to listen rather than quick to give advice (which may not always be welcome). Even when friends and family say, "What do you think about this situation?" they may not truly want advice. What most everyone is really seeking is a good and thorough listening to.

Your boss. Most bosses feel a bit misunderstood. Listening carefully to your boss before taking action is wise. It is better to understand her vision fully and to prove that you heard her than to give a fast response that may slightly miss the mark and disappoint her. If you take the time to thoroughly listen and make sure you have captured the ideas and details that are important to her, you won't have to suffer the consequences of disappointing her or getting it wrong the first time. Doing any task right the first time makes you an employee who can be trusted with more responsibility, and more responsibility usually leads to promotions.

Your customers or others you serve. Customers complain constantly that they explicitly state their needs and then get products or services they didn't ask for. A frustrated customer is even harder to please on the second try. Customers are so surprised at being served by someone who really listens and cares enough to make sure they heard everything correctly that they tend to be more supportive if anything does go wrong. Customers often say that it is not the failed product or service that angers them—it's that they didn't feel the employee listened to what they said.

Strangers and acquaintances. Stopping to listen will help you assess people and adjust your behavior accordingly. Until you know someone better, you don't know what will motivate, interest, or even offend them. Spend time listening while in the getting-to-know-you phase. You can avoid bad decisions and hasty commitments.

HOLD THAT THOUGHT

You may want to keep some people at the acquaintance stage rather than move them to the friend category. Protecting your time and security is important, so don't give away too much information too quickly. Instead, listen and receive the information you need to make good decisions.

How Do People Know You're Listening?

So how do people know you're listening? They need evidence. When communicating face-to-face, you give many nonverbal cues that you're listening. (These cues will be discussed more thoroughly in Part 2.) Following are some do's and don'ts of listening, as well as some other strategies you can use.

The Do's of Listening

First, the most important sign of listening has nothing to do with your ears, but with your eyes! Great eye contact is a must, but change your eye width once in a while to show your responsiveness. Widen your eyes in wonder or surprise when fascinating new information is offered (this information may only be fascinating to the speaker). You may have a background that makes establishing eye contact difficult or uncomfortable for you. You must learn to maintain relaxed, attentive eye contact. Eye contact may be broken briefly so as not to devolve into a vacant stare, but some eye contact should be given throughout the conversation.

Second, make listening noises. Do you know the sounds that a doctor makes as he examines you closely or takes a thorough health history? *Ah, uh-huh,* and *mmm.* These sounds are called *subvocals.* Subvocals are a powerful secret weapon in demonstrating that you're a responsive and caring listener. You can also use short phrases or words such as "oh," "really?," and "interesting" to show that you're listening (use these sparingly).

DEFINITION

Subvocals are sounds you make that let the speaker know you're alert and engaged without your having to interrupt her to ask questions or interject your own comments.

Paraphrasing and repeating are techniques that also offer your listener proof that you're listening closely. After you're sure your partner has finished her comments and it's your turn to respond, be sure to repeat a phrase she has just said or paraphrase what you think you heard her say. People love to hear their own words and comments coming back to them; it is very flattering to them to know you listened so closely and can repeat to them what they just said. For example, if your neighbor spends five minutes telling you about a new car she just bought, which she describes as an SUV that gets unusually great gas mileage and seats six people, you could say, "I can't believe you get that kind of mileage with an SUV that seats six." Those words are proof positive that you listened to every detail. Isn't that response so much more gratifying than the generic "That's great"?

Another sign that you're listening is your body language, particularly your facial expressions. Beyond eye contact, lively and interested facial expressions reflect great interest in the speaker's words. Sometimes when we're listening our face goes into "neutral," giving us a bored expression. This neutral expression could be mistakenly viewed as hostility or negativism, even if you've been interested and listening. Be aware that your face is sending a message at all times, even when you aren't talking.

And if you are gathering a great deal of information, be sure to take notes to capture facts and further demonstrate that you're paying close attention. If you have trouble paying attention, write down a key word here and there as your partner speaks. It helps you focus.

Finally, if you're really listening, you'll do two things: keep your remarks brief and ask questions. When your remarks are brief, you give the floor to your partner and you spend more time listening. Sometimes your remarks can be so brief that you don't even need to speak in complete sentences. And asking questions is your way of giving up the spotlight and asking your partner to talk more while you play the role of the attentive listener. People are so used to being interrupted or rushed through their explanations that when someone asks a question, they're really knocked out!

COMMUNICATION TIP

Asking a question says to conversation partners, "You are so interesting and what you're saying is so important that I want to know even more." People will feel that you're a brilliant conversationalist when you've actually contributed very little. Their own words sound golden to them.

The Don'ts of Listening

Now that you know the do's, consider some of the don'ts of listening.

Don't fiddle with pen or papers, or use any distracting gestures while you're listening. You may feel impatient, but hide it. Don't jiggle your foot or your loose change. Don't gesture constantly. When energy pours out of you like this, you appear to be impatient and not listening. Not only will your actions keep your receiver from concentrating on your response, but they may send a message that you are bored or annoyed. Maintain your composure and keep hand and body motions under control.

Don't relate everything to yourself. Do you constantly say things like, "The same thing happened to me one time …" or "That's just like my old boss, he …"? When you make these types of statements, you're really finding ways to steer the conversation away from your partner and back to your favorite subject—you. Everyone does this occasionally—the operative word being *occasionally.* Don't abuse.

Don't constantly check your phone or other electronic device. This breaks eye contact and says to your partner that she is of lower priority than anyone who is reaching out to you electronically. Just as you would never keep your phone turned on during a job interview, do not power on your phone during any conversation.

Don't be guilty of clipping. When your words follow closely on the heels of the last syllable of your partner, she feels "clipped." You would probably never actually interrupt. You may, however, wait with great patience until the last syllable is out of the other person's mouth and then jump in with your pent-up comment. You are like a dam bursting as you pour out the thoughts that have gone through your mind as your partner talks. (Clipping is closely related to scriptwriting, discussed later in this chapter.)

Don't abruptly change topics when someone is talking to you. This is like leapfrogging from one lily pad to the next. It shows no interest on your part in the current conversation. At least make a responsive statement or two about your partner's input. You can then try to link the current topic to the one you want to change to with a transitional statement.

COMMUNICATION TIP

Mark was guilty of topic-changing behavior, and it almost cost him his friendship with Elena. Elena was telling Mark about the new car she was purchasing. As Elena described the luxury features and the size of the engine, Mark's mind wandered. Elena ended her description with, "The brakes have special sensors that balance the braking on all four tires to improve control." Mark said, "By the way, what are the one-year CDs at the credit union paying?" His mind had skipped to auto financing and then on to his bank account. Elena was insulted.

Other Listening Strategies

In addition to the do's and don'ts, other strategies can help you develop the people skills of a great listener.

Be sure to use the speaker's name as frequently as comfortable, using a warm and friendly tone of voice. Whenever people approach or call, smile and greet them warmly. (Yes, smile on the phone. People can "hear" a smile.) Also, practice the art of embracing interruptions. How you handle the unexpected can make relationships stronger or hurt them. And when the conversation is over, say thank you verbally and in the way you follow up. Send thank-you notes or emails to follow up on conversations. Call a few days later to see how a situation turned out.

Learning to Be a Better Listener

You aren't born a great listener; you become one. Either someone, such as a forward-thinking parent, trains you or you train yourself. Listening is a skill anyone can acquire with a bit of patience and a sense of purpose to do a few necessary things.

Developing the Power of the Pause

First, develop the power of the pause. People underestimate the power of a tiny one- or two-second pause. Americans, especially, are rushing so intensely to be heard and to get their little sound bites of information into the conversation that they rarely pause. If you can train yourself to pause briefly after someone speaks, you will transform yourself into a much better listener.

When your conversation partner says her last syllable, wait one or two seconds before you begin speaking. What will happen next is one of two things. Your partner may start speaking again because, in many cases, she hasn't really said all she wanted to say! Most of us eagerly anticipate our turn in the conversation. When our partner pauses, we optimistically think she has finished speaking. We jump in because we have been *scriptwriting*. Most of us pay so much attention to scriptwriting that we are not sensitive to the fact that our partner is not finished talking. People find it refreshing to be able to finish all they wanted to say without your jumping in on the last syllable.

DEFINITION

Scriptwriting is the habit of thinking of what you want to say next while your partner is still talking.

Something quite different may happen as well when you pause. Your partner will think you're reflecting on what she has said. She will think you have found what she says worthy of mulling over for a second or two. This is very attractive and makes your partner feel you two are having an exciting conversation. When you begin speaking again, your partner will feel you have first listened to what she had to say and will listen more attentively to you in return. Soon, you actually are having a great conversation.

Pausing feels awkward at first, but stick with it. After a while, you will be pausing more naturally. Discipline yourself to insert these pauses for 21 days; after that, pausing will be part of your skill set.

The Art of Responding

The second step to take is to be sure to respond to whatever is said, even if it appears not to require a response.

For example, my brother-in-law is a brilliant attorney and very caring and generous. You wouldn't guess how caring he is upon first meeting him because he is very literal in his communication and often does not feel that a comment requires a response. When my sister attended his 20-year class reunion with him, she was mortified at his lack of response to others. Former classmates would come up and say things like, "I haven't seen you since we ran into each other at the beach five years ago" or "I meant to get in touch, but my wife died and I haven't been going out much." These comments would be met with a stony stare from my brother-in-law. He heard them as factual statements that needed no embellishment from him. After an awkward silence of 30 seconds or more, the crushed classmate would excuse himself and walk away with a completely wrong impression. I'm sure my brother-in-law was thinking about the time he encountered the friend at the beach and was also trying to remember the deceased wife, but all the speaker knew was that there was zero responsiveness to their effort to connect.

So a response, any response, is better than not acknowledging what was said. The subvocals mentioned earlier will work for only so long—you then have to *say something.*

Most of the time, when your boss or your spouse accuses you of not listening, what they really mean is you didn't respond in a way that proved you were listening. Responding like a good listener is 10 times more important than actually listening. You must learn the art of making people "feel listened to." That art is called *responding.*

COMMUNICATION TIP

What can 911 operators teach you about responding? Many of the phrases they use can also be helpful when you deal with the people in your life. Examples include: I understand; I'm sorry; I can help you ...; I understand you're upset and frightened, but ...; I don't know, but I can find out; and let me help you.

One of the best responses is the open question. A closed question requires only a brief answer, sometimes just "yes" or "no." Some examples of closed questions might be, "Did you finish your shopping?" and "What brand was it?" When you use an open question, you encourage the speaker to go on talking and tell you even more. Open questions are refreshing, as few people are ever encouraged to tell more of their stories and opinions. How flattering!

Open questions lend a much better feel to a conversation. An open question says, "I'm interested. Tell me more." Open questions encourage your partner to open up and tell all.

The following are some of my favorite ways to begin open questions and statements:

How did that come about?

In what ways …

Tell me about …

Describe …

How did it seem to you?

I'd like to hear your thinking …

Would you like to talk about it?

Let's discuss it …

Sounds like you've got some feeling about this …

I'd be interested in what you've got to say …

People will find they enjoy conversations with you and will probably never detect that it's because you continue to prime them with open questions. Because so much of the content came from their lives and experiences, they feel you had a fascinating conversation. After all, everyone's favorite topic is themselves.

Taking Listening to the Next Level: Empathy

You really cannot be a great listener if you only deal with the facts of a conversation and not the feelings. Every conversation operates on two planes at all times: the text and the subtext. The literal words are far less important than the deeper meaning and emotions the speaker is trying to convey.

How often have you heard people say "I don't mind" or "I would be glad to" when they actually sound as if they mind very much and are not at all glad? How do you find out these underlying feelings if your conversation partner does not offer them straightforwardly?

Years ago, you could have just said a generic statement, such as "I know how you feel." Today, people want more. They want you to show that you really get it. They want proof you detected the real meaning behind their words. The way you do that is through *empathy* statements.

DEFINITION

Empathy is the intellectual identification with or vicarious experiencing of the feelings, thoughts, or attitudes of another.

Even if you feel empathy, you may not be skilled at demonstrating your support in a way that makes your listener really notice your empathy. Also, we all have times that we do not have natural empathy or we don't know what to say. Having a go-to phrase that will help you be responsive and empathetic will be invaluable at times like this as well.

Anti-bulling expert Izzy Kalman discusses the concept of empathy for Psychologytoday.com. He says that it is our mirror neurons that trigger empathy: "What is the mechanism by which we feel bad when we hurt people? Neuroscientists tell us that our mirror neurons are the mechanism through which we feel empathy. Brain imaging has revealed that our brains actually experience what others experience. When someone smiles at us, we spontaneously smile. When someone screams in pain, we cringe. We know that laughter is contagious, which is why TV sitcoms usually have laugh tracks."

Demonstrating empathy means you show your partner that you feel her pain, so to speak. But you can also show empathy when you acknowledge the joy someone takes in her accomplishment or the hilarity someone felt when she viewed her toddler doing something funny. For example, if your friend tells you about the internship she served that resulted in her being offered a job before the internship was even half finished, you might say, "You must have been thrilled when your work was recognized and rewarded in such a short time" or "You had to be flattered that they did not even wait until you had finished the internship to offer you a position."

These statements acknowledge the specifics your friend told you but also acknowledge the underlying pride and excitement. The emotions are of equal or greater importance than the facts, so be sure to include both in your response.

Empathy Statements

Empathy statements are not difficult once you practice for a week or two. In fact, empathy statements can take an easy fill-in-the-blank approach. The basic formula, which can be paraphrased for variety, is as follows:

> You must be feeling very (FEELING WORD) (Examples: frustrated, disappointed, excited, upset, overjoyed, let down).

Because (SUMMARIZE THE SITUATION) (Examples: you don't have an answer yet; you won; I was late; this will be expensive).

The hard part is filling in that first blank. In this blank, you have to put the *feeling* that you think the other person is having. You have to guess what that feeling is, which is tricky. In the previous example, you could say:

"You must be feeling very *concerned* because you were left out of the loop."

or

"You must be feeling *frustrated* because no one consulted you before moving forward."

It doesn't matter if you guess the feeling word exactly right. In fact, in many cases, the other person loves to come back and change your feeling word like this:

"Well, not exactly *frustrated* but certainly *doubtful* about what to do next."

That's great! Now they're really opening up and communicating with you.

Choosing Your Words

Be careful not to choose feeling words that, although accurate, might be unflattering to the speaker. Although true, you wouldn't tell the speaker in the preceding example that she must feel "threatened," "petty," or "snubbed."

The following are a few more feeling words:

interested	confused	let down
ecstatic	concerned	disappointed
intrigued	doubtful	flattered
challenged	curious	satisfied
anxious	ambivalent	successful

No matter how you phrase empathy, your conversation partners will appreciate your trying to identify and show an interest in how they are feeling.

Do not be concerned if you have to practice this skill for a while before it becomes natural to you. The connection you make with people will be well worth it. Empathy deepens relationships more effectively than almost any other skill.

The Least You Need to Know

- Listening skills can completely change the relationship dynamics with anyone, from teenagers to octogenarians.
- Paraphrasing and repeating key words your partner just said give evidence that you have listened.
- Avoid clipping, or jumping in as soon as your partner says her last syllable.
- Don't underestimate the power of a pause after your partner speaks.
- Responding is even more important than listening, as it makes your partner feel listened to.
- Empathy statements must acknowledge the underlying feelings, as well as the facts of what was said.

CHAPTER

3

Developing Great Conversation Skills

Some people are just great conversationalists. They are welcome at any gathering and equally sought after for one-on-one conversations. But people define "great conversationalist" in many ways. This chapter will define and clarify the various qualities others desire from a great conversationalist. You then will learn how to develop into the type of conversationalist that is effective in conversations with family, friends, neighbors, and colleagues. Well-honed conversational abilities are a cornerstone of people skills.

In This Chapter

- What traits great conversationalists share
- Five factors that determine if you are a strong or weak conversationalist
- Perfecting your conversation skills through practice
- Conversation banks and how to build them
- Learning the art of rich conversation

Traits of a Great Conversationalist

What are some of the traits people think of when they think of a great conversationalist? They may expect one or more of the following attributes.

First, they can talk about a broad range of topics. Whatever the conversation, from sports to art, they can participate at some level in the conversation. They do not limit their interests to a few favorite areas but are open to hearing about areas outside their expertise and knowledge. Being "interesting" means being interested in diverse topics and people. Poor conversationalists can only engage when the topic relates to their jobs, interests, or experience. Great conversationalists may not be able to contribute extensively, but they seem to be able to keep the conversation flowing on many topics, even if they do so by asking questions and putting themselves in the role of the learner.

That leads to the greatest asset of great conversationalists: they listen more than they talk. Every person's favorite topic is himself. People find conversations that are all about them fascinating. Great conversationalists know how to ask leading questions and to listen attentively as people answer, which is very flattering. When you listen to someone who does most of the talking, he usually walks away thinking, "What a great conversation!" (Chapter 2 gives you valuable strategies for how to be a great listener.)

Great conversationalists also know how to draw others into the conversation skillfully. They proactively find ways to help everyone involved in the conversation relate to the subject and have an opportunity to contribute. If there are three or more people in the conversation, a skilled conversationalist will notice when one person is being left out and artfully include him. They can bring balance to a group conversation.

Allie's Story

Allie was a young management consultant on her first job with a large oil company in Louisiana. The oil company's vice president was displeased with the consultant he had been working with (another consultant for Allie's company), and Allie was to take his place. She knew nothing about the oil industry except for what she had read in preparation for the work.

Allie and her boss were scheduled to fly down from New York for an interview; they had had to wait for weeks since the vice president's schedule was so busy. The plan was for Allie to observe the interview and begin to learn the consulting skills and a bit about the oil industry at the same time. On the morning of the interview, however, her boss woke with the stomach flu. She called Allie at her hotel and said, "I can't go. You'll need to do this interview alone. We can't cancel on him or he'll be even unhappier with us. Just go and ask lots of questions."

Fortunately, Allie had excellent conversation skills, which was the reason the firm had hired her in the first place. She sat with the oil executive for over an hour and asked many open questions (see Chapter 2 for more on open questions). She was very responsive, paraphrasing what he said and encouraging him to elaborate on stories and topics he brought up. He did almost all the talking, but she responded enthusiastically to everything he said. The next day, the executive told one of the firm's partners, "We had a great conversation. At last you've brought in someone who understands the oil business."

The executive had loved the conversation because it revolved around his ideas and because Allie was a great listener. He didn't notice how little Allie contributed because she kept the conversation going with smart questions that proved she'd heard the specifics of each topic he brought up.

Other Traits of Great Conversationalists

In addition to knowing how to draw people out and keep a conversation going, great conversationalists look engaged. If you watch a great conversationalist in action, you'll see they are unusually animated and engaged. Great conversations are lively, even when the topic is serious. Skilled conversationalists are not passive but show a great deal of energy; they work at the conversation. Their faces, their sitting positions, and everything else about them are awake and alive.

You won't find negative people among popular conversationalists; they find ways to make the conversation upbeat and positive. Even if people agree with a negative person, they get tired of negativity. Pessimistic or critical conversations bring the mood and atmosphere of a conversation down, even if the content is factually correct. People look forward to conversations with positive people. In time, people will avoid someone who always has something negative to say. Avoid critical remarks. Is it really important to evaluate and criticize the person or topic under discussion? If not, leave out the evaluative or judgmental comments. Besides, people will think you're just as critical about them when they are not around.

HOLD THAT THOUGHT

Whatever you do, never gossip. Your peers may even participate for a while, but eventually you will develop the reputation of a gossip, which carries a negative stigma.

Great conversationalists are open and curious. They are excited at the prospect that each new day, each new conversation, and each new person offers them new things to learn. The opposite of being negative about topics and people is the extreme openness of a truly engaging conversationalist. They are willing to participate in conversations that may at first seem bizarre, alien, or even dull. They are open to people of all different cultures. Even if their belief systems don't align with their partner's, great conversationalists know that nuggets of value can come from unlikely people and topics and they are willing to be adventurous. With that kind of attitude, you embrace more diverse ideas and include a wider circle of people among your relationships.

Most people known as great conversationalists have a wonderful sense of humor. They are careful, however, to use humor appropriately. You can be a great conversationalist without being humorous, but you must have a sense of humor. Humor is a part of conversation, so you must be able to appreciate the humor of others. Great conversationalists never use inappropriate humor about sex, politics, religion, or other sensitive subjects. They never use sarcasm or make remarks at another person's expense. These remarks may work well short term, but they are not the basis for building a reputation as someone others long to have more conversations with. People just don't feel safe. Remember that humor varies based on many things, including culture, ethnicity, gender, age, and values. A sense of humor is an asset; inappropriate humor is a conversation killer. Hone your skills in this area, maybe not as a joke-teller, but as one who can appreciate the sometimes offbeat humor of others.

HOLD THAT THOUGHT

Humor can "make" a conversation or be a complete turn-off, so use it with caution. One person may like corny or slapstick humor and the other person may only respond to very dry, intellectual humor. Know your partner's presence. One thing that always works is to be a great audience for the humor of others. Show your appreciation for the sometimes quirky humor of others and watch how they warm to you.

Most great conversationalists are careful not to monopolize the conversation. If you view a conversation as a series of radio waves, the great conversationalist does not take up extended air time. He talks briefly, and then defers to someone else, asks a question, or pauses for someone else to contribute. The conversation goes back and forth so no one feels he is back in eighth grade being lectured to.

If you think about the great conversationalists you know, many are unpredictable. Great conversationalists will sometimes bring up a surprising fact or ask a stimulating question instead of just rehashing old conversations and facts everyone knows. They avoid clichés and truisms. If there is a lull in the conversation, talented conversationalists know how to shake things up with an unexpected question or viewpoint. They don't use shock appeal; they simply freshen a stale conversation with something new and slightly different from the status quo.

Most importantly, skilled conversationalists are aware of the person they're speaking to and tailor the conversation to him. They do not rehash old conversations, as those would be boring and nonproductive. They consciously try to steer the conversation to fresh topics that appeal to their partner. In most conversations, you will know several areas of interest to your partner. Can you find connections to those topics? Even with strangers, you can make educated guesses about what might interest them. Take into consideration their job, your mutual friends, the event you're attending, and any other clues to their identity. Connect them to the conversation and they will be gratified.

COMMUNICATION TIP

Great conversationalists spend more time asking and less time telling. The amount of time you spend listening and asking questions should far outweigh the time you spend speaking.

Have you ever experienced this situation? You go to a certain holiday party each year where you see someone you rarely run into. In fact, this event is the only place where you usually run into this person. You can predict what the conversation will be. The two of you always talk about the same subjects annually. Each conversation is really just an update from last year, but the content is pretty much the same.

Would either of you think the other wowed anyone as a conversationalist? Chances are, you didn't demonstrate many of the previous attributes. Next time, try to demonstrate some of these skills. Not only will your once-a-year acquaintance be wowed, you will enjoy the conversation far more yourself!

Are You a Strong or Weak Conversationalist? Signs to Look For

This section highlights some of the signs that you are a great conversationalist. As you read, think back to a recent conversation you had. Could the following traits describe you, or do you need to cultivate some of the following?

If you are a strong conversationalist, people seek you out for conversations. Even the best conversationalists are not liked by 100 percent of people, but there should be several people who seem to want to engage you in conversations either at work, in your neighborhood, or at social events. Are you the one engaging others most of the time, or do some people engage you first? Strong conversationalists are in great demand. Are you one of those in-demand people?

Another sign that you are a strong conversationalist is that you are invited frequently into situations where conversation will take place. Are you invited by neighbors or co-workers to coffee, lunch, or other social events where people meet to talk? Is your presence desired? You may go through times when you have to be the initiator—such as after a move or a lifestyle change—but if you always have to initiate, you may want to reevaluate your conversation skills. If you employ all the skills discussed in this chapter, you will be invited more often to share your gifts at opportunities for good conversation.

If you're a lively and strong conversationalist, you are usually the one who terminates your conversations with others. If most of the time other people say they have to go or otherwise end the conversation, you may need to brush up on your conversation skills. A small tweak may be all it takes to make people want to extend their conversations with you. You may actually be a great conversationalist but just like longer conversations than most people. Today, most people prefer shorter conversations.

COMMUNICATION TIP

Call it "Generation Text" or whatever, but the practice of long conversations is quickly going out of style. Therefore, watch that you aren't burying your listener in information. You may not like the idea that the preferred conversation mode for most people today is more succinct than in years past, but that is the reality. Shortening the length of your comments is a great first step.

During a conversation, do others ask you questions or try to delve deeper? If not, you may need to leave them wanting more. A sign that you have interested your partner is that he asks you questions and invites you to expand on something you said. If this never happens to you, you may have expanded too much already.

Every conversation should be a volley between two partners. Conversation should bounce back and forth between the two like a tennis ball between two well-matched players. There should be a steady back-and-forth between conversing parties. One person doesn't keep the tennis ball on his side for an extended time in a tennis match and no communication partner does either. Your conversation should be so interesting that it prompts a connection or observation from your partner. Stop talking after you bring up the topic to see if your partner wants to weigh in. Even if you could talk all day on a certain topic, pause from time to time to let the other person chime in.

Finally, if you're a strong conversationalist, your facial expressions and body language, as well as your partner's, will say so. Both partners will be animated and their expressions varied. No bored or neutral expressions here. A slight leaning in or inclination toward each other takes place. Eye contact is steady but not staring. Similarly, voice tone rises and falls. Neither speaker uses a monotone. At times, the rate picks up and the pitch is higher when excitement or interest kicks in. At other times, the tone is confidential and lower or serious for variety. These are signs of engagement and both parties should reflect that engagement.

You May Not Be the Best Judge

My friends and I once knew a nice, attractive young man whose father was a famous athlete and who had the potential to be an interesting conversationalist. His conversation topics, however, were maddeningly trivial. He would ramble on for seeming hours about how disappointed he was in a certain dry cleaner and then go on to itemize the strengths and weaknesses of each dry cleaner in town. We would look the other way, be nonresponsive, and try to change the subject, but our new friend would continue with his monologue. He was never aware that there was no volley, no response, no enthusiastic looks or noises; he just seemed mesmerized by the sound of his own voice.

Though he was a great person and very kind, we soon stopped going places with him, as the car rides meant we would be held hostage to a lecture about some trivia that was our friend's obsession of the week. What a shame that we could not have helped him make the conversation topics more inclusive, but we were young and we just moved on. That's what most people do.

Be aware that you are not the best judge of your conversation habits. Often, people who monopolize a conversation think they didn't talk "that much." They may even mistakenly think another person talked more! That is why you need to change your conversation habits instead of trusting yourself to improve through good intentions.

Practice Makes Perfect

If you've identified a trait you want to work on, the next step is to develop your skills in that area. I'd like to talk about some steps you can take to transform yourself into a better conversationalist.

First, ask a friend or acquaintance if you can use your phone to video a conversation. Pretend you're a scientist and observe objectively. Is there an even back-and-forth volley between you and your partner? Now, turn off the volume and just observe the moving mouths. You should actually measure the seconds you speak and the seconds your partner speaks in a log or list form. You may be surprised to find that the conversation is a bit more one-sided than you thought.

Next, continue viewing your video with the volume still turned off. Now watch your facial expressions and body language. Are you smiling and do you show a variety of expressions? Do you maintain good eye contact? Do you seem lively? How would you describe the various looks on your face? Are they inviting? Interested? Tuned in? Bored? Passive?

Now observe your partner's expressions. Does he seem interested, or is he giving you nonverbal cues that he's bored? Does he look away or tap his fingers or squirm as if the conversation has gone on too long? These may be signs that you need to adapt your conversation to his preferences a bit more.

Now look away from the picture on the screen and just listen to the audio. Is the topic of the conversation one you chose or your partner chose? If you chose it, do you ever move to a topic your partner prefers? Does the partner ever seem to try to end the topic and bring up another? Does he sound as if he is trying to end this topic in any way? Is he staying unengaged by saying things like "That's nice" or "Great" but not really making contributions equal to yours? If your partner is being passive in the conversation, you may need to work to engage him more the next time you converse.

Now view the audio and video together and note the following behaviors. When your partner makes a comment, are you asking him questions or responding specifically to what he says, or do you just jump in with your own observations? Are you connecting specifically to the point he brought up? Do you draw him out with open questions and ask him to tell you more, or do you take your turn as soon as possible?

Finally, are there long silences on the part of your partner? This is usually the sign that your partner has "checked out." He is not mentally engaged in the conversation any longer. There are exceptions to the rule if you're dealing with a profound thinker who may take longer to listen carefully and respond, but those individuals are a rarity.

Another way to develop great listening skills is to find role models and observe the way they apply any or all of the skills in this book. Identify three people you admire as conversationalists. Be very subtle in the way you observe them. In your next couple of conversations with them, note the way they bring up topics of interest to others in the group or with you. What do they do to include others in the conversation? What did you particularly enjoy about the conversation you had with your role model?

COMMUNICATION TIP

Although your best conversation role models are drawn from people you see frequently, you can also learn by watching celebrities. Be sure to model yourself after a style that works for you. Are you more like Jimmy Fallon or Jay Leno? Is your style more like Matt Lauer or Wendy Williams?

Next, ask yourself if any of these techniques would work for you. We all have different styles, and what works for one person might not work for another. Adopt only the approaches that you are comfortable with.

Talk shows are another example you can observe to gain ideas about how to keep a conversation going at a lively pace. Shows with multiple hosts offer you a wide range of styles and examples of how good conversationalists play off each other. Again, you don't want to copy anyone's style in a cookie-cutter way, but you can pick up pointers from professionals.

Building a Conversation Bank

Two people may be known as great conversationalists and have totally different styles. Some conversationalists earn that reputation with their great listening skills. Still others keep people coming back for more because of what seems to be their vast storehouse of knowledge. Building a conversation bank will help you appeal to those who want to be around interesting people who have something of value to contribute to their lives and conversations.

As I discussed previously, some people are always in demand for conversations. At parties or other events, they are sought out by people of all ages and types. Who are some of these people that are in demand? Athletes are popular. Investment professionals, such as stockbrokers and investment bankers, are often surrounded by listeners chiefly for their investment tips. Of course, celebrities attract a crowd. Newscasters often draw the greatest audiences of all at a social event because they are up to date on current events. These are all people who have a passion for something and who have deep knowledge and expertise in areas that interest people. Many people who attend events are into sports, their finances, and pop culture, so these popular newscasters, athletes, and others offer something of value.

It may be too late for you to be an athlete or to pursue a career in investments or entertainment, but it is not too late for you to develop a conversation bank that will offer interesting content in your conversations about these topics. You may not have deep expertise in any of these areas, but you can develop something to say about each and every one.

You develop a conversation bank by researching, by interviewing and questioning, and by experiencing. In today's world, you have no excuse for not knowing a bit about current events. Going online to sites like Google or Bing is fine, but find sites that offer particularly interesting stories so you have something unique to offer. For example, if you're going to be around a bunch of sports enthusiasts, sportsillustrated.cnn.com might be the way to go. If you're interacting with a more highbrow group who loves the opera, operamerica.org will give you the latest news in seconds.

Build your knowledge bank first with the things that you are passionately and genuinely interested in, but then broaden your scope. Add winsome stories from sports, current events, the arts, and finance. Even if you're in a conversation with a subject matter expert, he may not have seen today's breaking news, enabling you to contribute substantially to the conversation. When possible, think about the person you will be conversing with in advance and prepare to bring up at least one topic you know they'll be interested in.

Some people say you should study a company's website if you're meeting with one of its employees. A more interesting approach is to study the company's industry. The employee already knows about his company. Instead, tell him a story you read on one of his industry's websites. Often, these are sponsored by a professional organization the employee may be a member of. You'll have something fresh to talk about; he is probably tired of rehashing what his website says.

HOLD THAT THOUGHT

Don't fall into the trap of repeating your stories. Some people tell the same old anecdotes and make the same old comments year after year. If you find you've fallen into this habit, think of something new to talk about. While you may be tempted to stick with what has worked for you in the past, add to your conversation bank periodically. If you get tired of telling the same stories, your delivery will be bored and mechanical, which is not very appealing.

More Secrets for Rich and Interesting Conversations

So what are some practical first steps you can take today to become a better conversationalist?

First, remember that everyone's favorite topic is themselves. However, every person has different parts of his life he wants to share. Some love to talk about current interests or projects but are uncomfortable talking about their personal lives. Some people enjoy telling you the details of their personal lives but want to avoid talking about their jobs or other topics. They like to leave work at work and not be reminded of it. Find out how your partner wants to talk about himself. Every person differs.

If you hear "I" used over and over again in a conversation, that's a sign you're having an egocentric conversation. Similarly, any first-person pronoun, such as "we" or "us," should not be overused as the conversation sounds all about you and not the other person.

Prepare a list of interesting questions that are your go-to questions to draw people out. Don't overuse the same old questions. Your go-to questions should be different enough to pique interest but not so different as to seem weird. Your questions should be easy for the other person to answer without invading his privacy or putting him on the spot.

An easy-to-answer question for someone who lives or works near the event you're attending might be, "My wife and I are going to dinner after this meeting. Do you know of any good restaurants?" If you're at a work-related conference, you can ask about the topic or speaker. An example might be, "Your company must be like mine and really promoting sustainability. Is that what drew you to this conference?" If you're at a party, you might ask how the other person knows the host. You could say, "I know Mike through work. How do you know him?" If you're at a PTA meeting or other event related to your children, you can say something like, "I have a daughter who is six and a son who is eight. Are you here as parent or a teacher to hear this new information on the bond issue?" Even though that is a close-to-personal question, you're inviting the person to comment on his kids or on the bond issue.

HOLD THAT THOUGHT

It's best not to ask the ages or genders of people's children today. Unfortunately, people must be security conscious.

The number-one secret weapon for being a master conversationalist is to use the listening skills covered in Chapter 2. There is no shortage of talkers but there is a shortage of listeners.

The final tip relates to group conversations. Are you in a conversation with several people and one is monopolizing? Find ways to draw the quietest member in by linking to something the monopolizer said. For example, is one person droning on and on about his new computer and all of its features? You might say, "That is amazing that your new computer has all those features, Zeke. What kind of computer do you have, Linda?"

The Least You Need to Know

- Some signs that you are a great conversationalist include people seeking you out for conversations, being invited into conversational situations, participating in a steady volley with your partner, and being the one to end the conversation.
- Great conversationalists can talk about a broad range of topics, draw others into the conversation, are not negative, are open and curious, use humor appropriately, and tailor the conversation to their partner.
- Topics you should know a little about as you build your conversation bank are financial news, current events, sports, pop culture, and bestsellers.
- Use friends, video, and checklists to determine where you need improvement.
- Develop a conversation bank by reading, questioning, and interviewing.

CHAPTER

4

Meeting and Greeting Friends and Strangers

In This Chapter

- Meeting someone for the first time
- Great first impressions
- How to have a perfect handshake
- The correct way to make an introduction

Whether you're meeting someone for the first time or having coffee with an old friend at Starbucks, the initial moments of any encounter are critical. With each meeting, you are either establishing or building a relationship. How you handle the opening of any encounter can make the conversation positive and successful or lead to a relational disaster.

Many popular expressions have evolved to describe the importance of these critical first moments. Examples include "You never get a second chance to make a first impression" and "Always trust your first impression." Whether these sayings are true or not, many people put a great deal of stock in a first impression. A good first impression can carry you for a long time. A bad first impression can be hard to come back from. This chapter will help ensure you make a favorable first impression with new acquaintances, as well as make the opening moments of conversations with friends memorable.

The Background Story of a First Encounter

When you meet someone for the first time, many communication dynamics come into play, including gender, age, location, timing, situation, expectations, and perceptions. If you're being introduced by a mutual friend, the new acquaintance may already know much about you and may even be prejudiced warmly or not-so-warmly toward you based on what has been said.

When you meet someone for the first time, remember that they may have preconceived notions based on gender—for example, that females should be treated deferentially. Is the person you are meeting the type who thinks in gender-neutral terms, or does she have some subtle prejudices? Does the person you are meeting feel that females should be treated with greater courtesy or respect based on gender? If not, you have nothing to consider here, but if you are dealing with a person with traditional views about the roles of men and women, you can't ignore their expectations. You also must decide if you will adapt to their views or maintain your own. For example, if you sit before the female you have just met sits, you may have unwittingly gotten off to a bad start if she holds more traditional views and believes it is courteous to allow a female to sit first. It is up to you whether you want to demonstrate modern or traditional courtesies and values, but you should be aware that gender can play a role in that first impression.

Similarly, does age play a factor in your first encounter? Traditionalists believe that the older person should be granted more attention and opportunity to speak than a younger person. Courtesies are sometimes expected by the Greatest Generation or even the Baby Boomers. Do you need to be sensitive to this?

Location can also help shape a first encounter. If you meet at a professional conference or in the cafeteria of a large company you both work for, there will be expectations that you have much in common and that you both have some knowledge of your industry. Your conversation partner will have some idea of the money you earn and probably think you share some of the same corporate values. If you work for a traditional, conservative company, such as a utility, the expectation may be that you are attracted to a stable lifestyle. If you work for a more modern, laid-back company, the assumption may be that you have more flexible attitudes.

Timing affects that first encounter dramatically. For example, Shari, a young accountant, met Brent, who was as conservative about money as she was. He talked a lot about being cautious with investments, and she liked this as his professed beliefs aligned with hers. They fell in love and married in just a few months. Unfortunately, he turned out to be terrible with money and was, in fact, a gambling addict. He also lost a great deal of money in get-rich-quick schemes in the stock and futures markets. How did this happen?

As it turns out, Brent had lost about $200,000 shortly before meeting Shari. He was in shock and had vowed never to gamble or invest foolishly again. In fact, part of his attraction to Shari was that he felt she would help him stay disciplined. Before Shari found out what was happening,

Brent had lost tens of thousands of dollars and the equity in their new home. When she confronted him, she said, "But I thought you were so committed to conservative investments and not taking risks. What about all those things you told me when we met?"

Brent was shamefaced as he said, "You caught me when I was still reeling from a huge financial loss that was so disastrous that I almost went bankrupt. I meant what I said at the time, but the temptation to try some of the high-risk and high-reward types of investments again just became too great. Just like the last time, I felt these opportunities could not lose. I should have learned from past experience that nothing is a sure thing."

Shari learned the hard way that the circumstances and situation around a first encounter can greatly influence what you see in the person you're meeting for the first time. What you see is not always what you get. Every conversation has a background story and situational dynamics that affect how each person perceives what is going on.

HOLD THAT THOUGHT

Remember that some wonderful people do not make great first impressions. They may be shy and unable to project their qualities and values easily at first. Truly, you cannot rely on first impressions.

So first meetings are full of perceptions that may or may not be accurate. With that in mind, we do have to take people at face value to some degree as we first begin to get to know them. Just be cognizant that, as people present themselves to you, they are presenting the best version of themselves that they believe to be true. Move cautiously as you get to know people better and observe their actions and their interactions with you and with others.

First Encounters

Because every person you meet is unique and, as you have seen, because the circumstances of a meeting are always a factor, it is impossible to set down a pattern that every first meeting should follow. This section, however, gives some guidelines for how most first encounters should play out.

You never have a second chance to make a first impression. Often, people talk about the first time they met a friend or co-worker in vivid detail, so in the end, it's important to make each first impression a positive one.

Being Introduced

Ideally, you will be introduced by someone you both know. An introduction by someone you both know makes the first conversation easier. You may have to prompt your friend or host in advance to make this introduction. Say, "I've never met your friend. If she comes to your party, would you be sure to introduce us?"

Having someone make that introduction also takes some of the pressure off of you to carry on a conversation with a stranger. That third party can offer topics that both you and your new acquaintance can relate to.

Introducing Yourself

You may not always have the luxury of being introduced, however. Certain times require you to step up and introduce yourself. Perhaps you're at a gathering and notice someone who seems a bit isolated and not talking to anyone, so you step forward. Or you have wanted to meet a specific person and you spot them. Perhaps no one is available to make the introduction at that moment, so you take the situation into your own hands. Maybe you have planned to meet someone in person whom you may have met only online. Or maybe the meeting has been arranged through someone else who can't be present at that time—a friend, co-worker, recruiter, or family member.

If you decide to approach a stranger, don't let timidity or other uncomfortable feelings show on your face. Smile as you approach the person. If you feel awkward, shy, and uncomfortable, your acquaintance-to-be may read your discomfort as hostility, negativity, or disapproval. The only antidote is a smile, so be intentional about smiling as you approach. Don't wait until you speak. Even the seconds before you speak can influence a person's opinion of you.

After you smile, determine whether a handshake is in order. (Handshakes will be covered in detail in the next section.) If you think your partner will be comfortable with a handshake, extend your hand, smiling all the while. Human response to a smile is hard to resist.

Then say your name, enunciating very clearly, and give the stranger some context about you. Here are three examples:

> "Good morning! I am Elise Goode, a friend of Bobbi, our hostess."
>
> "Hello, I am Elise Goode. I'm new to this school's PTA."
>
> "Hi, I am Elise Goode. My company sent me to attend this lecture because we're in the early stages of developing green space."

Be sure to keep your opening remarks short. Often, people are taken by surprise when a stranger approaches and don't really hear a lot of what you say anyway. Also, a longwinded first remark may make the other person think you will be too much of a talker to spend time with, and she will start thinking of excuses to edge away.

HOLD THAT THOUGHT

If you're at an event, remember that most people don't want to be monopolized when there is a crowd. Even if the conversation is going well, at some point, you will need to end the conversation and move on. Hanging on to the same person you just met at a party or other event seems needy and desperate. Watch for clues that your acquaintance is ready to move on. Is she looking around? Does she say she needs to be somewhere else soon? Graciously end the conversation and move on.

In an ideal world, your first short remark will prompt your new acquaintance to offer a name and to continue with the conversation you started. Unfortunately, so many people are poor conversationalists that you must be prepared to carry the burden of the conversation. If you get little or no response when you share your name and a brief remark, don't be put off. People are unresponsive for a variety of reasons:

- Painfully shy people may freeze and their minds may go blank, resulting in a failure to respond warmly to your first remark.
- People who have few friends may get that deer-in-headlights look because they aren't used to the volley of back-and-forth conversation. Give them another chance.
- Some people process words slowly. The stranger may actually be thinking about what you just said. We aren't used to people pausing to consider our remarks before responding. This person may actually prove to be a good listener and eventually a friend.
- The person may have been brought up to be cautious about talking to strangers. Even as an adult, this habit can be difficult to overcome. Do your best in this conversation. The next time you see this person, you won't be a stranger, and her memory of you will be pleasant.

The Next Steps

So now you have introduced yourself and either have or have not received a response. If you did receive a response and the stranger offered a name, be sure to tell them how pleased you are to meet them. Either way, go to the next step. You must say something pleasant and positive. Your remark doesn't have to be brilliant, but it does need to demonstrate a positive attitude. Examples may include traditional remarks, such as "Deena has really given Ted a nice birthday party,"

"This conference has had some excellent speakers so far," or "They couldn't have picked a better day for an outdoor event."

Your next remark should be designed to draw the other person into the conversation. It may even be a question. Try to think of an easy question or a topic that the new acquaintance can easily relate to. You want to make it as easy as possible for the acquaintance to respond and add a remark of her own. You might begin by mentioning your host: "How do you know Deena?" Or you might mention something about the event: "How long have you been attending these PTA meetings? Is the attendance always so good?" If there is a topic of discussion at the event, try to draw your acquaintance into a discussion about that: "Are you developing a green space, or is there some other reason you were drawn to this lecture?"

If your first question only requires a "yes" or "no" answer, follow with an open question that requires more elaboration, such as "How did you meet Deena?," "What are some interesting points you have heard made in the breakout sessions you've attended?," or "What do you think about the increasing interest in green space in our city?"

If your new friend indicates a desire to talk, be sure to clear the way for her to do so. Allow the other person as much as 75 percent of the conversation "air time." If they enjoy talking, and most people do, they will enjoy the conversation far more if you are a good listener than if you are a good talker. Listen for tidbits she offers about her job, hobbies, and other interests. Follow up on those remarks and try to steer the conversation toward that topic so the acquaintance will continue to talk. If she mentions her job, you might say, "Working there must involve some long hours, but I hear it's a great company to work for." If she mentions her children, you might say, "My kids are really into soccer. What kinds of activities do yours enjoy?" Encourage your friend to talk by not interrupting, by making listening noises such as "ah" and "mmm," and by asking questions about the specific things she says.

HOLD THAT THOUGHT

Be careful about asking questions that are too specific about someone's children. In this age of stranger danger, folks are hesitant to offer too much specific information about their kids. Do not ask for what league the children play in, their names, or anything that could help track them down.

When you end the conversation, reiterate how much you've enjoyed talking to her. Most people are flattered that talking to them was such a treat! Don't be pushy, but mention that you hope to talk to them soon. You might say, "This has been fun. I hope our paths cross again," "Meeting you was a real pleasure. I hope to see you at PTA next month," or "I've really enjoyed talking to you as we have so much in common."

Developing a Great Handshake

Earlier in this chapter, I discussed the need for having a good handshake. Many men, in particular, judge others by their handshakes. Handshakes are an appropriate means of making contact at an early stage of the relationship. In fact, some very tactile people will warm up to you faster if you shake hands during your introduction.

When you meet someone new, you must try to determine if the situation requires a handshake. All business introductions require a handshake. Today's business etiquette does not differentiate between greeting a male or a female. You shake hands with everyone. However, social situations are a different matter. You must size up the situation and decide whether a handshake will be welcomed by your partner.

COMMUNICATION TIP

Etiquette exists to enable us to show consideration for others and to help them be more comfortable. If you sense that a handshake will be awkward for someone because of their culture or any other factor, don't force the issue.

In general, we follow the rules of the Court of England for handshakes (no joke). When people are introduced in a royal court, the person of lower status is presented to the person of higher status. It is up to the person of higher status to decide to extend a hand or not.

Similarly, these guidelines apply for most handshakes in social (as opposed to business) situations, but watch for cues in case your partner wants to do something else:

- Wait for an elderly person to extend a hand first.
- If you are a male, wait for a female to extend a hand first.
- Wait for a dignitary or person of higher status to extend a hand first.

When it comes to the handshake itself, a great handshake is a four-part process that happens simultaneously.

The first part relates to the loose skin that stretches between your thumb and index finger, known as the web. Your web should touch the web of your partner as you engage hands.

Second, you should grip firmly, but without squeezing so hard as to cause discomfort. Grip your partner's hand in such a way that your fingers barely wrap around the edges of her hand. Nothing says "wimpy" like a weak handshake, but be careful not to squeeze too hard.

COMMUNICATION TIP

You may be surprised at some of the people who think your grip is too hard. For example, NFL football players often complain that fans squeeze their hands painfully hard, because most fans don't realize that those seasoned players have often had broken bones or suffer from arthritis. Ask people around you to give you a good assessment of your handshake. Would they say your grip is too soft or too hard? Do you touch webs or do one of those dainty end-of-the-fingers handshakes? Ask several people to get a consensus because one assessment may be wrong and just the opinion of one peculiar person.

Next, shake your partner's hand twice; don't continue shaking and talking. Two shakes gets the job done and doesn't leave your partner standing there feeling awkward as you shake and shake.

The final part of the handshake is the most important: look your partner in the eye!

As with anything, handle handshakes with thoughtful consideration and watch for positive or negative responses from your partner. If you extend your hand and the other person withdraws a bit, quickly drop your hand without comment. The refusal to shake hands may be for many reasons. Increasingly, people are foregoing the handshake because of the many viruses being transmitted through physical contact. Far more often, the reason people don't shake hands is that they are self-conscious because they have never been taught the correct way to shake hands. So if someone refuses to shake hands, don't draw attention to the refusal. Instead, continue to smile pleasantly.

Making Introductions

The same rules apply to introductions as apply to handshakes. Pretend you are being presented to the queen or someone royal when you meet someone or introduce someone. The person of lower status is presented or introduced to the person of higher status. The following are some examples of introductions:

- Presenting an entry-level employee to a CEO, Mr. Gilchrist: "Mr. Gilchrist, I would like for you to meet John McEntyre, who started his job here today."
- Presenting a man to a woman (a social rule that is still observed in some communities): "Michelle, I would like to introduce Eduardo."
- Presenting a young person to an elderly person: "Grandmother, I would like to introduce my friend Kim to you."

After the names have been stated, always try to think of something the two might have in common so they can begin a conversation:

"Mr. Gilchrist started in customer service just as you have, John."

"Eduardo is a Braves fan also."

"Grandmother, Kim is the friend I told you about who enjoys playing Hearts."

Introductions are often awkward, so your friends will appreciate the confident way you take charge of the exchange of names. You will be perceived as gracious when you give the two strangers a link by sharing some small thing that they have in common.

Mastering the art of linking people through introductions will enhance your people skills and broaden your network. Introducing yourself and others is one of the most visible people skills you can demonstrate.

The Opening Moments of an Encounter with Someone You Already Know

When you encounter someone you already know, you still need to be attentive to the opening moments of the conversation. With the exception of the introduction, almost everything recommended for meeting strangers applies to a meeting with a friend or acquaintance. Relationships show wear and tear because we fail to extend the same interest and courtesy to friends as we do to new acquaintances.

Greet a friend or acquaintance with a pleasant, positive remark and tell them how glad you are to see them. You should still tailor the opening of a conversation to topics you know are of interest to the other person, even if you need to get to your agenda items later. Work at drawing your friend out and strive to give her 75 percent of the air time in a conversation.

With those you've known for some time, it's more important than ever to take into consideration your history. What was the last conversation you had with this person? What was she excited about or bothered by? Usually, that topic is a good place to start. Your partner will appreciate your remembering what was important to her. What is your partner's feelings or prejudices related to the conversation you're about to have? Be sensitive to touchy areas regarding the conversation topic.

In short, treat old friends as considerately as you do someone you're trying to impress for the first time. Old friends are worth even more valuable investments of your time and effort.

The Least You Need to Know

- When meeting someone, remember that many communication dynamics come into play, including gender, age, location, timing, situation, expectations, and perceptions.
- Draw your new acquaintance out with cordial pleasantries and by talking about topics she has shown an interest in.
- Try to give your conversation partner 75 percent of the air time in a conversation.
- The rules for handshakes and introductions differ for social settings as opposed to business settings.
- Eye contact is the most important part of a handshake.
- In handshakes and introductions, the person of lower status is presented to the person of higher status, as if you are presenting a commoner to the queen in the Court of England.

PART

2

The Number-One Communication Skill: Nonverbal Communication

Do you realize that your success with people depends more on the look on your face than the words you choose? Nonverbal communication is twice as critical to how well we connect with others, yet we worry more about what to say.

Chapter 5 helps you explore your wide range of "nonverbals" and how they are working for you—or not. Chapter 6 is devoted to other forms of this powerful form of communication, such as energy, presence, posture, and gestures. The final part of your nonverbal skillset is your voice. No matter what your words say, the wrong tone of voice can completely change your message. Chapter 7 will show you how to use your voice like an instrument to convey exactly what you desire to communicate.

CHAPTER

5

What Is Nonverbal Communication?

Although most people worry about *what* to say, *how* they say what they say makes more of an impact on their conversation partner. The tone and the look on your face as you speak to your co-worker or friend is the greatest factor in determining whether the listener receives what you say positively or not. Every word you say is delivered with a nonverbal message that influences what the listener thinks of you and your message.

This chapter gives you a deep understanding of what nonverbal communication is and shows you how it operates in your life every day. To help you master this powerful factor in your connection with people, I discuss the broad scope of what your nonverbal communication covers and how to be more intentional about making it work in your favor in your relationships.

In This Chapter

- Why nonverbal communication matters
- The dangers of sending mixed messages
- How facial expressions communicate more than you know
- Three smiles you must practice
- Looking fascinated and other winning facial expressions

Understanding Nonverbals

Nonverbals are either working for you or against you 24/7. These are just a few of the key nonverbal elements of communication:

- Facial expressions
- Hand gestures
- Fast or slow tempo of speech
- Intonation and inflection
- Fast or slow tempo of movement
- Eye contact
- Posture and how you hold yourself
- Context, location, and other peripheral elements
- Types of emotions behind the words

DEFINITION

Nonverbal means literally everything about the way you communicate beyond the literal message of the words. People communicate with their voices, their bodies, and particularly their faces. Surprisingly, most experts agree that the nonverbal message is far more powerful than the verbal message.

Why Are Nonverbals Important?

Why is it important to master nonverbal communication? Because when your words send one message and your face sends another, the nonverbal part of the communication will win every time. Since, according to Albert Mehrabian, 55 percent of your effectiveness as a communicator is based on your facial expression, working on this part of your nonverbal communication is critical to your success with people.

Carolyn's Story

Consider this example. Carolyn, a college student, began to think about graduate school; however, she knew no one who had a Master's degree to discuss what graduate school might be like for her. Because she lacked confidence, she even thought she might just audit a course, but the advisor she talked to at her local college encouraged her to enter a master's program offered in the evenings for credit.

Carolyn was terrified on her first night of graduate school, and for every night for the rest of the semester. She sat on the edge of her seat, leaning forward with an intense focus on what the professor said. Her eyes would narrow in fierce concentration. Because she felt other students were smarter or better prepared for graduate work than she, Carolyn did not volunteer answers in class for fear of looking foolish.

COMMUNICATION TIP

The response the receiver of a communication has may have little to do with the verbal message but more to do with the context of the nonverbal messages accompanying the words. Albert Mehrabian of UCLA, one of the foremost authorities on nonverbals, says that up to 93 percent of your partner's response can be attributed to your nonverbal communication! In his article "Silent Messages," he offers this breakdown of the "liking" the receiver feels for the message:

- 7%: Spoken words
- 38%: The way that the words are said
- 55%: Facial expression

At the end of the course, she was stunned to find that she received an "A." For the first time, she approached her professor to talk to him. "Professor Griffith," she said, "this class has been one of the most interesting experiences of my life, and I have enjoyed learning from you so much."

The professor said, "You have your grade, so you don't have to flatter me. I've seen you there every week going to sleep in my class. You clearly already knew the material. The expression on your face showed how miserable you were as I spoke."

Carolyn had never considered that her facial expression had been telegraphing a message to her professor every week—a misleading message. She had been communicating even though she had never said a word!

The 7 percent of her message that was verbal had told the professor that she admired his work and his teaching. The 55 percent that was nonverbal suggested another story entirely.

Are You Sending Mixed Messages?

That's the problem with nonverbals. If they don't match your words, you can send mixed messages to others. *Mixed messages* lead to frustrating conversations and misunderstandings.

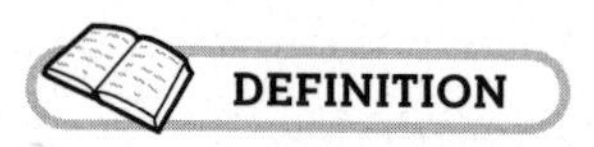

Mixed messages happen when a person receives verbal and nonverbal cues that seem to contradict each other. This can lead to the person becoming confused, angry, and unwilling to communicate with the other person.

Consider this scenario: You have an appointment at the bank to seek a loan and want to make a good impression. Just before you leave home, you have an argument with a family member that leaves you in a bad mood. Those emotions will show on your face and may make you seem untrustworthy or as if you are hiding something. What if the decision to loan you the money could go either way and the loan officer is asked to use his discretion to decide whether you should be approved for the loan? That look on your face may cause him to deny the loan. All your banker knows is that your facial expression is more negative than positive and that something appears to be going on that he can't quite put his finger on.

Therefore, you must perfect your nonverbal communication just as you work to perfect your verbal communication. When you realize that being hungry, tired, or stressed affects your nonverbal communication, you can take action to change any negative nonverbal cues.

So what can you do to make your nonverbals consistent with your verbal message? The following sections give you tips for altering facial expressions, body language, and even your voice to project the message you want to express and not the message you don't.

COMMUNICATION TIP

Remember, when your nonverbal message conflicts with your verbal message, your communication partner will believe the nonverbal message almost every time. Facial expressions, mannerisms, and the way you come across are all more powerful forms of communication than the words you choose.

Communicating with Facial Expressions

Look at the list of facial expressions in the left-hand column and compare them to the ones in the right-hand column:

Showing seriousness and respect	Boredom
Listening attentively	Hostility
Trying hard to understand	Disagreement

All of the facial expressions on the left can be misread as the facial expressions on the right. Additionally, when you feel physical discomfort, your face may show it. Your face may be saying, "I'm hungry" or "I'm sore from basketball," but your friend may think you're in a bad mood because of something he said. Our friends and other communication partners tend to personalize what they see. They usually feel that the look on your face is projecting your feelings about them and not your feelings about your empty stomach or aching muscles.

Keep in mind that you're either controlling the message your face is sending or your face is sending its own message—a message you aren't even aware of.

Being Intentional About Smiling

Our faces are never in neutral; they are sending messages to others every waking minute. Imagine that your face is a billboard. When you walk into a room, your face sends a message. The message your face sends might be one of the following:

- "Hello! I'm glad to see you!"
- "Oh, no, I'm dreading this conversation."
- "I'm feeling pretty sexy today."
- "I'm unworthy and feel I have nothing interesting or valuable to offer in this conversation."

There is never a time that your face is not sending a message. The safest facial expression is a smile. The smile is universally understood as a message of peace and agreement, and shows an eagerness to please and get along. Conversations will almost always go better if you begin by smiling.

You must put an enthusiastic, inviting, and confident look on your face. If you don't intentionally put a smiling expression on your face, an unfriendly or defeated look can take over without your realizing it. You wouldn't enter a room and say "I really wish I weren't here." But your face can send that same message, and even more dramatically. The nonverbal message on your face has the potential to hurt your image and the other person's feelings just as much or more than the verbal message.

People see a smile as your message that you like them and mean well. If you are not intentional about interjecting an occasional smile, people may read you as aloof, arrogant, hostile, unfriendly, or full of attitude. Therefore, make a point to smile at these key times:

- At the beginning and end of a conversation
- As you approach someone
- When you are listening to someone
- When you enter a room, especially if it is an event or gathering

COMMUNICATION TIP

You may think no one notices you, but you might be surprised. Just because no one comments on your expression doesn't mean they didn't read a message there—whether they read it correctly or incorrectly.

When people see you smile, they also think that your smile is all about them. They are much more motivated to offer you help or to accept even bad news if they feel you regard them highly as a person. Your facial expressions can help you convey that regard.

Smiles relax the face and actually influence how positively you communicate—even if you are faking it at first! A smile on your face actually improves the friendly tone of your voice, your stress level, and your attitude.

Develop These Three Smiles

Not all smiles are broad, toothy smiles; some are shy grins, some show contentment, and others are downright sexy. You should develop a variety of smiles to suit the occasion and the mood of the conversation.

For example, the *Mona Lisa smile*—named after the small, enigmatic smile in da Vinci's painting—is a barely perceptible smile for encouraging and supporting someone when a huge smile would be inappropriate. The Mona Lisa smile is also excellent for when you're listening and want to avoid a neutral expression; the Mona Lisa smile will help you look friendly and avoid an unconscious scowl.

The *amused smile*, on the other hand, gives your listener a knowing look that says that you get his point but the content of the conversation is not funny or sunny enough for a broad smile. This smile can be conspiratorial. Be careful, however, not to look seductive with this smile—unless that is your intention.

Then there is the *"Oh, I am so glad to see you" smile.* This look says that you are delighted to have the good fortune to run into one of your favorite people. You can also use this surprised smile when your partner says something interesting or revealing.

Pauline Phillips, better known as the advice columnist "Dear Abby," said, "There are two kinds of people in the world. Those who walk into a room and say, 'There you are' and those who say, 'Here I am.'" Be a "There you are" type of person with the third type of smile. Smile while looking deeply into your partner's eyes to say that you acknowledge his existence and are glad he is present. People warm to that type of welcome.

HOLD THAT THOUGHT

If you are not intentional about interjecting an occasional smile, people may read you as aloof, arrogant, hostile, unfriendly, or full of "attitude."

Smiles to Avoid

One reason to practice your smiles is that smiles can be interpreted wrongly by your conversation partner. Be sure that none of your smiles can be misinterpreted.

Be especially careful to avoid the *sneer.* This smile is lethal to friendships and conversation. The sneer occurs when you lift one part of your upper lip higher than the rest of the lip.

Similarly, the *sarcastic smile* may make you appear to be laughing *at* someone and not *with* them. The lips may be more pursed or twisted.

At rare times, you should avoid smiling at all. Funerals and job terminations come to mind. Use your judgment. Though most conversations will be improved by a smile, be sensitive to times when a smile will look out of place. If your partner is not smiling in a situation, you probably should not either.

The Genuine Smile

Smiles should gently appear on your face from time to time; don't smile so continuously that it appears to be a mask. Part of the charm of a smile is for your partner to see it breaking forth like the sun because of something he said or at the first sight of him. Use the smile like a punctuation mark, punctuating happy and interesting moments in the conversation.

The most basic smile means that you turn up the corners of your mouth. When you smile wholeheartedly or at someone you care about greatly, your eyes get more involved. The crinkles or crow's feet deepen at the outside corners of your eyes when you smile with your heart in it.

A genuine, wholehearted smile will break down communication barriers and make the other person want to accept your words more, and therefore accept *you* more. These smiles are highly effective in opening doors into people's lives, their circle of friends, and their businesses. A great smile is an asset in everything from flirting to interviewing.

Training Yourself to Smile

You may feel awkward smiling on purpose at first, and your first intentional smiles may not be your most successful. Do it anyway. Propose to smile before starting a conversation or before entering a party. This is a transformational habit that will improve your people skills greatly over time.

As the months go on, that smile you had to remind yourself to do will become natural. And you will notice something interesting: People will begin to smile at you more. They will like you more and respond to you better.

Colin's Story

Colin was often described as "too serious" by his peers. He didn't feel as much a part of the group as others at the large retailer where he worked. He wasn't invited to parties or lunches, and it hurt. A colleague gave him some great advice: "You have to be a friend to have a friend." The colleague suggested that he start by greeting each person he encountered at work with a friendly smile and a "good morning" or "hello." The colleague told Colin not to expect anything in return, but to be consistently friendly, even if others were not.

Colin decided that he had nothing to lose and began following this colleague's advice. At first, he felt awkward and believed his smile looked weird, but he made himself keep it up for six weeks. At the end of the first week, he was discouraged because he often received no smile in return. The strategy didn't appear to be working.

But at the end of six weeks, Colin noticed something different. When co-workers approached him, they began to smile sometimes before he did. They had a connection with him now because they knew he was going to smile at them, and that felt good to *them.*

As the awkwardness Colin felt began to melt away, people became more comfortable with him and began to invite him to coffee and lunch. In time, Colin developed a circle of work friends, and it all started with his smiling at them.

COMMUNICATION TIP

Smiles are reflective; if we smile at people, they tend to smile back, even if they don't have a rational reason for doing so. It is almost a reflex but is more closely described as reflective.

Like Colin, practice some everyday pleasant expressions for neighbors, people you meet at parties, and co-workers. Your smile will be twice as effective as the words you speak.

The Art of Looking Fascinated

Fascination as a facial expression is a powerhouse tool to have in your communication tool set. People would much rather have a friend who thinks they are fascinating than a friend who is fascinating. The look of fascination is like catnip, and people cannot get enough of those who have mastered this skill.

So how does one look fascinated? First, look into the other person's eyes as if looking for an answer there. Then very slightly cock your head as if you're carefully considering what the other person is saying. (Don't overdo this part.) Once in a while (not often), widen or narrow your eyes. These eye movements must be subtle and infrequent. When your conversation partner says something you can tell he thinks is interesting or surprising, widen your eyes in interest. When your partner says something that causes concern or provokes thought, narrow your eyes in concentration. And, as always, smile when appropriate.

Even though you're listening and not speaking, you have to show proof of engagement in the conversation, so some occasional eye movement or head movement will show that you find what your partner is saying compelling. How flattering! Everyone loves to feel as if he is the most interesting person in the room, and your face will confirm that your partner is just that.

Other Winning Facial Expressions

There are a couple other critical parts of facial expressions you should work on in order to better communicate with others.

First and foremost is eye contact. As discussed previously, eye contact is the single most influential part of your facial expression. Are you meeting someone for the first time? Look into his eyes. Are you trying to make a friend? Look into his eyes. Are you trying to convince someone to cooperate with you? Look into his eyes.

HOLD THAT THOUGHT

What does it mean if you don't establish eye contact? Some people think that if you can't meet their gaze, you are actually saying "I don't respect you," "I am lying or hiding something," "I don't like you," or "I have no confidence."

But now let's talk about eyebrows. Try the following exercise. Gaze into a mirror with a neutral expression on your face.

Now, raise one eyebrow. What message does that send? Suspicion? Arrogance? Negativity? Next, raise both eyebrows as high as you can. Is the message surprise? Excitement? Then lift your eyebrows ever so slightly. How does this message differ from the high-raised eyebrows?

You see that the emotions projected by raising one eyebrow are very different from the ones projected by raising both eyebrows. The intensity of the expression changes the message as well. Every part of your facial expression, from your smile, to your eyes, to your eyebrows, sends powerful messages.

COMMUNICATION TIP

In a *Los Angeles Times* article by Kathleen Kelleher, the "eyebrow flash" is described as shorthand for any number of nonverbal messages, adding emphasis like a facial exclamation point or question mark, according to psychologists, sociologists, and ethologists. Raised brows also are used to flirt; to express agreement, surprise, fear, disbelief or disapproval; and to send a silent greeting.

The "eyebrow flash" is another universal nonverbal form of communication. When you briefly raise both brows in eagerness or expectation while simultaneously showing a friendly look, you are silently trying to establish friendship or at least a pleasant basis for conversation. When someone gives you the eyebrow flash, it is important that you flash him back or you will appear unfriendly and unresponsive to an overture of friendship.

Only rare people like Michael Keaton or Jack Nicholson can make the eyebrow flash look intimidating or creepy—and they had to work at it. For most people, the eyebrow flash works as a move to break down communication barriers and to connect with others.

Be Observant of Others

Fred Leland, a trainer of law enforcement and security professionals, places great value on reading the body language of people suspected of crimes. He says in his blog series "Dangerous Body Language: A Thousand Words … None Spoken," "… the thousand-yard stare … may indicate aggression and gaze avoidance [may] indicate deception or avoidance. The face and eyes tell us the story if we are first observant."

Leland shows officers how to be more observant of the nonverbal messages suspects are showing rather than listening to their words, which may be deceptive, covering up true motives and facts.

Although you may not deal with criminals, all kinds of people hide their true feelings for a variety of reasons. Therefore, when you try to establish eye contact with your conversation partner and that person drops his eyes, you should ask the following questions:

- Does he feel intimidated? Does he lack confidence in general? Is he shy?
- Is there something he is hiding for my sake or his own?
- Is my timing off?

You may not know immediately why your conversation partner can't look you in the eye, but you should begin to observe or ask questions to find out. Finding out that your partner is simply shy will direct your behavior to being more encouraging and supportive. On the other hand, if your probing questions reveal discrepancies or deceptive behavior, you know you should be cautious about revealing information or sharing resources. This behavior may mean you need to be protective of yourself and establish boundaries rather than encourage further conversation.

COMMUNICATION TIP

According to the book *Communicating Globally: Intercultural Communication and International Business*, there are seven different nonverbal dimensions as identified by Judee Burgoon, Professor of Communication and Professor of Family Studies and Human Development at the University of Arizona: 1) kinesics, also known as body movements that include facial expressions and eye contact; 2) vocalics, or language that includes volume, rate, pitch, and timbre; 3) personal appearance; 4) your physical environment and the artifacts or objects that compose it; (5) proxemics, also known as personal space; (6) haptics, or touch; and (7) chronemics, or time.

The Least You Need to Know

- A smile tells others that you like their message and are engaged in the conversation.
- Your face is never in neutral. Be sure your facial expressions match your words.
- Like any skill, great nonverbal behavior takes lots of practice.
- Reading others' nonverbals is as important as controlling your own nonverbals.

CHAPTER

6

Other Nonverbal Ways You Communicate

In This Chapter

- How to enter a room with presence and energy
- Mien, posture, and head motion: what it means to hold yourself distinctively
- How to use gestures that are engaging and not distracting
- Becoming aware of hidden messages
- Using electronics while you interact with people
- How to conduct a nonverbal assessment

Everyone has seen T-shirts and bumper stickers that feature a message the wearer or driver wants you to know about who she is. These messages may announce a hobby ("I love fly-fishing"), a lifestyle ("It *is* easy being green"), a philosophy ("Coexist"), a personality trait ("To know me is to love me"), or some happy news ("Just married").

Not only do your facial expressions send messages, but many other nonverbal factors send messages as well. You want to make sure the messages are positive. This chapter shows you how to send the nonverbal message you want to send and to project a more confident and winsome image.

Energy and Presence: How to Enter a Room

Like those T-shirts and bumper stickers, when you enter a room you also send a message before you even say a word. Pause for a moment and think about that. Just the way you walk into a room sends a message. When you're about to enter a party, a classroom, a meeting, or any other gathering, imagine you're wearing a T-shirt printed with the message you want to send. Think of the last time you entered a room full of people. What would your T-shirt have said if words could capture how you looked that day? Would it have said any of the following?

- I am excited about seeing you and you and you, and this is going to be a great experience for all of us!
- I am wilting with lack of confidence and am, therefore, miserable. I will probably make you miserable, too.
- I am probably the smartest person in the room.
- I feel a connection to you and am looking forward to this time so I can get to know you better.
- I am worried about something.
- I am critical and do not approve of something I am seeing or experiencing at this event.
- I am an angry or troubled person.
- I am desperate for approval.
- You are lucky I graced this event with my presence.

You may not have said any of these words out loud, but you may have said them nonverbally.

One factor that influences what others think of you is the energy you project. When you enter a room with a great deal of energy, there is an excitement you bring with you and the vibe is very positive. People feel an air of anticipation when you enter the room in a high-energy way. They think that good conversation and enjoyable times will follow and are therefore drawn to you.

COMMUNICATION TIP

Do you look energetic and lively? The signs of a high-energy person include a fast pace, animated facial expressions, use of hand gestures during conversation, body language that "leans in," and frequent head nods and inclines.

When you enter a room with low energy, people may feel that you are depressed or even that you feel negatively about them. They avoid negativity and therefore avoid you. Even high-energy people report that low-energy people seem to drain the energy from the room with their presence. Even if you have much to say and an interesting way of saying it, if your energy is low, people will disengage with you fairly quickly.

So what are the attributes of high energy?

- The movements of your hands, arms, and legs are a bit faster, with more frequent gestures and an animated body language. However, these gestures and movements are not distracting.
- You take the lead and engage with people by walking up to them rather than waiting for them to approach you; you do not hang back. Not only are you approachable, you approach others in a lively and cordial manner.
- Your voice is not too loud but it is definitely not soft. There is a lilt to your voice and your speaking pace is slightly faster than average.
- You connect with more people per hour than lower-energy people. You don't latch on to one person at a party but you engage for a while and then move on to greet more people.

Even lower-energy people will want to talk to you because there is something lively and magnetic in your demeanor. You are sending out all the right signals that you are there to connect and engage with as many people as possible, even them! This high-energy style makes it easier for people with low confidence to converse with you since they feel you will carry more than half the load of the conversation. You are willing to put the work and the energy into a good conversation. You are open and enthusiastic.

Posture and Mien

Many people will judge your attitude by your posture. Though that is not rational, it is true. In this case, your mother was right when she harped on good posture because it makes a statement about you. Some people even see a slouching posture as sending this message:

> I have an attitude and not a good one.
>
> I don't care about anything or what you think of me.
>
> I am lazy.
>
> I am untrustworthy.

This same group of people (and it is a large section of the population) think the following when they see you standing tall with excellent posture and a regal bearing:

> Now, that is a leader.
>
> You can count on this person to do the right thing.
>
> That person has the character and the training to make this project or event successful.

Developing an engaging *mien,* or overall impression of who you are, starts with this work on your posture. By working on your posture, you affect the way you carry yourself and the aura you give off to others.

DEFINITION

Mien is a composition of personality, confidence level, presence, and posture. Do you walk into a room as if you know everyone is glad to see you? That way of bearing yourself is different from someone whose mien shows lack of confidence or negativity.

Dillon's Story

Dillon was a young man of great character. His natural integrity was well known in the small community in rural Ohio where he grew up. When he was 18, however, he left home to go to a large state university. No one there knew him. Everyone he met, from professors to students, sized him up. Dillon did well in forming relationships with his peers and his social life went well from the beginning. His experience in the classroom was not as successful, however. His professors did not seem to like him. Dillon didn't realize that his slouching posture and his habit of hunching over his desk were creating a negative opinion of him in some of his professors' eyes.

When Dillon's English professor saw him with one hip slung out and standing in a lazy posture, she thought Dillon had an attitude problem. She was not as friendly to him when he asked questions as she was to some of the other students and he could not understand why. The same posture made his history professor think he was lazy, so when he graded Dillon's first paper he looked with more scrutiny for any shortcuts. The math professor wondered if the way Dillon draped his upper body far over the desk was part of a strategy to hide answers and cheat.

Naturally, in time Dillon proved himself and won the respect of his professors, but it took longer than it needed to. So as you can see, great posture and the way you carry yourself can make better first impressions, and better first impressions make the rest of a relationship go easier.

Developing Your Posture

So how do you develop the posture and bearing that inspires admiration and confidence? Whatever you do, don't throw your shoulders back in an awkward and uncomfortable stance. You will look pained and unpleasant.

Instead, use the technique of leveling. Every part of your body should be level. Your left shoulder should be level with your right shoulder; your left hip should be level with the right hip. If you're standing, your left knee should be level with your right knee.

Have doubts? Try this experiment. Stand with your hips, knees, and shoulders level. Now bend one knee and make one hip go higher than the other hip. What message might the person opposite you think this stance sends?

I am bored.

I have an attitude problem.

I am disrespectful.

Whatever.

The following are other posture problems that may send a message you never meant to send:

- Stooped shoulders may say, "I lack confidence."
- Overly stiff posture with shoulders thrown too far back may say, "I am trying too hard because I want to hide my deficiencies."
- Crossed feet while standing may send the message, "I am young or inexperienced or think I am cute or am trying to be sexy, but I am not the poised person I want to be."
- A body hunched inward says, "I want to be as small as I can and would even disappear if I could because I feel unworthy."

HOLD THAT THOUGHT

Unfortunately, most people think they are excellent judges of other people. Many will even say they know instantly if they like someone or not.

It's important to stand in a straight but relaxed posture with a confident manner in order to let people know you're a person with assets to offer in a conversation or relationship.

How Head Motion and Tilting Send a Message

Have you ever been driving in traffic and realized that the couple in front of you is having an argument? You may not be able to see their eyes or mouths, but you can see the backs of their heads. Just from the head motion, you can read their anger. The male may lean in aggressively and invade the space of his partner. The female may jerk her head in short, staccato movements that punctuate each sharp remark she makes. Even without facial expressions, you can read an underlying message into their movements.

To a lesser degree, subtle motions of your head can enhance or detract from your spoken message. If you're truly engaged in great conversation, there should be some head motion.

When you're engaged in conversation with someone, don't forget to slightly tilt your head from time to time. Even animals cock their heads when they pick up on a noise that interests them or the voice of someone they love. Similarly, people who are genuinely interested in listening to a story or conversation naturally tilt their heads. They don't sit there with a perfectly still head throughout several minutes of conversation. Nodding "yes," shaking your head "no," and tilting your head are some basic starter moves for sending the positive message you want to send.

Try this experiment. Stand far back from two people who seem to genuinely enjoy and admire one another and who love to talk to each other. Observe them as if you are a scientist watching animals in the wild. Watch their heads move slightly throughout the conversation; the head tilt will happen naturally. Be intentional about emulating these head motions when listening to others.

HOLD THAT THOUGHT

Don't overdo the head tilt or you will look uncomfortable or fake. The subtle nuance of this head tilt is important, as is changing positions occasionally.

Be sure to nod from time to time, but not continually. If the other person makes a statement that requires a negative response, turn your head left to right. For example, if your partner says, "Of course, we would never mean to overload the circuit and leave the entire block without electricity," your shaking head affirms that you know she would *never* do this intentionally.

Hand Gestures That Engage, Not Distract

Hand gestures can be small or large, depending on the circumstances.

When you are seated at a table, your hands will be folded and resting most of the time. A little hand movement is good to show energy, but too much is distracting. Keep movements confined to a very small space directly in front of you. Only occasionally move your hands when you're in a seated conversation.

When standing, you should gesture more. Still, keep gestures close to your body and around your ribcage zone. You must find a good balance for how many gestures to use. A lack of gestures makes you look like a wooden soldier, whereas too many gestures make you look out of control. You may appear to be making a dramatic dance move!

Ask your friends and family to let you know if you have any distracting gestures. You can also practice some basic gestures and find the ones you're comfortable with. If you're asking someone for their opinion or support, you can turn your palms up. If you want to say "never," you can cross your hands back and forth subtly, the way an umpire calls someone safe. Do this gesture very gently and reserve it for noncontroversial topics. For example, you could use this gesture if you were saying, "We finished moving all of our furniture into our new house and are finished at the apartment. We will never have to go back again!"

HOLD THAT THOUGHT

Be careful not to use some gestures. In general, avoid pointing. Also, don't tap a table with your index finger as it appears you are being demanding.

Hidden Messages You May Be Sending

Joyce Johnson is a fashionable, fun, and active woman in her seventies. She decided to treat herself to a really sporty SUV. She felt so young and energized driving it—until one day when she had to pick up her 4-year-old granddaughter from school. The little girl had to stand in the carpool line for a long time and watch as her grandmother's car and all the cars of the young moms picking up their children filed slowly to the curb. When it was finally time for the little girl to get into the car, she got in but didn't say much. A few miles down the road, she told Joyce, "Memom, you aren't 'spose to have a car like this 'cause you don't have the right kind of face!"

"What kind of face am I supposed to have?" asked Joyce.

"You 'spose to have a mommy face … and your face does not look like my mommy!"

Even at 4, she knew that the 20- and 30-something moms who usually drove sporty SUVs did not have faces that looked like a grandmother's! Despite our heart's intentions, we start developing expectations and stereotypes at a very young age.

Factors such as age, relationships, emotions, and much more color the way people perceive us, view our actions, and receive our spoken words. In turn, your perceptions and belief about someone's age, gender, or other factors may cause you not to connect with some people.

The safest strategy is to observe your conversation partner for clues about their preferences. When you communicate in a style that your partner demonstrates, you will be on safe ground. Because your style matches her style, she will feel more comfortable, even if there are differences in age, gender, or other aspects. That way, everything "matches" according to your listener's expectations.

Mirroring

If you're interviewing for a start-up high-tech company, you might dress differently than if you were interviewing for IBM or Delta Airlines. In other words, you want to mirror the style of dress most accepted by the employer. Dress is just one nonverbal factor that can be *mirrored.*

DEFINITION

To **mirror** is to reflect, represent, or depict faithfully. Just as a mirror reflects what it sees in a person, you should adapt your communication to reflect what you see in our partner. Mirroring is like dancing. You have to change your rate and style of movements to adapt to those of your partner.

Picking up on cues regarding what your listener wants helps you tailor your way of responding. If you're speaking with someone who is very high-energy and excited, you should sound more excited and be more energetic in your body language. In this case, you are mirroring voice tone and rate.

If you're speaking with someone who is more laid back, very still, and self-contained, rein in your gestures and body movement more—in other words, mirror her movements.

For example, I recently was hired by a company to coach a talented professional who had been passed over several times for promotions even though he was the most qualified person. I asked him to get feedback from the last couple of people who declined to hire him. It turns out that he was working in a very staid and quiet corporate culture. He was so high-energy and aggressive about how much he wanted the job that he was overpowering the quiet, almost timid managers. One person who attended the interviews said, "Andy, you're scaring people."

Every word he had said was perfect; it was his manner that put them off. Andy should have taken into consideration the culture he was in. That was a hidden factor that influenced the expectations of the people he was conversing with. They were expecting a quieter demeanor that reflected the culture they were accustomed to. Andy disregarded the cultural context.

You know how you feel when someone "comes at you." Don't be too aggressive. Like the way a car salesman approaches as soon as people enter a car lot and throws one reason after another at them why they should buy, you could potentially make people back off and get some space—even if they're interested in what you're "selling." Be sensitive to the style of the other person. It's all about being assertive, not aggressive.

Other Nonverbal Factors

Many other nonverbal factors are operating while you hold a conversation.

Consider emotion. When you enter a conversation with a strong emotion such as anger or love, it will color and influence your words and how they are received by your conversation partner. Partners sense the emotion you bring, even when the feelings are subtle. Be sure to get your emotions under control before you enter a conversation. Be aware of how your emotions can prejudice what you say and hear, either in favor of the speaker or against her.

You should also consider the history you have with your conversation partner. Have you had similar conversations in the past? If you have, you may have a bias about what you think will be said and thought by your partner. Has this topic come up before? All past exchanges of information will be a hidden context for this conversation.

I mentioned corporate culture earlier, but social culture is important to consider, too. If you're dealing with someone whose culture you have reason to believe is quite different from yours, take that into consideration. If you're dealing with a person of the opposite sex, you may have to factor in different cultural views of gender (see Chapter 19 for more on this subject). If you have strong religious beliefs or if your partner does, and they differ, these beliefs can color your conversational experience.

Similarly, deal with your expectations and try to sense those of your partner. Without realizing it, we usually bring some expectations to any conversation we begin. We often make wrong assumptions. This element is perhaps the most dangerous of all. When you or your partner enters a conversation with definite expectations, then the conversation can become uncomfortable if the expectations are not met or are not met fully. For important conversations, be sure to establish the expectations. Let your partner know if a conversation about a problem is just to define the issues. Otherwise, the partner may be disappointed in the progress made to define a problem when his expectation was that the problem would be solved at the end of the meeting.

We mentioned dressing appropriately earlier in this chapter. But grooming also plays a role in the success or failure of a conversation. If your hair or nails are not groomed, some people will disrespect what you have to say.

COMMUNICATION TIP

Some listeners just can't get past physical appearance. Although this factor seems irrational to some, it is a very real barrier to connecting with many people.

Similarly, some people almost shut down if you are standing too close or too far away as you communicate. They are uncomfortable unless you respect their space or "zones." The following are some general zones people tend to have:

- **Public zone (12 feet):** What most people are in when they are walking down the street
- **Social zone (4 to 12 feet):** Close enough to talk to someone without shouting but far enough to feel safe
- **Personal zone (1 to 4 feet):** Allows people to focus on the person in front of them
- **Intimate zone (0 to 1 foot):** Reserved for people they have a lot of trust in

Keep in mind, this is a general guideline. In the end, you should take your cues from your partner. If she is inching backward occasionally, you may need to give him more space. If she seems to be inching toward you, she may be the type of person who feels that the best conversations are up close and personal. You may need to stand a bit closer than is ordinarily comfortable for you, but your listener will feel you are more engaged.

COMMUNICATION TIP

Sheryl Sandberg, former CEO of Facebook, encourages communicators to lean in. These words can mean intentionality and self-advocacy, but they can also mean to literally lean in to a conversation—that is, to lean in slightly toward the speaker.

Being Present

Be sure to be present in any conversation you participate in. Sometimes, we're tempted to be unengaged and just let a conversation run its course. In most conversations, try to use active listening and look responsive to your partner's input. Don't hang back, literally or figuratively. Be there. Be a fully committed conversation partner. You may be surprised at the value you take away from all kinds of conversations you might ordinarily have been tempted to "check out of" mentally.

People usually sense when we are vacant intellectually and emotionally, so you need to work at being engaged.

For example, Thanh had a problem connecting with people, but she did not know why. Her main problem was a very weak presence, but not knowing about this issue cost her relationships and greater satisfaction from her work life. Thanh had been raised to be very quiet and not to promote herself and her interests strongly. She took that too far and did not project herself, her opinions, her feelings, or her desires very much at all. She withheld these things from colleagues and acquaintances. They felt she was aloof and did not want to connect. On the contrary, Thanh was waiting for someone to draw her out. Unfortunately, most people will never take the time. Most people are waiting for the other person to make the first move.

Della worked as a corporate trainer at a large accounting firm where Thanh also worked as an accountant. The company had very few professional women. Because Della wanted to have a work friend to go to lunch with and to perhaps share office gossip with, she was always looking for someone who seemed a good match for her—someone young and single and preferably female. Whenever Della would attend or lead an orientation seminar or her professionalism seminar, she would try to identify someone who would be fun to hang out with. Thanh had been in both of her classes in the past and Della would have loved to have begun a friendship with her. Thanh, however, never responded. In class, when Della opened a topic up for discussion, Thanh would never participate. She looked at Della with a completely blank face and never returned her smile.

In time, Della was offered a better job with another company in another state. About a month after she moved, she was surprised to receive an invitation from Thanh to connect on LinkedIn. They began to email and text and became long-distance friends.

Della finally asked Thanh, "I didn't think you liked me. You never seemed that impressed or engaged with me when you were in my classes."

Thanh explained that she came from a culture that respected teachers greatly. They did not ask questions in class or take the floor. They let the teacher always have the floor as she is the acknowledged expert.

Della regretted that she did not know this sooner. She could have started her friendship with Thanh while they were in the same state!

Thanh had just not seemed to be engaged or present. Thanh was actually very lonely and desired friendship as much as Della did. Thanh needed to demonstrate nonverbally that she was engaged by smiling more and asking questions. Just as Della should have learned more about Thanh's cultural background, Thanh should have learned to adapt to her current corporate culture.

Electronics vs. People

It goes without saying that incoming texts, tweets, and calls prevent you from fully engaging in productive conversations. The most important person is the person you are face-to-face with, not the person trying to send you a message electronically.

COMMUNICATION TIP

For important conversations, turn electronics completely off. If you have limited time with someone or have had a hard time scheduling a lunch with her, consider not giving up that valuable face time to check incoming messages. Most incoming messages can wait an hour.

Even the buzzing of a vibrating phone is distracting to those around you. Many people will not tell you that they are offended as you check to see who is calling or glance at the occasional text, but they are. The rule is that the more you respect someone, the less you check your electronic messages. For example, if the president asked you to visit the Oval Office, would you keep checking your texts during your presidential visit? I hope not. People want that kind of respect. And the people we break this rule most with are the people closest to us. When they are trying to tell us something that is important to them, step away from the phone.

Asking for a Nonverbal Assessment

It's hard to be impartial when judging your own nonverbal quirks and bad habits, especially when you aren't the one seeing them. Therefore, it's important to bring in others who do get to see them pretty frequently, such as your friends and family, to help you improve your nonverbals. For example, you can ask four or five people who see you regularly or know you well to help you. Tell them you're working on improving your facial expressions. Ask if there are situations when you sometimes give a blank look, a negative look, or other nonverbal that could be improved. Do they ever have trouble "reading you" based on your nonverbals? What are some recommendations they could give you? Do they think you should smile more?

You can also ask a friend if you can video yourself as you have a conversation with her. Most phones and tablets today have excellent recording capabilities. Set the phone on a stack of books or other materials so that you capture your facial expressions only. You want a good look at your face as you talk. When you replay your video, do you look fascinated by what your friend is saying? If not, determine to work on your facial expressions using the tools and tips I discussed earlier.

The Least You Need to Know

- Slouching makes some people think you are lazy or untrustworthy.
- Slightly tilting your head occasionally indicates that you are interested in the other person's remarks.
- Respect people's "zones" or the amount of space they need when communicating.
- Be present emotionally and intellectually and engage with your partner.
- For an important conversation or appointment, power off any phone or electronic device.
- Ask a friend to video you in natural conversation and watch yourself for an instant lesson on nonverbal communication.

CHAPTER

7

Why Tone of Voice Matters

The tone of your voice can completely change the meaning of whatever you are saying. Sweet tones, harsh tones, sexy tones, or weak tones convey a message parallel to your words and sometimes have far more meaning. Similarly, the inflection of your voice can change your meaning. If you say to someone, "I guess you were right," you can sound admiring, sarcastic, or resentful, depending on how you say it.

This chapter covers the nuances of the voice and helps you use your voice to engage people in a more pleasant and attractive way. You will learn to identify speech habits that may be annoying to listeners and ways to correct those habits. Your voice is a powerful tool. Don't neglect to develop this part of your communication skills.

In This Chapter

- How your tone of voice affects your communication success
- The importance of enunciation and pronunciation
- Developing a voice that sounds engaged and interested
- Voice habits you should avoid
- How to improve your voice

Don't Take That Tone!

Have you ever observed a young child who has been told to apologize to a friend? A child may say "I'm sorry," but his tone may make it perfectly clear that he is being forced to say the words. The child will still convey his resentment or his lack of sincerity in delivering the apology through the *tone* of his voice. The tone trumps the actual words as no one, especially not the recipient of the apology, misses the fact that the child is not genuinely sorry.

DEFINITION

Tone is a quality or character of sound. It is the modulation or intonation of the voice as expressive of some meaning, feeling, or spirit.

Likewise, tone of voice is the cause of many conflicts between adult communicators. Like other nonverbals, tone of voice is unreliable and open to interpretation.

Ria and Molly's Story

A haughty or negative tone of voice can destroy the good will the words should have conveyed.

Ria, 25, and Molly, 27, work in the same office. Ria is extremely gifted in using technology and is an innovator. Molly has been the star employee in the office for two years, but now she is sharing the spotlight with Ria. Often, when Ria has a new idea, Molly will shoot her idea down. Molly prefaces her negative comment with the word "dear," said in a condescending tone. She will say, "Dear, we don't do it that way in Corporate." Aside from the fact that you should not call anyone "dear" in the workplace, the real venom in Molly's message is conveyed in the demeaning tone she uses when she says "dear."

Another word Molly completely changes with her tone of voice is the word "really." She imbues this word with so much doubt and sarcasm that she can shake Ria's confidence with just one word. For example, Ria recently came into the office and said, "I've found a way we can all attend the upcoming meeting at the same time. The employees who need to stay in their cubicles and attend to the phones can view the meeting through videoconferencing." Molly looked at her and said, "Reeeaaally?" This word was so laden with skepticism and negativity that Ria immediately knew that Molly was opposed to the idea. Molly's words had not conveyed her opposition, but her tone certainly had.

Afta's Story

But it's not just a speaker's use of the wrong tone that can be a problem; the receiver of the communication is capable of hearing sarcasm or resentment where none may be intended. If a receiver lacks confidence, he may not believe a compliment and instead think the sender is mocking him.

For example, Afta is a very self-conscious young woman. Even when people like her and support her, she often reads negative motives into their words—motives that simply are not there. Recently, Afta's neighbor said to her, "You certainly chose a cheerful color to paint your house."

For the rest of the afternoon, Afta wondered, "Did she mean what she said? Was she trying to tell me the color is too cheerful and even loud? Was she saying that the old color was really ugly and that I was overdue to paint my house?" None of these negative thoughts were intended by the neighbor. Afta is just prone to believing people disapprove of her. This thinking colors everything she hears and is an impediment to her making friends and being happy.

COMMUNICATION TIP

A voice that thins out and becomes squeakier than usual is conveying stress. A voice that is excited may go higher in pitch as well. A voice that grows huskier may be showing deep emotion.

Inflection and Volume

If you don't believe that your voice is part of your image in the eyes of others, think about how the voices of some celebrities help define their images. Gilbert Gottfried is a comedian who is considered funny primarily for his harsh and whiney voice. Marilyn Monroe was considered ultra-feminine for her extremely soft and breathy voice. James Earl Jones's voice was so commanding that he became more famous for his role as the voice of Darth Vader than for any other role. The famous actress from the 1930s, Mae West, and her sometimes co-star, W. C. Fields, are still parodied today for their distinctive inflections, especially when conveying sexual innuendo. When companies select actors as spokespersons, they choose men and women with deeper and more authoritative voices. Go online and listen to some of these voices to get a feel for what voice tone can do for your personal power—or not. You'll find many differences not only in tone, but in inflection.

Inflection is part of the nuance of meaning in your tone of voice. For example, take the statement "I guess you were right." If you emphasize a different word each time you say it, you get a different meaning entirely:

- If you emphasize "guess," it can sound as if you're unsure of your statement or even what your partner said.
- If you emphasize "you," it sounds as if you're saying that your partner was right instead of you.

- If you emphasize "were," you firmly place the event in the past tense, which may suggest that at present your partner may not be quite as "right."

As you can see, inflection is the way many people insinuate meaning into a conversation beyond the spoken words. That's why you should be sure to use a positive tone; otherwise, some people may read negative innuendo into your voice.

Other factors that can influence your message are volume, huskiness, and mellowness. Speaking loudly can make someone feel yelled at. If you have even the slightest hearing impairment, your voice may be louder than other people's voices. Constantly speaking in a loud voice may make people think you're trying to draw attention to yourself or are bullying them. You may come from a family or a region of the country where the norm is to speak in a loud voice. When you move or are around people whose culture encouraged them to speak softly, your volume puts them off and causes them to back away—literally and figuratively.

HOLD THAT THOUGHT

Even simple statements such as "You're next" or "May I help you?" can sound impatient if said loudly. Conversely, the same words can sound solicitous, caring, helpful, and polite if said softly.

A voice that is too quiet and soft, however, can present a different set of problems. If you speak so quietly that people have trouble hearing you, you send a message that you lack confidence and may not feel worthy of being listened to. If you think this habit is coy and charming, think again. Note whether people are constantly asking you to repeat yourself. If so, be courteous enough to speak a bit more loudly.

Volume is not the only indicator of stress or other problems. If your voice is so tight that you sound strangled, your listener will know something is wrong even if your words are "Everything is fine." These same words said in a very clipped way can also make you sound as if things are far from fine. Quite often, when people are angry or fearful, they will bite off the ends of their words very sharply, and their sentences will have a staccato sound. Listeners may not know exactly what is wrong but they do know the speaker is not relaxed and confident.

Enunciation vs. Pronunciation

These two terms probably bring back memories of English class. Whether you were learning how to sound out words or being made to give speeches to the class, you got a lesson not only in how to pronounce and enunciate words, but also in how to communicate with others. But what's the difference between them, and how can they help your people skills?

Pronouncing Words

Pronunciation can be very telling. If you pronounce words incorrectly, others may think less of your experience, education, or sophistication. This may not be right, but it is a common occurrence. For example, students in business school find it humorous when less sophisticated students pronounce the "Ernst" in Ernst & Young as the two-syllable word "earnest." This mispronunciation could be very costly if someone were judging a young accounting student's business savvy in a job interview.

Naturally, you should be sure to pronounce your words correctly. Pay extra attention to pronouncing names of people you meet correctly, as some individuals are offended if you mispronounce their names. If you continue to mispronounce someone's name repeatedly, you may be perceived as disrespectful and rude.

Enunciating Words

Just as important as pronunciation is enunciation. Being attentive to sharply pronouncing your words, especially the consonants, is key to good enunciation.

Crisply enunciating the first and last sound in a word improves your communication skills. The opposite of good enunciation is mumbling. Many people have an aversion to mumbling. Some perceive that mumbling is a way of being evasive and less straightforward. Good enunciation is similar to good eye contact. This skill will help you come across as honest, direct, and confident.

For instance, Lianna took a job as an administrative assistant. Her word processing skills were excellent and she had an impressive résumé. She almost lost her new job, however, due to her habit of mumbling. When she was hired as the assistant to a top executive, Lianna had at first felt excited; however, she quickly began to feel panicky. She had worked for a lower-level supervisor and now felt she was in over her head working at such a high level. She was fearful she would say the wrong thing or have the wrong answer. When her new boss asked her something, she would mumble and talk softly. She would not strongly assert her information for fear she might be wrong and look foolish; her mumbling was her way of hedging her answers. It drove her boss crazy. He had to ask Lianna to repeat many things she said. She felt Lianna was balky, uncooperative, and disrespectful. As the boss became more annoyed, Lianna became even less confident and her voice became weaker and weaker.

Fortunately, the executive brought Lianna in for a developmental session that began with questions about the issue instead of accusations. Once the problem was on the table, the boss gave Lianna 30 days to make mistakes with no repercussions. With the fear factor gone, Lianna felt empowered to speak up. Both the boss and Lianna felt the next 30 days were a success.

In the case of Lianna, learning to enunciate helped her confidence and improved others' impressions of her.

Speaking to People with Hearing Loss

Pronunciation and enunciation is not just about sounding better; it's also about being clearer, particularly if you're speaking to someone who can't hear very well. More people than you realize have minor degrees of hearing loss. No one knows why hearing loss is on the rise, but some attribute it to loud music and monster speakers that create greater vibrations on the eardrums. Whatever the reason, be aware that some people's hearing is not as good as yours. Many people don't want to admit that they can't hear something. Pay attention to clues as people ask you to repeat things. Some will not ask you to repeat, so you will have to observe whether they are missing parts of the conversation. People with nerve-damage hearing loss will hear volume fine but will not distinguish some of your words. These people may honestly feel that you are mumbling.

If anyone has ever suggested that you speak up or stop mumbling, work on your enunciation. When you speak, open your mouth more widely and be conscious of carefully pronouncing every word. The epidemic of minor hearing loss is just one more reason to articulate and enunciate clearly.

Smiling and Conveying a Pleasant Tone

What are some things you can do to make sure your voice is as winning as your words? Make sure you sound engaged, enthused, and interested.

One way to do this is to smile before you answer a phone or enter a conversation. Yes, a smile has been proven to change your voice quality. Even during a phone conversation, when the person you're calling can't see you smile, he can hear your smile in your voice—really! And a smiling person entering a room is perceived positively from the beginning as friendly and confident. So before you step into a room or pick up the phone, smile!

COMMUNICATION TIP

In his book *All Too Human*, Friedrich Nietzsche wrote, "We often contradict an opinion for no other reason than that we do not like the tone in which it was expressed."

You can also improve how you're received by planning the first and last words of a conversation, particularly a phone conversation. I stress phone conversations because the listener can't see your face and gain a better understanding of your emotions and intent. No matter the case, though, your voice must sound upbeat and pleasant from the start of the conversation in order to set the positive context for your verbal message. To do this, think of something pleasant to say beforehand. For example, ask about an event the listener attended or something he mentioned the last time you spoke. Choose a friendly topic and make your voice friendly.

Energy and Pauses

Voice energy is a huge component of a winning tone and makes people think you are interesting. You must sound lively and enthusiastic if you want people to find you interesting. People are drawn to those who radiate energy, not those who drain it. If your voice sounds alert, strong, and peppy, you will be more attractive to people, and more people will want to be around you. If you sound draggy, like Eeyore in the *Winnie the Pooh* books, most people will feel you are a downer and avoid you.

Draggy and depressed Lacks energy Perfect voice tone Energetic Lively and enthused Fast talker
0............1............2..............3.............4..............5................6...............7................8................9..............10

Voice speed can convey anything from high energy and enthusiasm to disinterest and depression. On this scale, aim for a high score but stop just short of seeming like a fast talker.

You want to have a pace that is energetic, but you don't want to be a fast talker. You can control your speed through the use of pauses.

HOLD THAT THOUGHT

Talking too fast brings problems of its own. People don't trust fast talkers. Often, there is a subliminal feeling that someone who is talking too fast may be hiding something. The stereotype of a fast-talking salesman portrays a less-than-honest persona. People who talk too fast may also be perceived as lacking confidence. There is a style of talking too fast that says, "I know you don't want to listen to me, so I will cram all my words into this little space and get it over with really quickly so you won't have to listen to me because I am not valuable enough to listen to." Don't be one of those people.

When it comes to pauses, they can be as powerful as words in a conversation. Be sure to pause at key times to punctuate your conversation the same way you would punctuate an email or letter. When speaking, imagine where the commas and periods would be and pause briefly in those spots. If you want to emphasize a point or be more dramatic when you're about to tell the exciting part of a story, pause just before you get to that point. Great conversationalists don't speak nonstop. They understand how to use a pause for great effect.

Another technique for improving your tone is to learn from great role models. If you know someone who has a pleasing tone, practice imitating their inflection and *lilt*. Consider leaders, teachers, politicians, and other people you have known who have voices you love to listen to.

You can also listen to audio or ebooks to hear examples of great inflection and tone from professionals. Some voices have distinctive tones that convey joy, dignity, power, or humor. Find a style you admire and try to emulate it. You don't want to sound exactly like another person, but you do want to give your voice greater variety. A voice that offers highs and lows, soft moments and louder moments, and other variations is much more interesting to listen to than a monotone.

DEFINITION

A **lilt** is a rhythmic swing or cadence in a person's speech.

Voice Habits to Avoid

In general, lower voice tones carry more authority. For that reason, women who want to establish authority should avoid what is sometimes called the *little girl voice.* For some reason, some highly intelligent and confident women will adopt some of the cadences and tonal qualities of a child. Although this can be overcome by demonstrating competence over a long period of time, this type of voice can delay the respect and cooperation due a female professional.

Similarly, what is called *valley voice* can also diminish the perceived power of a male or female. The key indicator of valley voice is that the speaker makes a declarative statement, but his voice rises at the end as if asking a question. So the speaker would say, "So my team and I are going to Los Angeles?" This should be a statement with a period, but valley voice makes it sound like a question.

As I have discussed, for both males and females, a soft voice can diminish your power if you need to sound confident and authoritative. Soft and quiet voices can, however, be assets in handling conflict or in meeting people under difficult circumstances.

So when it comes to tone, play your voice like an instrument. Lower your voice and speak firmly when you want to establish power and authority. Soften and quieten your voice if you want to sound more agreeable. Whatever you do, remember that the tone of your voice is part of your verbal message.

Another speech habit that annoys listeners and diminishes credibility is the *uhs* and *ums* people use as fillers in conversation. When speakers pause slightly to think of the next word or to focus their thoughts, they often say "uh." That doesn't sound particularly intelligent, does it? This habit is so annoying that some people actually count the number of times they hear them in speeches and conversations. This not-very-nice behavior is a clue to how distracting this seemingly harmless habit can be with some listeners.

COMMUNICATION TIP

Voice rest is the remedy most doctors recommend for a strained voice, but other remedies may help as well. Tea and honey, sometimes with a bit of lemon, is said to soothe a scratchy throat. Many over-the-counter lozenges can also aid in restoring your voice before an event where you know you will be expected to hold a conversation or talk to many people.

If your confidence is low because you aren't familiar with the topic or the person you're speaking to, you may hear yourself saying more than your usual number of *uhs*. In prepared speeches, the solution to get rid of *uhs* is to practice. That is not always possible in conversation. Instead, try to discipline yourself with another method. Every time you start to say "uh," pause instead. Because these subvocal sounds are just fillers, allow yourself to just wait and not fill that empty space.

Other annoying fillers are "you know" and "like." Both of these speech habits diminish your image as a confident and articulate conversationalist. Work toward eliminating them from your speech. Invite friends to give you a signal every time you say one of these fillers. Reward yourself when you go a day or a half day without saying one. These habits are deeply ingrained and will not disappear overnight. Give yourself plenty of time and don't become discouraged. Remember, just being conscious of your habits is the most important step to improving.

Bringing It All Together

In the end, these tips and tricks I've shared are about making your voice even more appealing. But how can you bring everything together to get the most out of your voice?

Your voice is an instrument you learn to play by ear. That's why finding a role model, like I discussed earlier, is so important. It's key to focus on a voice you find attractive and appropriate for your gender and age; after all, you shouldn't be trying to aim for a really deep and aged voice when you naturally have a higher and younger-sounding voice.

When you listen to the voice role model, try to repeat whatever he says and copy his timing and pauses. This way, you can add variety to your voice based on a voice that's similar to yours without sounding awkward. For example, when your role model's pitch is higher, make sure yours is higher on the same syllables. You can also listen for the moments when the voice model's voice becomes lower and huskier. These differences will teach you to make your tone softer and more lilting at times, excited and more intense at others. When it comes to tone, you can listen for how the role model says *o, a,* and *e* and imitate that.

If you have problems with an accent or pronunciation, you can even use the model to help you overcome any habits. Be sure to pronounce the endings of your words exactly as your model does. Other problem spots to look for are the letters *s*, *r*, and *t*.

COMMUNICATION TIP

Practicing to sound like someone you admire will gradually affect the way you sound. You won't sound exactly like your model at first, but you will improve.

But don't let an accent, such as a regional accent, make you self-conscious; you don't have to change it. Many people find listening to accented conversations more appealing. You must, however, be courteous and do your best to be understandable. If you have an accent, slow down a bit and allow your listener to understand each word distinctly. Pause ever so briefly between words. At the end of each word, pronounce the last sound and separate with a mini-pause before you start the next word. This allows your listener to fully comprehend one word before you move to the next.

If you want to engage in a more intensive approach to improving your voice or pronunciation, ask the speech teacher at your local college if there are speech therapists in your area who can coach you. Many universities now have excellent accent-reduction programs. If you feel your accent is impeding your career or social goals, consider investing time and money in one of these programs.

Finally, all that work you put in on your voice isn't going to mean anything if you don't take proper care of it. Care for your voice as you do for your skin, muscles, and other physical assets. Don't force your voice to do more than it was designed to do. Don't yell, especially for a prolonged time, as some do at sporting events. In extremely cold weather, don't strain your voice, as your vocal cords may be tighter than usual. If you feel that your throat is getting scratchy from talking too much, stop!

And whatever you do, don't whisper if you feel you're losing your voice. Strange as it may seem, whispering is even harder on your vocal cords than speaking normally. Many people prolong their bouts of laryngitis by straining their vocal cords by whispering!

The Least You Need to Know

- Before you answer the phone, smile—the caller can hear the smile in your voice.
- Choose voice models like you choose role models for other life skills.
- Open your mouth wide and carefully enunciate each word to avoid mumbling.
- Avoid "uh," "like," or "you know" by simply pausing when you get the urge to use a filler.
- You can transform your voice and speech patterns if you are willing to ask for feedback and are willing to work on changing some habits.

PART

3

Handling Routine Conflict, Difficult People, and Awkward Situations

Even the most wonderful communicators run into conflict and difficult people. Part 3 prepares you to handle challenging situations and people with grace and ease and to achieve the best possible outcome.

Chapter 8 shows you tactics for avoiding conflict in your life. You will learn strategies for handling conflicts such as word choice and having the all-important best first response. Sometimes you know in advance that a conversation is going to be difficult. Chapter 9 teaches you how to prepare for conversations that you might even dread. Chapter 10 addresses specific types of difficult conversations such as apologizing, breaking the news of a death, leaving a situation, offering constructive criticism, and asking for anything such as money or time. Chapter 11 shows you how and when to be assertive, and you will learn how to stop short of being aggressive. Chapter 12 completes this part by looking at specific types of difficult people. You will learn how to deal with people who are prickly, critical, or overly emotional, as well as the know-it-all, the person who changes his mind constantly, and other types.

If you're dealing with a difficult situation or person in your life, this part will give you meaningful steps to improving things for yourself and your partner.

CHAPTER

8

Dealing with Conflict

Presidential press advisors do one thing really well: they know how to avoid conflict by preparing for controversial questions and topics. One of their strategies is to anticipate potentially problematic situations or conversations. They know it is far better to head off conflict before it starts.

With just a few minutes a day, you can incorporate this useful habit into your approach to people, too. This chapter makes you aware of the effect conflict can have on your people skills and gives you greater control of situations that have the potential for conflict. You will learn to prepare for conflict more effectively, and how to handle those critical first words when conflict occurs.

In This Chapter

- Learning to anticipate and prepare for conflict
- Making your first response appropriate and effective
- How doing is more important than saying
- Managing conflict resolution and delivering bad news

Anticipating and Preparing for Conflict

You can take some proactive steps to avoid *conflict*. When you look at your calendar to see the appointments and social events you have coming up, take a few moments to ask yourself the following questions:

- What is the topic or purpose of this meeting?
- Is there anything my partner might want from this meeting?
- Are there differences in the way I see the situation?
- What is my history with this person?
- Have we ever held different opinions over a social issue or a project or anything else?

DEFINITION

Conflict refers to a battle, fight, or struggle. Anytime there is discord, antagonism, or opposition, you have the potential for conflict.

There are many things that equally moral and caring people can see differently. Naturally, you avoid the obvious topics people disagree on: politics, religion, and most social issues. But there are other topics you should either avoid or plan in advance how to bring up.

Be careful when discussing topics that your conversation partner may be sensitive about, especially if they broach some loss of power, status, or authority on the part of your partner. Changes in leadership and the hiring of new people are examples. When talking about tasks or practices that are part of a person's identity, handle these topics with care. If your friend has always headed the community clothes drive and you mention that some people are talking about handing that task over to a local charity, you may be talking about taking away a position that your friend felt was part of her identity. Finally, lifestyle changes, such as divorces, moves, and deaths, must be handled with great compassion and sensitivity.

All this is not to say you shouldn't mention these topics, but plan your remarks so you bring these up thoughtfully and diplomatically. The time you spend identifying potential sensitive spots in the conversation and planning your phrasing will help you keep some conflicts from ever arising.

Your First Response

When a sharp word is spoken or an unwelcome action is taken and the potential for conflict rears its head, the first moments are the most important for determining how successfully things will be worked out. Your first response will tell your partner how supportive you will be at arriving at a solution that respects her needs as well as yours. What you say first shows you care about the other person, even if you disagree with her position. Otherwise, you may come across as not only being against the person's position but against the person.

Some people have stored-up emotions on certain subjects and are the proverbial ticking bombs. For example, an employee who has not been given a raise in years might explode when asked to work overtime with no compensation. She may have been angry for months or years about her lack of reward, but she had not had the courage to press the issue. When an insensitive boss asks for more time and no more money, the emotions spill over and an avalanche of resentment flows out.

If your first words are too direct, you may sound confrontational, even if you don't intend to. When you make a statement that sounds too blunt to your listener, she may feel attacked or threatened. Her response may be to strike out verbally. After an emotional start like this, it's much more difficult to get the conversation and the relationship back on track. Though not impossible to come back from, these situations make relationships and trust harder to build, so watch your first words.

Breaking Bad News While Still Avoiding Conflict

The saying "Don't kill the messenger" is used frequently, because so many times people take their disappointment out on the deliverer of the message. Even if you are not the cause of the bad news, you may experience a bad reaction aimed at you personally.

So what's a good plan of action when you must bear bad news?

Consider this scenario. You always go on vacation with your friend Kerri. This year, you have the opportunity to go to Italy to visit some relatives who are living there for one year. They have invited you but not Kerri. You very much want to go but know that Kerri will be disappointed. Use the following format to bring this emotional topic up with Kerri:

Begin with a neutral or noncontroversial comment about the topic. "Kerri, did I tell you that my uncle's family, the Martins, are living in Italy for a year while my uncle is doing an assignment in Rome?" You then allow your partner to do most of the talking. Keep your remarks succinct. The more you talk, the more opportunities you have to say something that your partner won't like.

Bring the topic up in a way that doesn't sound adamant or inflexible. "Actually, they said I could room with my cousin Alden if I visit them." This statement only says that the invitation has been issued. It does not say that you have made a choice. If your partner's reaction is too emotional (hurt, angry), consider postponing the rest of the conversation for a day or two. Let your partner digest the news and deal with her emotions. She may call you and encourage you to go if she has time to think. Make sure she doesn't hear this as you saying that you are going with no regard for her feelings.

When you feel emotions have calmed down, proceed to the next step. Say that you've been thinking about the subject in order to let your partner know that your decision is a well-considered and thoughtful one—for example, "I've really been thinking about this invitation." Next, describe the facts you both know already about the topic. At this point, don't say you've made a decision or give an indication that bad news is coming. Say something like, "Even though the family will be in Italy for a year, the invitation is for July only."

Offer something caring or complimentary to the person who is no doubt disappointed. "Even though in the past we have enjoyed vacationing together, I hope you will understand."

Break the news clearly but not bluntly. "Unfortunately, I can only take one vacation, and this is an opportunity to see Italy that I may never get again. I hope you understand if this year I forgo our usual trip in order to take this trip." This response gives an honest, direct explanation but also takes into consideration Kerri's feelings with words like "unfortunately" and "understand" to soften the message.

In closing, offer something positive, rewarding, or consoling after you break the news. "I do hope you will want to plan a vacation with me next year, as I would like nothing more than to do one of our trips then." Bookending bad news this way, with positive and encouraging wording before and after, may not take away the disappointment, but it can help tone down the potential for conflict.

Actions Speak Louder Than Words

Just as with your verbal message, the most important nonverbal moment is the moment the conflict arises and how you physically respond. This is very challenging, as your physical reaction may be to let your emotions show in your facial expression.

When conflict begins, it is often escalated by someone giving someone else "the look." The look may say "You're crazy," "That ticks me off," or "What are you talking about?" The look is a barrel of gasoline you don't want to open when you have a tiny spark of conflict unfolding.

COMMUNICATION TIP

Remember to practice all the nonverbal skills described in Part 2. If you recall, nonverbals account for more than 90 percent of your effectiveness, as opposed to the words you say.

You should therefore develop a facial expression that is neutral and nonjudgmental for those moments when you are surprised, angered, or shocked by something someone says. Practice self-talk to calm yourself and tell yourself that you are just going to look blank rather than express what you are actually feeling in that moment.

Give your partner caring and understanding looks in order to buy some time until you can talk through the issues. Controlling your emotions is a sign of a mature person, and self-control of facial expressions requires a high level of maturity. Work at it as practice is the only way to acquire this skill of a master communicator.

I have practiced control of nonverbal reactions and can tell you that you can control them most of the time. In a recent meeting, however, an attendee was so insensitive to a minority member of the group that I was shocked. Despite my usual ability to appear implacable, I wondered if my shock showed on my face. I know that we are not good judges of our own nonverbals, so I asked someone who is a keen observer if my face had betrayed me. She said, "You looked startled." Knowing that having someone look startled at something you say is not flattering, I went to the person who made the remark to talk through what had happened. The person was unaware of the problem, so we were able to talk it through and leave with a more amicable relationship. No one is perfect, so you will need some strategies for those moments when, despite your best efforts, conflict arises.

Strategies for Conflict Resolution

No matter how hard you try, sometimes conflict just happens. You may bring up a topic at the wrong moment or you may be unaware you are being insensitive. Sometimes, the other person is just being irrational, and the conflict may have more to do with something going on with her than with anything you said or did. No matter where the fault lies, resolving the conflict is almost always in your best interest.

COMMUNICATION TIP

Ask.com defines conflict resolution as "a wide range of methods of addressing, alleviating, and eliminating sources of conflict by use of nonviolent methods as opposed to armed struggle." While your conflicts with others typically aren't at such a high level, the process of conflict resolution generally consists of the same steps at any level of conflict—negotiation, mediation, diplomacy, and creative peace building.

Resolving conflict does not start with going to the other person but with an honest look at your own behavior. Review your conversation and your history with this person to see if there is anything you can think of that they could interpret as insensitive. You may not hold the same values or sensitivities, but this part is not about you. It is about the other person's perception. If your partner is predisposed to feel certain topics are controversial or off-limits, then, in her view, you really were insensitive. You have to accept that, to her, her view is valid.

How to Begin Resolving a Conflict

The conversation for resolving conflict is very much like the example in the previous section in which you practiced breaking bad news about a cancelled vacation to your friend Kerri. What if, despite your careful approach, Kerri "blew up" and was very angry with you? What would you say to help resolve the conflict once it was out there?

First, review the empathy statements in Chapter 2. Showing empathy is the most effective way to soothe angry people like Kerri. Also, the person will want to vent and tell you her concerns, so be sure to let her talk as much as she needs to in order to put this event behind you. Your only job is to empathize while she talks.

Second, scour your memory (you can use the following writing exercise to do so) to face whatever role you might have played in the conflict. There really are two sides to an issue. Even if you did nothing overtly wrong, what could you have done differently that could perhaps have helped you avoid the conflict?

Writing Exercise

One of the most effective ways to understand the other person's perspective is to write her a letter from her point of view. Pretend you are the person you're having conflict with. Put yourself in the other person's shoes, so to speak. Now imagine that she has a close friend or cousin in another state and she is writing to that person. If she were to pour out her heart to someone she was very close to, what are some of the small things, big things, or even minor annoyances she might mention? Take the filter off and let your imagination run wild to think of how she might describe you and the incident that took place.

HOLD THAT THOUGHT

Don't write this letter in the form of an email. You are never going to send this letter to anyone, and email is dangerous. After you write this inflammatory letter, you might accidentally push **Send**. So write this on paper only!

The following is a sample of a letter written from another person's point of view about a neighborhood conflict:

> Dear Jean,
>
> I hope you're doing well and that things have calmed down around your house. Personally, I have my hands full right now and a neighborhood situation is not helping my stress level. You wouldn't believe this neighbor of mine named __(Put your name here)__. It all started because __(State first events or words)__. Then __(State phrases or events that escalated the conflict)__.
>
> Anyway, thanks for always being there and understanding.
>
> Warmly,
>
> (Sign with your communication partner's name)

Writing this letter will not solve your problems, but it will help you get closer to seeing the other person's viewpoint. You will be better able to empathize if you put yourself in her shoes through this exercise. You may even recall a few facts that you had forgotten that may be part of the reason your partner is in conflict with you.

Now write a second letter to someone who always supports you and is a good listener. This letter is your chance to pour out your heart, frustrations, and observations about the other person's words and actions. Get it all down on paper. Why? Because you need to be honest about any hidden resentments you have or any judgmental attitudes you have toward the other person. If resolving conflict is truly your goal, you may need to face how small some of these irritations are. Are they worth the conflict?

Review the letter and ask yourself, "Can I let these things go? Is there anything in here we have to address or can I live with it?"

Ask yourself if there are areas of the letter that have a negative or critical tone. Plan ahead not to sound negative in your upcoming conversation. Plan, instead, to use some supportive statements that will offset any undertones of negativity.

Put the faults of the other person in context. Everyone has faults, and everyone needs some latitude and leniency. Can you extend graciousness to this person? Think of a time someone did not bust you for a mistake you made. Think of the flood of relief you felt when they simply let it go. Is this your chance to be the bigger person?

After you have learned more about yourself by studying this letter, shred it! You don't need to revisit and rehash this negative information. Learn from it and go on to the conversation you need to have with the other person.

HOLD THAT THOUGHT

Be sure you set a time and a location for this conversation that is agreeable to the person you're trying to reconcile with. Don't play power games, such as insisting on having the conversation on your "turf."

Conflict Resolution Model

Now that you've looked at your conversation partner's perspective as well as your own, it's time to confront the issue. Fist, follow the steps for presenting disappointing news while avoiding conflict described earlier. Bring the topic up in a neutral way, do not antagonize by taking a strong position at first, allow your partner to do most of the talking while you empathize, and define the options or situation in an unemotional and factual way. Be sure you stress the positive relationship you have had in the past. Talk about the parts of the situation that the two of you are in agreement about.

Next, instead of breaking the news, address the conflict. Your partner already knows the bad news or whatever started the problem. Check in with your partner after you've defined the problem and say, "I understand that when I said X it was hurtful (disappointing, surprising, cause for concern). What I want from this conversation is to make things right and to resolve any problems between us. I hope you feel the same."

If your partner agrees to wanting to work things out, you are already successful. At this point, you can offer an apology and suggest anything concrete you can do in the future to help you avoid this problem. If your partner is not ready to put differences behind you, you might try saying, "I value our friendship so much and want to do what you think is right. How can I make things better?"

If your partner makes demands or says something you cannot agree to, try one of these responses:

- "I do agree that ___A___ (say what you can do first), although I didn't arrive at the same conclusion about ___B___ (state the issue)."
- "I do agree that ___A___ (state the issue) and I am very sorry, but I want you to know that ___B___ (say what you can do)."
- "I can ___A___ (say what you can do first), although ___B___ (state request) may be difficult."

For instance, using the Kerri example from earlier, you could say, "I do agree that my changing the plans for our vacation has been a hardship for you and I am very sorry, but I want you to know that it was not intentional or meant to make you feel that I don't value your time."

COMMUNICATION TIP

When breaking bad news, it's usually best to start with the good news and state the bad news second. The only message you should ever deliver is good news-good news or good news-bad news. Never deliver a bad news-bad news message. Find one good thing to tell your listener, even if it's just that you're going to help them deal with the bad news in some way.

When you feel you have resolved things as much as you can reasonably expect for one conversation, express relief for the points of resolution and gratitude for your partner's willingness to work things out with you. If there is any follow-up you can offer, end the conversation by telling your partner what you plan to do and when.

Naturally, you will tailor all of these conversations to your unique situation. No formula can guarantee a successful resolution with all people, but this approach usually works. Many people find that when two friends go through a bad period and work through it successfully, they become much closer.

Conflict is actually healthy and productive in a relationship. You should desire to have people in your life who see things differently from you; their different perspective will give you added insight and keep things interesting. Try to stay objective about your differences and remember that it is the issue you don't like and not the person.

The Least You Need to Know

- Head off potential conflict by preparing your phrasing to avoid sensitive areas.
- It is a given to avoid the topics of politics, sex, race, or religion, as they frequently lead to conflict.
- Your first response to conflict is the most critical and demonstrates whether you care about the other person's feelings.
- Start with a buffer before breaking bad news, because being too direct may sound confrontational.
- Develop a neutral facial expression for delivering or receiving bad news.
- Bookend bad news by starting with something noncontroversial, ending with an optimistic look at next steps, and sandwiching the bad news in between.

CHAPTER

9

Preparing for Important Conversations

In This Chapter

- Having important but positive conversations
- Knowing your partner's preferences
- How to close the gaps between your preferences and your partner's
- How to prepare for important conversations
- Identifying conversations that deserve preparation

An important conversation is one that simply must go right for you or for your partner. Negotiations, announcements, changes, disagreements, and many more exchanges can all be critical conversations. In a critical conversation, the stakes are higher and there is usually potential for gain or loss to one or both parties. If everyone does not hear and understand the information in a way that is constructive, anger or hurt feelings could result.

This chapter gives you an action plan for approaching a critical conversation so that you increase your chances of having a successful outcome.

Taking the Time to Prepare

When you take the time to prepare for an important conversation, such as a negotiation, changes are embraced and complied to more readily and disagreements are more likely to be resolved sooner rather than later. Preparation ensures that the announcements you are asked to make are clearly understood and that you give each topic the importance and consideration it is due. By the way you prepare for an important conversation, you may be setting in motion a positive turning point in your relationship with a friend or acquaintance.

Assessing Your Partner's Communication Style

How do you make a critical conversation as rewarding as it can possibly be? The best move you can make is to invest some time considering your partner's preferences. Rushing into a delicate conversation runs the risk of hurting feelings or angering your partner and increases the odds of a bad outcome. The first thing to do is ask yourself, "How would my partner like to receive this news and what are his communication preferences?" In other words, you assess your partner to determine his style and his preferences.

Consider the communication basics discussed in Chapter 1. How would your partner prefer to receive information? Would he prefer to receive it verbally or through an email or letter? If a conversation needs to take place, would he be more comfortable with a phone call or a face-to-face talk? Serious conversations generally need to be held in person. After all, would you propose marriage by phone or text?

COMMUNICATION TIP

We've all heard horror stories of managers who fire people by text or email. So carefully consider the mode of conversation you think your partner will prefer. If you really can't figure it out, ask! Most people will appreciate your thoughtfulness in wanting to cater to their preferences.

Similarly, if you need to ask your partner to send information, consider how he would be most comfortable sending it. For example, if your friend has spent what appears to be an excessive amount of money on the supplies for an upcoming charity ball, you may need him to give an accounting of where the money went. You may feel he will be more comfortable if you discuss the event over coffee. When you bring up the topic face to face, you will have the opportunity to answer his questions and to be a calming force if he is offended. These relational aspects do not happen as successfully in a phone conversation or an email. On the other hand, you may want to give him the opportunity to pull the information together and send it to you by email.

We all have friends who want to communicate only by text or who do not text but prefer to email. Other friends are telephone talkers. Some people, as in the preceding example, prefer to receive information one way but to send it another. With new acquaintances, try to pick up on cues about their preferences. Watch what they do. If they tend to text more than email, try to respond using text, even if email is your preference. You will be more successful in getting the information and response you need if you use their preferred mode of communication.

Considering Personality Type

If you decide that a conversation needs to take place instead of a text or email exchange, consider the type of person you're dealing with. Is your partner the type who prefers specific information with exact numbers and facts, or is he more interested in the back story, the context, and the reasons a decision has been made? Some people like a situation to be told to them like a story. They find all the nuances that lead up to a decision as important as the decision—the "why" behind a decision, who said what, and any curious related events. Conversely, another type of person wants just the facts, hard data, and the bottom line. From past conversations with your partner and the types of questions he tends to ask you, you can usually pick up on this preference.

Next, consider that some people are open about their emotions, while others like to keep the conversation objective or businesslike. Do you think your partner would like you to ask about his health, family, vacation, and personal topics he brought up in previous conversations? Does he like to share and hear a lot of personal anecdotes and information? Or would he consider these topics invasive or rude? Tailor your conversation accordingly.

COMMUNICATION TIP

Remember that some people will respond to you with a great deal of empathy and some will not. Some people have been brought up to keep emotions hidden, so be prepared mentally in case you think someone is being cold or unreceptive. Decide how much empathy this person will be comfortable with as well.

Setting the Tone

Next, consider what type of tone you want to create. Would it be better to make this a casual communication, or do you think the occasion requires more formality in your partner's view? Is this is a conversation with a friend and you are working through some differences that need to be negotiated or is this a more business-oriented negotiation?

Set the tone with your choice of location first. Where would your friend be most comfortable for this conversation? Would your location or his be his preference? A word of caution here: some people feel that when you set up a meeting at your house or office, you are getting the upper hand in a "turf" battle. If your friend is a tough negotiator and a bit controlling, you might want to give him the option of meeting either place, according to his preference. Also, you want to make sure that wherever you decide, it's neat and tidy. For example, if you arrange a meeting in your home and the breakfast dishes are still out and newspapers are strewn about, your partner may feel disrespected.

If you have chosen to create a casual atmosphere for your conversation, be sure your opening words are casual and friendly. Don't start with the stereotypical, "I suppose you wonder why I've asked you here today." Friendly small talk at the beginning is a better way to keep the mood relaxed and easy.

On the other hand, if this is a group meeting and your partner is a real traditionalist, he may lose respect for you if you don't follow a structured meeting that lays out the agenda early. Consider the tone your partner wants.

Remembering Your Nonverbals

Next, plan to use the appropriate nonverbal communication (see Chapters 5 through 7). You want to use the type of facial expressions, mannerisms, and other nonverbals that will improve your communication.

Physical distance is another nonverbal factor to consider. Does your partner like a lot of *personal space?* Give it to him. Does he feel that communication is stronger when you're physically closer? Adjust your physical distance based on your client's cues.

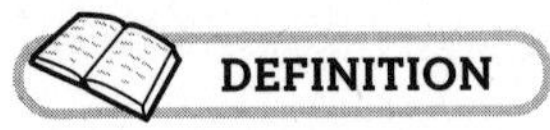

DEFINITION

Personal space is the distance between two people that's considered comfortable for a conversation. Negotiating personal space is ongoing. As the name implies, this is different for every individual. What may be considered fine by one person may be considered too intimate or too impersonal by someone else.

Try to determine whether your partner is a hand-shaker. If so, extend your hand in a friendly manner. Plan where you both will sit so that the sharing of information will not be awkward or uncomfortable. Finally, plan a smile for your greeting and for your goodbye. If there are other appropriate times to smile in between the two, remind yourself to smile graciously.

Being Aware of Status

The next factor to consider is the status of your partner. We all like to think we're not status conscious, but almost everyone is. If you work for a huge corporation and are going to have a conversation with the CEO, you might prepare a bit differently than if you're having a conversation with a temporary worker. One factor to consider is whether you believe your partner feels his status is somewhat higher than yours. If so, be sure to express gratitude for his sparing the time and for his lending his expertise or insights. Strangely enough, you use the same technique with someone who may feel his status is far below yours. If your partner appears self-conscious because he believes you are better educated, wealthier, or more knowledgeable, it is even more important to thank him for his time, his opinion, or anything else that will make him feel valued.

Asking Questions

Next, what is your partner's comfort level with questions? Some people feel threatened if asked one question after another. These people are usually your less-confident friends and acquaintances. They might say they feel they are being "grilled" when someone asks them too many questions. Other people like the fact that you're interested enough to ask questions. If you do ask questions, be sure to ask primarily the open questions described in Chapter 2. Open questions invite dialogue and good communication.

Capturing the Right Tempo

Every conversation also has a *tempo*. What type of tempo does your partner prefer? Some people like the conversation to move fast, while others want a more measured, thoughtful pace. If you're preparing for a conversation with someone who likes a fast tempo, be sure to give the most important facts early in the conversation. You can always elaborate as you go along. First, however, you need to demonstrate that you are not going to waste your partner's time. Don't be repetitious. Answer exactly the questions you are asked.

DEFINITION

Tempo refers to speed—in this case, the speed of your conversation. Some people like a very dynamic tempo with words bouncing quickly back and forth, while others like a lovely, slower tempo with more dramatic pauses.

For partners who appear to desire a slower pace, break your conversation into several parts and move through each slowly. Allow time for your partner to ask questions.

In the earlier case, where you were going to meet with a friend to discuss how he spent the charity's money, the conversation might have four parts. Part one might be some pleasantries and the exchange of personal information. Part two might be a general discussion of the progress of the committee and the event, including a compliment for your friend. Part three might be an explanation of what took place at the last meeting and the request that your friend submit the details of his expenses. Preferably, you will be able to say that everyone is being asked to submit this information so your friend does not feel singled out. Offer your friend the option to submit the information the way he feels most comfortable, by email or letter, in a table or a bulleted list. Finally, be sure to plan to close on a high note and bring up something pleasant or neutral.

The Stress Factor

This brings us to another factor to keep in mind as you plan an important conversation. How sensitive is your friend to stress? Is he highly reactive or not? Is he so immune to stress that he might not realize the urgency of a situation and a need for immediate action? Will you have to be clear about that?

If your friend is easily stressed out, what parts of your upcoming conversation might he find stressful? How do you plan to deal with a reaction to this stress?

Similarly, does your friend tend to have more optimistic or pessimistic leanings? Is there anything in your conversation that he might see too pessimistically? Conversely, is there any danger that he will be overly optimistic about something and hear something incorrectly?

Accomplishing Goals

Now consider exactly what you want from this conversation. Do you want to walk away with a decision, an agreement, money, support, or what? You can't expect people to give you what you want if you haven't clearly asked for it. Think of how you will ask specifically for what you want. Do you need to provide an action step or two? Do you need to volunteer to do the next step?

Are you trying to persuade someone to do something? Be aware that some people are unable to make fast changes based on one conversation. Even if you are successful in making progress toward changing your partner's mind, he may not say "yes" in this first conversation.

COMMUNICATION TIP

Don't let your disappointment show if you don't get everything you want at first. Thank your partner for the concessions he does make, even if he simply says, "I'll think about it."

Are you asking your partner to do something that requires lead time? Some people need more lead time than others. They don't like to have requests sprung on them. To ensure success, plan your conversation far enough in advance that your partner doesn't feel rushed or pressured.

On the other hand, some people work better under pressure. If you ask too far in advance, they might ignore or forget your request. With these last-minute types, approaching them closer to the time you actually need their help will yield a better result.

Even the Happiest Conversations Deserve Preparation

Many people may think that extremely important and potentially stressful conversations require preparation. However, that's not true. Even the most joyous ones can require thought and planning.

For example, Harvey Biggs was a supervisor known for being able to get work done. He was fair to his employees and they were basically satisfied with their jobs. Joe Saxon had worked for the company for 35 years and for Harvey for the last 10 years. When it came time for Joe to retire, Harvey had planned to mention it in the regular monthly staff meeting that Joe and his peers always attended. Harvey didn't put it on an agenda and almost forgot about it until the end of the meeting. He actually dismissed the meeting and then hurriedly said, "Oh, one more thing. Joe Saxon is retiring in two weeks. He has done a great job for 35 years. That's all."

Joe was left thinking of all the sacrifices he had made and accomplishments he had achieved with the company, and not one was acknowledged. His farewell was generic enough to apply to anyone. He was hurt.

Even worse for morale, the rest of the employees were appalled at Harvey's lack of thoughtfulness for such a faithful colleague. One of them said, "It really shows how much they realize and appreciate what we do around here. I don't know why anyone should knock themselves out the way Joe did."

HOLD THAT THOUGHT

As much as we are tempted to be humorous at these times, most people would prefer that the occasion be treated with a little bit of dignity. Also, humor can be taken the wrong way and can diminish the joy of the occasion.

All communication is important, but there are times you know that a conversation may be a turning point. A few minutes of planning can offer you a result that may benefit your partner and you for years.

Thinking through all the communication dynamics will give you a greater chance for a successful outcome. Planning and preparing are worth the investment if the conversation is an important one.

Closing the Gaps Between You and Your Partner

After thorough preparation, assess yourself and your conversation partner on these same style and preference issues. Look at your preferences side by side and see where you differ. Where you see gaps and style differences, you need to prepare to adapt more to your partner. The following table is an excellent tool for assessing your style and your partner's.

Sender–Receiver Inventory

Attribute	Rating Scale
Sender Style: Mode Would your partner prefer an email or a conversation?	Speaking Writing 1 2 3 4 5 6 7 8 9 10
Sender Style: Content Does your partner prefer facts and statistics or reasoning and explanations?	Hard Data Exposition 1 2 3 4 5 6 7 8 9 10
Sender Style: Tone Is your partner's style more traditional or loose and casual?	Formal Informal 1 2 3 4 5 6 7 8 9 10
Receiver Style: Mode Do you prefer an email or a conversation?	Listening Reading 1 2 3 4 5 6 7 8 9 10
Receiver Style: Content Do you prefer facts and statistics or reasoning and explanations?	Hard Data Exposition 1 2 3 4 5 6 7 8 9 10
Receiver Style: Tone Is your style more traditional or loose and casual?	Formal Informal 1 2 3 4 5 6 7 8 9 10
Nonverbal To what degree does it impact you?	Strongly Little Impact 1 2 3 4 5 6 7 8 9 10
Empathic vs. Nonempathic How responsive are you to someone's emotions?	Very Responsive Nonresponsive 1 2 3 4 5 6 7 8 9 10
Emotions To what degree do you reveal them?	Guarded Unguarded 1 2 3 4 5 6 7 8 9 10
Physical Distance How much space do you need?	Close Distant 1 2 3 4 5 6 7 8 9 10

Attribute	**Rating Scale**
Status Awareness To what degree does your level/position impact how you communicate with someone?	Little Influence Much Influence 1 2 3 4 5 6 7 8 9 10
Interpersonal Distance Do you like to share incidents and experiences with friends you make at work?	Close Distant 1 2 3 4 5 6 7 8 9 10
Nonverbal Expression To what degree do you express and control your nonverbals?	Expressive Nonexpressive 1 2 3 4 5 6 7 8 9 10
Questioning Stance To what degree do you question new information?	Intensely Very Little 1 2 3 4 5 6 7 8 9 10
Tempo Do you like fast-paced oral communication or a slower pace?	Fast Slow 1 2 3 4 5 6 7 8 9 10
Change Profile Do you change your mind easily in one conversation?	Changeable Conservative 1 2 3 4 5 6 7 8 9 10
Reaction to Stress How sensitive are you to stress?	Sensitive Insensitive 1 2 3 4 5 6 7 8 9 10
Attitude What viewpoint do you tend to have on issues?	Pessimistic Optimistic 1 2 3 4 5 6 7 8 9 10
Lead-Time Orientation Do you prefer people to approach you well in advance or spontaneously?	Present Future 1 2 3 4 5 6 7 8 9 10

Naturally, you may not know all of the information in the inventory about your partner, but complete what you can. Observe your partner to see if you can get clues about his preferences. For example, if, when you talk to him, he edges back a bit, he may need more physical distance than you. Listen to determine if his tempo is faster or slower than yours. Have you noticed his reaction when you give him very little lead time, and does it indicate that he likes more, or is he very spontaneous and responsive to a little time pressure?

After you compare your self-assessment to the assessment you complete on your partner, you will see your differences and can begin to plan accordingly to make an important conversation as pleasant for your partner as you can.

The next step is to plan the conversation and adapt all the variables you can to your partner's comfort zone. Be sure you try to accommodate all the differences you noted in the table. For example, if your partner likes a methodical, step-by-step pace, slow down your tempo. If you are a fast-temp type, be conscious that you will have to be very intentional about closing this gap and getting more aligned with your partner's style. If you like to stand very close to someone in a conversation but your partner wants more physical distance, be intentional about backing up a bit and watch that you don't get closer as you get more animated in your speaking. Go item by item and try to accommodate your partner in every way that is in your control. When you have thought through how you will match your style to his, you can then proceed to planning the appointment or encounter.

COMMUNICATION TIP

Keep in mind that this is a gap you have with your partner. Do you really want this gap to shut out the message you are trying to convey? Adjust accordingly.

Setting Yourself Up for Success

A few simple steps may make the difference in whether you're able to complete the conversation in one session or if you will need to meet again. Especially in the case of an important conversation, no one wants to have to visit the topic multiple times. The following table will you help ensure that you're setting the conversation up for success.

Question	Answer	Action to Be Taken
Have I removed all obstacles (within my control) to my listening (cell phone, noises, and so on)?		
Have I prepared my mind to listen empathically?		
Do I have positive or negative feelings toward my partner? Have I prepared myself to be objective by factoring in my feelings?		
Am I committed to true shared communication?		

Question	Answer	Action to Be Taken
Can I accept that my partner may not like me and still communicate effectively on this topic?		
Do I want to say what I have to say?		
How do I feel it will be received?		
What do I expect him to bring to the situation?		
Do I know the best way to say this?		
Do I know my role in this situation (authority, peer, subordinate)?		
Is this the right time and place for this communication?		
Is my facial expression encouraging communication?		
Am I listening for central themes?		
Have I faced up honestly to feelings and prejudices I may have brought into this communication?		
Do I feel safe to take the following actions:		
Say I don't know?		
Say I don't understand what is meant?		
Make suggestions?		
Express gut feelings that he can later substantiate?		
Have I correctly identified the feelings behind his message?		
Am I able to pick up on his nonverbals?		

You don't have time to plan this extensively for every conversation, but if a conversation is extremely important, it's worth taking the time to review the items on this form. The time you spend in setting the stage for a productive conversation may save you hours or even weeks in some cases.

The Least You Need to Know

- Remember when disagreeing that it is the person's ideas you don't like, not the person.
- Understand your partner's preferences for tempo, personal space, and other factors before communicating.
- Set the stage for a productive conversation by preparing the location, timing, and, most of all, your attitude.
- Happier conversations, such as announcements and congratulations, require just as much planning as more serious conversations.

CHAPTER

10

Handling the Five Most Difficult Conversations

In This Chapter

- How to apologize effectively
- Appropriate ways to announce deaths and disasters
- What to say when you resign a job or leave a situation
- How to offer constructive criticism
- How to ask for money, time, or other resources

Your life intersects in all kinds of ways with others, and you will eventually be faced with having to communicate with sensitivity about a variety of difficult situations. You will make a mistake and have to apologize. You will need to discuss a life event, such as a death. You may need to resign a position. You might need to offer someone some constructive criticism. You might need to ask for someone's time or money. All of these conversations are challenging for different reasons. In this chapter, each type of difficult conversation is examined, and you learn strategies for handling each.

Delivering an Effective Apology

You cannot get through life without needing to apologize from time to time. Even if you are not primarily at fault in a situation, an apology may be a good choice anyway. Often, your apology prompts your partner's apology and good relations are restored all round.

The art of an authentic apology is vital to your people skills. Learn to make the kind of apology that turns a bad situation into one that builds your relationship with the other person and increases mutual respect.

DEFINITION

An **apology** is an expression, either spoken or written, of regret for having made a mistake, hurt someone, or omitted something. It's an expression of concern for the feelings of someone you have let down, hurt, or caused difficulty for.

In the last few decades, we've seen example after example of politicians who were vilified after making mistakes because they did not do the two things that today's voters desire: They did not take responsibility for their wrongdoing quickly enough, and they did not offer a heartfelt apology.

Historically, leaders were not as answerable to the public. But in today's era of transparency, owning up and apologizing are vital to any person's image and reputation. Public figures are not exempted.

For example, in the last several years, we have seen popular athletes such as Lance Armstrong lose the support of fans because they did not confess their use of performance-enhancing drugs soon enough. After years of worldwide popularity, Armstrong saw the tide of public opinion change and go against him with tsunamilike momentum. Most media experts believe that if Armstrong had confessed his use early, the public would have forgiven and forgotten fairly quickly. Much was in his favor. His use occurred when many athletes were not as knowledgeable about the difference between nutritional supplements and steroids. To further create sympathy for Armstrong was the fact that he had cancer in those years. But it was Armstrong's vehement and repeated denials that made the public lose all faith in him.

Contrast that with Charley English, director of the Georgia Emergency Management Agency. He was vilified by the media nationally for failing to warn and prepare Georgians for what came to be known as the Snowpocalypse of 2014. Most of Atlanta was furious with him, as many of them or someone they knew had spent 10 to 13 hours trapped in their cars in an ice storm when an unusual series of events jammed the interstates all over the metro area. Charley's first press conference was a disaster and reinforced the fact that he had underestimated the scope of the storm and its effects. The next day, however, a contrite Charley faced the public and the press again and said, "I made a terrible error in judgment" for not opening the emergency response center earlier than he did. His apology took full ownership and his demeanor was so sincere that the animosity toward him began to turn to sympathy for some. Plus, he kept his job.

I am a firm believer in saying "I am sorry" clearly and succinctly right up front. The words must be said with sincerity and compassion or the conversation will leave you worse than you were before the apology.

When you apologize, say what you are apologizing for, but don't limit the apology too much. Don't make it sound as if you are not apologizing for some parts.

Second, use an empathy statement like the ones in Chapter 2.

Next, tell the person how much you value her, because often people want an apology because they feel that what you did devalued them. People who feel disrespected or slighted are angrier and less prone to receiving your apology. Take care of their feelings and their egos first so they can hear what you say.

Finally, if there is anything you can offer in the way of restitution or help, please do. For example, did your oversight cause your friend to have to pay additional parking; make special arrangements; or cost time, delays, or missed opportunities?

In all, this creates an effective apology. Let's take a look at how the pieces come together. Say you forgot to pick up your friend to take her to her outpatient eye surgery because she asked you six months ago and didn't remind you, your apology might sound something like this:

> "I am so sorry I forgot to pick you up for this surgery. Surgery is stressful enough, and you must have felt hurt that I didn't remember. You are someone I care very much about, and I would not have put you through this intentionally. I hope you will allow me to make amends by taking you to your rescheduled surgery tomorrow."

COMMUNICATION TIP

Not everyone accepts an apology graciously at first, but apologies are a great start to mending a relationship.

Don't be concerned if your apology is not received with warmth and reconciliation when first delivered. Hurt feelings are like bruises; they may just need time to heal. Give your friend time to consider what you've said and to realize that you had the character to apologize. Sometimes, seeing you demonstrate that you have the courage and consideration to apologize can actually raise someone's estimation of you. You may find that this temporary breach in your relationship, if handled correctly, may bond you closer.

Announcing Deaths and Disasters

No one wants to be the bearer of bad news, but when it falls to you to make such an announcement, be sure you do it thoughtfully. Emotions may run high with regard to the subject you are addressing, so proceed with tact and a sense of decorum.

Announcing a Death

If you're breaking the news of someone's death to a relative or close friend, don't lead with the announcement; take an indirect approach. Bring up the topic first, such as "As you know, John has been very ill for some time" or "You know that John has been serving in Afghanistan." Follow that with the news but avoid sounding blunt. You might say, "Sadly, this morning I was informed that John has died." Or another example might be, "After three days of heavy gunfire in which John fought heroically, he was hit and died on Thursday."

If the person will be emotionally affected, you might add, "I am so sorry. I know this is a great personal loss." If the receiver of the news is very close to the deceased, consider offering to do something for them. Ask them, "Is there anything I can do?"

COMMUNICATION TIP

Difficult conversations can lead to great success. Many successful people have found that the turning point for them in a relationship or a career was a difficult situation. People may not be thrilled with the news or feedback you have to deliver, but most will be sympathetic with your role of messenger. In time, they may come to admire your tact, wisdom, and sensitivity in handling a difficult conversation.

It is usually preferable to announce a death face to face, especially if the receiver of the news is a close friend or relative of the deceased. Phone calls are the second choice. There are times, however, that you need to send an email because of geographic distance or other logistics. The following is an example of an email to an individual announcing a death:

> "As you know, John has been critically ill for days. I realize you have been very concerned and have called often. Thank you. I am sorry to tell you that he passed away just a few minutes ago. He was in no pain and his children were there. I will be in touch about what the family wants to do about the arrangements."

At other times, you may need to send an email to a group of people to let them know quickly so they can arrange to attend a funeral or memorial service. If you are sending an email to announce a death, it is permissible to lead with the announcement. Finally, ask yourself if there is anything people will want to know. Put as much information as is appropriate in the announcement since you want to be as helpful as you can:

> Early this morning, John Simon passed away after a short illness. He was much admired as an illustrator, friend, and family man. [You can include a very short biography here if you wish.]
>
> Arrangements will be Monday, January 27, at 2:00 P.M. The funeral will be handled by Dewey's Funeral Services and details can be found on their website at zzz.deweyco.com.
>
> I have been asked if John named a charity to donate to in lieu of flowers, and he did. Please send donations to Leading the Way at leadingtheway.org.
>
> Thank you for all the concern for John and his family in this difficult time.
>
> Respectfully,
>
> Jim Marsden

Be sure to respond to the emails you will receive in return, as people are especially sensitive at a time like this. Thank the sender for her response and offer your condolences for her loss.

Announcing Other Unwelcome News

If the news you need to share is not related to death, you have a decision to make about the opening. In general, you should start with a *buffer,* such as a summary of the events leading to the news or a neutral fact related to the event.

DEFINITION

A **buffer** is a sentence or two of pleasant or neutral information that should be stated before you deliver bad news. It postpones the bad news briefly while you establish rapport with your listener or reader.

For example, if Mary Stevens writes to you saying she wants free installation of her internet service because her neighbor down the street received free installation, you could break the news of your refusal like this:

> "Thank you for writing us and explaining the reason for your request for free service. The apartment complex down the street from you paid for the installation of internet service to their residents several years ago. They paid a one-time fee to make every apartment internet ready for our service. We want very much to serve you as your internet provider. Like the apartment complex you mentioned, we will need to make your home internet ready. That service has a one-time-only charge."

If, however, there is urgency or a compelling reason to leave out the buffer, you may consider doing that.

Leave off the buffer if immediate action is needed and you're concerned that your message may not be read thoroughly. The following is an example of an email announcement of unwelcome news that should not have a buffer:

> Tenants,
>
> The water main has broken and you should immediately cut the water valve to your individual townhome off. If you do not shut down your access to the water pipes, you may experience costly flooding. The shutoff is usually located near the bathroom in the water heater closet.
>
> We apologize for any inconvenience you may experience and are working diligently to shut down the flow of water to the property. The property manager is going door to door now to alert homeowners who may not be online. Your help would be greatly appreciated if you could contact your neighbors.
>
> We will give you an update when we have further information from our plumber and from City Water Department.
>
> Best regards,
>
> Alex Zane

In this case, the gracious apology is given in the second paragraph, because the first priority is to get the water shut off and avoid further damage.

Resigning or Leaving

An old saying goes something like this: "All good things must come to an end." Even positions you hold in service organizations you love may end due to conflicts in your schedule or lifestyle changes. At various points in your life, you may find you need to end a job, a tradition, or a relationship. The key to having conversations about these types of transitions is to be objective and to focus on the positives.

Stay focused on the constructive reasons for leaving. You may have some hard feelings or bad memories from this relationship, but in the good-bye, stay positive. Rarely is anything to be gained from offering criticism or parting shots. And many people deeply regret leaving on a down note, even when they are completely justified for their negative remarks. In the end, you want to make these discussions win-win situations.

Ending a Relationship

When you decide to end a relationship, you are usually dissatisfied in some way. In the conversation or letter ending the relationship, it is important that you don't dwell on the disappointments. Focus on the positives. Even if you feel you will never again see the person or company you are leaving, try to end the relationship with respect and appreciation for anything of value you experienced.

HOLD THAT THOUGHT

Life is full of boomerangs, and you never know when you may work with or encounter people again. Leaving behind people who think well of you is better than leaving hurt, angry, or resentful people in your wake.

This type of conversation definitely requires a buffer. Begin by saying what you value in the relationship. Be specific and even consider giving a brief example. You may buffer the news further by describing the facts leading up to your decision, but don't include facts that are controversial or critical. Announce the news and then offer to help make any transition easier for your partner.

For example, if you've decided to leave your longtime roommate because you've purchased a condominium, the conversation might go something like this:

> "I remember how excited we were to find this house to rent and all the good times we've had over the last two years. I have loved living with you because you're generous with your time and are always willing to help with the chores or give me a ride when I need one. Recently, a co-worker offered to sell me his one-bedroom condo because he's being transferred. I would like to purchase it and move in when our lease is up in May. I want to give you a two-month notice so you can find another roommate or another place. I would be glad to put a notice on the board at work or help you if I can."

Resigning from a Job

Even though resigning from a job should be a business-as-usual step in a career, emotions sometimes come into play. Just as you would try to avoid making an acquaintance feel rejected, you should avoid making your resignation sound like a rejection of your company or your boss. For those left behind, you need to show that you value your soon-to-be former employer and the people you worked with. The following example is from an employee who is leaving his present firm for a better job.

"Thanks to your help, I have learned a great deal about auditing over the last two years. Recently, I was offered a position at Hastings & Hastings that will be a very good opportunity for me to work more in the commercial area. Naturally, I will give you at least a two-week notice, although they want me to start as soon as possible. I have written up instructions for training a new employee for my position, and I will be glad to spend time training the new hire before I leave. Thank you for a great first job experience."

Offering Constructive Criticism

Quite often, friends or colleagues do not realize that they are making a mistake or being inconsiderate. They may not know that they don't currently have the skill or knowledge needed for a task. At those times, you need to point out an area of improvement in a person or a process. This is known as *constructive criticism.*

DEFINITION

Constructive criticism is giving a friend or colleague information that will make her better in some way. The information about her performance or habits can lead to more success and better outcomes for her. This type of criticism is not about blame or judgment, but about factual ways this person can improve.

Unfortunately, when we say the words *constructive criticism* or the more popular *constructive feedback,* people tend to view this and the process negatively. There are many reasons for this. Because we are human, our egos are involved. It may make us self-conscious to think that someone has observed something about us or our performance that is less than perfect. Giving the feedback is awkward and so is receiving it.

Still, the best relationships benefit from mutual constructive feedback. If there is freedom and trust in your relationship to help the other person to better herself, and to be able to hear feedback that will help you better yourself, your relationship will be a huge asset in your life.

Plus, most people who are highly successful have learned to give and receive constructive criticism. The best seminar speakers ask audiences to complete an evaluation after each presentation. That feedback helps them continually change, improve, and keep up with what audiences want. They value the constructive feedback, and so should you.

How to Provide Feedback

Like the other challenging conversations in this chapter, constructive criticism should start with a buffer. Give some background information or describe the part of the process that is being done right prior to saying what is being done wrong. Be sure to mention your purpose in offering the criticism so you don't sound negative. You can say that you're helping prepare your partner for an upcoming event or for building her skills so she benefits in some way. Perhaps your feedback will make her a better tennis player, wife, server, or friend.

HOLD THAT THOUGHT

Evaluate the words you are about to use in a difficult conversation. Some words are so emotionally charged that saying them can shut down communication. Some people hear nothing after you say a loaded word like *feminism* or *bureaucrat*. Even words like *poor, mistake, shouldn't, must,* and *wrong* can evoke resistance. When you use them, they throw your listener's mind onto another track and she may not hear what you're saying. Worse, she may be offended and determined to reject whatever you suggest.

For example, a conversation telling a new employee that she is overstepping her authority and that she needs to avoid making executive decisions might go like this:

> "One of the things I like best about you is your energy and proactive approach to this job. I have prepared a chart that outlines your responsibilities and mine. As you can see, I am required to authorize all media. I do appreciate your trying to take some of these tasks off my plate, but I do need to sign off on any media requests and to approve the other items on this list. I would rather have someone like you who tries to take on more responsibilities than someone who avoids responsibility, so please know I appreciate you. Still, we need to stick by our assigned responsibilities as described here. Does that make sense?"

This approach lets the employee know the parts of her performance that are going well and the parts that are not. The feedback is so specific that she knows exactly what she needs to change. It even offers the feedback both orally and visually. Giving someone a list or visual aid can often help her more than just describing in sentences the situation or improvement you desire.

Being Thoughtful

When delivering constructive criticism, your desire should be to change the behavior, not to prove you are right or better and not to punish or put down the other person.

Telling your boss that she doesn't need to be so tight with marketing dollars is a mistake. Brainstorming with her on ways to identify opportunity costs and then suggesting that she could spend money in a specific area that would have a good return is much more effective.

Telling your spouse that you've noticed she is getting love handles is not nearly as effective as asking her to join you in a health regimen.

Constructive criticism can be delivered successfully if you are thoughtful and have the right motives.

Asking for Money, Time, or Other Resources

You may be in charge of fundraising or asking for volunteers for community service. You may need to ask a relative for money. Whatever you're asking for, the right approach will help you avoid a fast "no."

When requesting money, time, or other resources, your buffer should be extended and descriptive. Describe the project or need in a way that will appeal to your audience. Make it exciting. Stress the parts that may be of unique interest to them: that it is a green project, that it will save them time or money, that they may meet someone they want to meet, that it will help a group they have a special interest in, and so on. Get their buy-in before you make your request.

For example, let's say you're asking local businesses to buy ads to support your local Little League Baseball organization. The conversation might sound like this:

> "Hello, I am Judy Daniels. In our community, one out of eight families have had a member play Little League and most have played with the Metropolitan League. This group makes the community better by building the character and physical fitness of young people and offering them a positive way to spend their time. You can get your business's name in front of all those people and help the young people at the same time if you purchase an ad in our program. Do you have five minutes so I can show you what we have to offer that can help build the community and your business at the same time?"

Be sure you ask explicitly for what you want. Amazingly, some people never really ask clearly for exactly what it is they want. Their listener might have complied without knowing what they were being asked to deliver. Try to use the word *please* and then use a verb that describes what you want your listener to do. Say, "Please send me," "please email," "please change this," or whatever action you need.

Also, be prepared to ask more than once. "No" does not necessarily mean "No, never." It usually means "No, for now." Studies of sales professionals have proven that the more times they ask, the more times they get what they want.

Getting people to say "yes" is a skill you can use all the time. You will be better positioned for success if you get someone to say "yes" to something small and nonthreatening first. Judy Daniels has a better chance of the business owner's saying "yes" to giving her five minutes than she does to asking for the money up front. As the owner converses with her about baseball and the program, she can build on that first "yes" and ask him what size ad he thinks would be best for his business. This incremental approach to getting people to say "yes" is highly effective.

Don't take "no" as a rejection of you. "No" means "no" to your request or maybe some part of your request. Stay objective and ask what part of your proposition is the hold-up. Often, some minor adjustments or help on your part will turn a "no" into a "yes."

The Least You Need to Know

- Use an indirect approach in conversations that involve apologies, announcements of tragedies, and other difficult subjects. Buffer the negative information.
- Communicating a death is best done in person, but circumstances may require an email that is respectful, traditional, and sensitive.
- When leaving a relationship or resigning, focus on the positives and leave the door open for future opportunities.
- When offering constructive criticism, be specific about what is being done right as well as what needs improvement.
- When you ask for money, time, or resources, mention the benefits to the person you're making the request of.

CHAPTER

11

Being Assertive vs. Being Aggressive

People sometimes cross the line from being appropriately assertive to being inappropriately aggressive. People may not even know how to distinguish aggressiveness from assertiveness. Aggression may include behaviors such as forcing one's will on someone else, being obnoxiously opinionated, or acting with hostility to ensure one gets his way. Aggression is not a behavior anyone would aspire to. On the other hand, everyone should aspire to be assertive and needs this trait to deal effectively with all kinds of people.

This chapter will give you insights into exactly what assertiveness is and why it is such a desirable people skill. You will learn to think and speak with assertiveness without crossing the line into aggressiveness. As you read, ask yourself whether you see qualities of assertiveness or aggressiveness in yourself.

In This Chapter

- What is the difference between assertive and aggressive?
- Identifying passive-aggressive behavior
- Having great timing
- How to set boundaries
- Learning to make assertive statements

What Assertiveness Really Means

Being *assertive* means you go forward with your plans and ideas because you know they are valid, ethical, and considerate of all parties involved. Assertiveness means confidence in yourself and in your abilities. When you are assertive, you can lead as a collaborative thought leader, conversation leader, or participant. You can energetically put forward your plans and suggestions because you have listened and communicated with others before sharing.

Whether you desire to be a leader in your community, circle of friends and family, or company, assertiveness is an asset. *Aggressive* behavior, on the other hand, can alienate you from the very people you most want to influence and connect with. Knowing the difference is crucial. How can you tell when you, perhaps unknowingly, have become aggressive rather than assertive? The following table has some differences.

DEFINITION

Being **assertive** means initiating ideas and opinions in an appropriate and considerate way when needed. When you are assertive, you are able to voice and support your stances and needs to others in a measured and effective way. Being **aggressive** means crossing the line from being assertive to pushing for a stance, need, or desire. Taken too far, it can be a win-lose attitude wherein you want to win your point at any cost.

Aggressive vs. Assertive Behavior

Aggressive People	Assertive People
Push their agendas	Are curious about the agendas of others
Have an "I'm right/You're wrong" attitude	Believe "win/win" is always possible
Don't listen to ideas of others	Intentionally listen
Are not flexible	Can change their minds if needed
Create a competitive atmosphere	Believe in teamwork

The following also gives you an idea of how someone can cross the line from assertive to aggressive.

Alejandro's Story

Alejandro was appointed to serve on the board of a local nonprofit that served the underprivileged youth in his neighborhood. He was energetic and full of ideas. He had lobbied to be appointed to the board because he felt the nonprofit had been too slow to build a playground, offer new after-school programs, and provide counseling for at-risk youth. At his first board meeting, all the group did was review the decisions from the previous year. The only thing on the agenda for the next meeting was to create a list of goals for the current year and to prioritize them for funding. Alejandro couldn't wait to make the changes he believed were overdue. So he didn't.

Instead of waiting until he could get to know his fellow board members, work with them to define the top goals, and discuss his ideas with them, he came to the second meeting with a plan for going forward. He said to the other board members, "We don't need to do the goals because I have already laid them out for the year. I have also defined the projects that will satisfy those goals and created a timeline."

The board was shocked because they knew they had accomplished much in the past through collaboration. The chairman said, "Alejandro, your plan has some great ideas and I suggest we use these as a starting point for our discussion."

Alejandro said, "You all have been discussing for too long. It's time for action. I move that we adopt this plan as our action plan going forward. It is complete and ready to go as is."

Shocked, the chairman said to Alejandro, "That is not how we make decisions. We learn a great deal in the goal-setting process through listening to others' ideas. Your ideas will be considered, but we need to hear from everyone."

Alejandro looked around the table and then said in a challenging tone, "These are the ideas that have been talked about in the neighborhood for months. Everyone knows I'm right. Why do we need to wait and have more meetings? Again, I move we use these goals and start on an action plan. I don't want to have to tell the neighbors that I presented everything they wanted to you and you refused to vote on it. Do I have a second to my motion to accept this action plan and timeline?"

At that time, the chairman called for a break. One of the other board members took Alejandro aside and assured him that his ideas would be considered that night, and that action would take place in a matter of weeks. He did say that Alejandro needed three of the five board members to vote for his ideas, and that his actions had just alienated at least two of the members, possibly three. He encouraged Alejandro to be more patient and to allow others to present ideas since he now risked receiving no support for the items on his plan due to the highly aggressive way he had presented his ideas.

COMMUNICATION TIP

Aggressiveness scares people. It produces the opposite effect of what the aggressive person wants because many people automatically apply their mental and emotional brakes when they sense aggression. Assertiveness, on the other hand, inspires confidence. No one is intimidated by a person with good ideas.

Alejandro thought he was showing strong leadership and assertiveness, when, in fact, he was just being aggressive. Being assertive would have been to come with a list of the goals he thought were important and to save the activities and timeline for the appropriate meeting. He was to be commended for figuring out the details, but since the goals had not been approved, he was presumptuous to try to get everyone to agree on his plan of implementation. The assertive move would have been to wait until the chairman asked for goal suggestions and to present his goals articulately while asking if these were in line with what the existing board members thought. Alejandro could have presented everything he wanted—in due time—if he had not steamrolled over his peers and the chairman. If he had been open to the ideas of others, his ideas would have received instant support, and he would have won over the other members to be receptive to his activities and timeline when the proper time came to present those items.

As it was, Alejandro's ideas always met with resistance for the rest of the time he was on the board. He never received the support he deserved for his excellent ideas because his aggressiveness alienated people who would have been his allies. Some of his ideas were eventually adopted, but it took much longer because the board felt it had to be very cautious after Alejandro's reckless approach in the beginning. After his disastrous start, whenever Alejandro brought up an idea, some members went into caution mode. His bold and aggressive behavior scared them a little bit. They felt they had to be careful and did not trust that Alejandro had the same concerns for caution that they did.

Paying Attention to Your Style of Delivery

As you can see from the case of Alejandro, when it comes to versus aggression, the style of delivery makes the difference. When you are assertive, you deliver your suggestions in a polite way that shows openness and respect for others. You demonstrate that you like your ideas and believe in them strongly, yet you are open to the good ideas of others as well. You are flexible and willing to hear others who may have points to make that may require you to modify your position, and you are open to modifying your position. You are collaborative instead of adamant and unilateral.

What you are trying to achieve is the perfect balance of assertiveness. If you lack enough assertiveness, you will be viewed as passive and lose the respect of your peers and leaders. If you go past assertiveness and cross over into aggressiveness, you will alienate people and create resistance to your ideas and to you personally.

Prepare for important conversations by asking friends for advice about how to be assertive in certain situations. Plan the best words to use for the person or persons you will be addressing. While you are holding the conversation, look for verbal and nonverbal cues that you may be coming across as too aggressive. Dial down any aggression you may feel you are demonstrating by doing more asking and less telling.

Consider the "ask/tell ratio" as you plan your remarks. This simply means you should have about a 2:1 ratio of questions you ask versus the points you are making. You want to ask for your partner's or team's input twice as much as you tell them what you think. If you have a point to make, be sure to ask at least two questions that invite the ideas and input of your team or partner. By keeping the dialogue going by asking, you don't seem so dogmatic and bossy. You make the conversation seem like a group discussion rather than you talking down to the team and telling them what they are going to do. If you talk down to your team, your ideas may be rejected even if they are very good. Adults don't like being told what to do.

HOLD THAT THOUGHT

Even the nicest people can be aggressive. These folks are well meaning. Their goals may be worthy. Still, in their quest to achieve even an unselfish goal, they can cause anger and resentment. These "nice aggressors" don't take "no" for an answer. They can't take hints that people are resisting their ideas. They seem to be impervious to the wishes, feelings, and objections of others. They may hear someone say they disagree, but they do not recognize that "no means no." To combat the nice aggressor, you simply need to bring the difference of opinion out in the open, with questions such as "Would you be open to compromising on any part of the changes?" Once the two sides of the issue are identified, you can begin working on a fair compromise.

Avoiding the Aggressive Mind-set

Without meaning to be, aggressive people can be "me first" people. They want to speak first, go through the door first, get recognition first, and be served first. In order to not become one of those people, you want to make sure you're taking into account the feelings of others; otherwise, you'll end up alienating others.

For example, Butch, a management consultant, was bright, fun, and talented. He was also a "me first" person. In his view, everything revolved around him. He heard each person's comments and viewed each situation solely from the standpoint of how it would affect him. In fact, his friends Sal and Katie, who worked with him, nicknamed him "It's All About Me." It was funny to them at first; then something happened that made them reevaluate Butch and their relationship with him.

One day, Katie came into work excited. She had been working on consulting projects related to time management and managing multiple priorities. She had just been assigned a project that aligned perfectly with her interests. She ran into the cubicle area where the three friends worked. She said, "I got the account! I can't believe it."

Butch seemed to consider this for a moment. He did not say, "Congratulations." He did not ask her questions about when she would start and how she had found out the news. Instead, he looked at her and said, "Hmmm. I wonder why they didn't choose me? I am soooooo organized."

Katie was crestfallen. She couldn't believe that her friend was not happy for her. His complete focus on himself blinded him to her feelings and made him think only of what Katie's promotion meant to him.

That day, Katie made up her mind that Butch was not a friend but simply a co-worker. Sal, who had observed the scene, was also influenced by what took place. He knew that Butch would have been equally oblivious to him. Their relationship was never as close after that. Sal and Katie laughed about it at the time and teased Butch about it, but his self-centeredness diminished his credibility.

HOLD THAT THOUGHT

Aggressive people are especially wearing to their families and longtime friends. Aggressive behavior is difficult enough to endure for the short term; in long-term relationships, the partners or families cease to endure the aggression at some point. Many relationships are broken over this behavior.

Passive-Aggressive Behavior

Perhaps even more difficult to deal with, and an attitude you should avoid cultivating, is *passive-aggressive* behavior. People who are passive-aggressive are just as strongly motivated to do things their way as their aggressive counterparts. Their methods of getting their way are more subtle and behind-the-scenes. A passive-aggressive person may not tell someone he minds something, but his behavior will communicate his bad feelings.

For instance, Kathy and Tina were friends and both members of the homeowners association. Both wanted to be president of the organization, but Kathy went after the position more aggressively and was elected. Tina said she was happy for her friend, but her behavior thereafter demonstrated her lack of support. For example, Tina was always late for homeowners meetings or did not attend at all. If she was asked to do something for the association, she would agree but then cancel at the last minute. Once she was in charge of bringing the pizza for a neighborhood children's party. She had it delivered to her house instead of the clubhouse. By the time she brought it to the clubhouse, it was room temperature. People complained about Kathy's mismanagement. Tina did not try to set the record straight.

DEFINITION

Passive-aggressive behavior is behavior that promotes the agenda of one person who desires to hide that agenda. In fairness, a passive-aggressive person may not even recognize he is pushing behind the scenes for his self-oriented agenda. He accomplishes his goals obliquely and subtly, and he may see more forthright styles as too aggressive. Make no mistake, however; this personality style still can achieve goals through wearing or waiting you out.

In Tina's case, she's being passive-aggressive to fight back against the person she feels is overpowering her. Feeling too weak to combat an aggressor face-to-face, the passive-aggressive person uses emotional and social guerilla tactics to level the playing field. Their tactics are not as obvious as others, but they are just as effective.

For some, the passive-aggressive behavior doesn't seem to be about fighting back, but rather about playing defense, with rationalizations for the behavior. So unlike aggressors, who are a bit more self-aware and know what they are doing and tend to take ownership faster, passive-aggressive people may be in a state of denial, making solving the problem much more difficult.

If you see yourself in these passive-aggressive traits, work on being more open and honest in your communication, rather than stewing silently. It can be uncomfortable at times, but in the end, it'll allow you and whomever you're talking to or working with to deal with issues in a mature and efficient manner.

Timing Is Everything

Sometimes what you say is not offensive to others, but your timing is. Stating your opinion up front is just too aggressive for some people. Some people need to be given time to warm up to an idea or even you at first.

If you remember from Chapter 9, it's important to consider your listener carefully before a conversation. Consider whether a listener may find what you say risky or controversial and buffer it. Start with safer, less controversial statements and ask for your listener's thoughts and ideas. Offer one idea at a time and don't download a raft of must-do's all at once.

Timing is also important as it relates to scheduling. Scheduling may be the most strategic part of your planning. Consider whether your listener is a morning person or whether you should time your conversation for the afternoon. Is this the time of year that your accounts receivable is closing out accounts and is totally swamped? Can you delay the conversation until the employees' minds are fresher and they are more receptive? Consider whether your conversation partner has just experienced a major disappointment. Is this really the right time for a challenging conversation?

If the conversation will take place in a meeting, ask ahead of time for the agenda. Ask the leader for his suggestion for an appropriate time to bring up your ideas in the context of the agenda. In short, be considerate and courteous of the leader and of everyone in the room.

Setting Boundaries

Even the most congenial person has to set some limits on his time, willingness to yield, and resources. Other people may not fully understand the full scope of favors they may ask of you. They will ask you to do something that will take far more time and effort than they realize. Still other folks do know they are asking too much, but they will continue to do so until you say "no."

If you allow someone to burden you too much, it is not all the other person's fault—it is yours. You are responsible for setting forth what you are willing to do and what you are not willing to do, in polite, positive, and assertive language. This is known as *boundary setting,* and it is not a bad thing. You must educate some people about how much you can do and what things you cannot do. Boundary setting can be a positive experience, and you should not feel guilty about this necessary part of building a healthy relationship.

When you do realize that you are doing more than your share on a project or in a relationship, it is your responsibility to communicate the boundaries of the relationship. Sometimes just understanding the issue from your perspective is all another person needs to adjust and start sharing an equal part of the load. You have to start by communicating using assertive language.

Using ESP

Assertive language is respectful and constructive. It contributes to the goal of solving the problem and mending what is wrong in a relationship or situation. For a problem to be corrected, the problem must be stated. You need to be clear and tactful when you approach someone to set a boundary. Your intent should be to find a solution that will improve the situation for you while respecting the needs and feelings of your partner. One formula for an assertiveness statement is the Emotion, Situation, and Proposal (ESP) approach:

COMMUNICATION TIP

Aggressive wording says, in effect, "I'm right and you're wrong." With assertive language, on the other hand, you're keeping an open mind and not pointing fingers.

Emotion. First, state in an undramatic way the emotion you are feeling when the unwelcome behavior happens. Don't say you feel abused, victimized, or taken advantage of. These are emotionally charged words that could inflame the situation. Say that you feel your time is not being taken into account or that you find the situation stressful. Saying that you find a situation stressful sounds far less accusatory than that you feel abused. An example might be "A situation I am running into lately has been causing me a surprising amount of stress" or "I have been experiencing something lately that is having a greater impact on my time than you or I could have anticipated, but it has reached the point that I need your input."

Situation. Second, very briefly and objectively describe the situation that is bothering you. Try to avoid highly accusatory words or motives to the other person. Try to describe the situation as a scientist would describe what she observes. For example, you might say something like this: "On Mondays when I teach late, the office is often locked when I finish, preventing my being able to turn in my tests. This requires that I return to the campus on Tuesday, which is my telecommuting day."

Proposal. Finally, describe what you would like to have happen next. If there is a way to state the proposal that shows that it will be a better approach for you and your partner, try that phrasing. For example, "What would work better for me and save me money on parking and gas would be for you to give me a key to the office. I could leave my tests to be processed and lock up at around 7:00 P.M."

COMMUNICATION TIP

Some people leave out the "Proposal" part of the assertiveness statement because they feel that allowing the other person to make the proposal is preferable. They may also prefer to bring the proposal up later after a good discussion of the first two parts. Feel free to apply this formula to each situation differently. Choose what you think will be most effective based on the person and the communication dynamics.

The following are applications of the ESP assertiveness statement:

Gardner is resentful that his roommate Eddie leaves dishes in the sink, never takes out the garbage, and never cleans the bathroom. He might say to his roommate:

> "Eddie, I become frustrated when you don't take out the garbage or clean the bathroom. We could get along much better as roommates and enjoy living together if you would clean the bathroom and take out the garbage once a week."

About once a month, good friends Kim and Deanna go to an outlet mall that is 40 miles from their homes. Kim always assumes that Deanna will drive. Deanna could say to Kim:

> "Kim, I am anxious about all the mileage I am putting on my car from so many trips to the outlets. I really have fun on our outings but would feel better if we could take your car next time."

Tilda is overweight and her slim friend Anna tries to help her by dropping suggestions and hints about what Tilda should and should not eat. Recently, Tilda has been on a high-protein diet. At restaurants, she eats none of the bread while Anna indulges. When the entrée arrives, however, Tilda eats all of her meat because it is all protein and is part of her diet. Because she is full from the bread, Anna often says things such as, "These portions are just far too large. I'm going to take half of mine home" or "I couldn't eat all that." Sometimes, Anna does not use words but just looks at Tilda's plate in a judgmental way. Tilda does not enjoy her meal, and the implied criticism is beginning to spoil the outings entirely. Tilda could say to Anna:

> "I feel uncomfortable when you talk about portion size when we go out to eat. This is an unusual diet that requires more protein than bread or other carbohydrates. I have always enjoyed our evenings out very much, but would enjoy our dinners so much more if we could avoid discussing the protein portions for my diet or how large the entrées are."

Preparing for Negative Reactions

No matter how cautious you are, the other person may react negatively out of embarrassment, anger, or resistance to change. They may lash out with angry words, or their reaction may be more subtle and take the form of giving you the silent treatment or giving you a look that says they are shocked at your words. They may defend themselves and their actions or even argue about the validity of what you have said.

Most relationships can weather those reactions if you continue to convey your respect and appreciation for the person. Don't let the possibility that your partner may react negatively keep you from saying what you need to say to improve the quality of your life. Most relationships grow stronger when this type of honest dialogue takes place. If the relationship can't take an uncomfortable conversation here and there, it probably was not going to be a long-term relationship anyway. You may not have lost as much as you think.

The Least You Need to Know

- Assertive behavior is not pushy or intimidating; that is aggression. Aggression scares people and may actually make them more resistant to your ideas.
- Assertiveness inspires confidence and makes people want to support your ideas.
- Passive-aggressive people are just as focused on getting their way as their aggressive counterparts, but their tactics are not as obvious.
- Timing is important in planning when to schedule a difficult conversation and in choosing at what point you will bring up the difficult topic.

- You should have about a 2:1 ratio of questions you ask versus the points you are making. Ask for your partner's or team's input twice as much as you tell them what you think.
- Set the boundaries you need by having a conversation based on the ESP model: Emotion, Situation, and Proposal.

CHAPTER

12

Coping with Conflict and Difficult People

If you are part of any community, family or organization, you are going to run across someone who is just difficult to communicate with, work harmoniously with, or get along with. With no provocation, these people bring challenges or even hostility into any situation they are a part of.

This chapter covers most of the challenging personalities you will encounter. Even if you don't see someone who is exactly like the difficult person in your life, try to use the techniques and strategies offered for a similar type described. You may be feeling you have tried everything and that there is no hope for you to coexist peacefully or productively with your nemesis. Read this chapter to see if there may yet be hope for you to improve the dynamic between your difficult person and you. She may never be your favorite person (and you may not ever be hers!), but you may be surprised at how much better the situation can be if you apply some of the techniques I give you.

In This Chapter

- Dealing with difficult people
- Different types of difficult people
- Gaining an understanding of other people's and your own difficulties

Understanding Difficult People

People can be difficult in a wide variety of ways, as you'll see in the following stories. When you find someone unpleasant, uncooperative, unkind, or challenging, you need to take steps to make sure their behavior does not have a negative impact on you.

Deirdre and Joanito's Story

Deirdre and Joanito worked together as volunteers on a committee for their service organization to staff a local soup kitchen. No matter what Deirdre suggested, Joanito voiced reasons for opposing her. Joanito was also very ambitious and liked to take credit that was not always due to her. Recently, Deirdre suggested they ask the Boy Scouts if they would like to assist as part of the staffing solution for the soup kitchen. Joanito disdainfully said that the Boy Scouts would not be as reliable as the adult volunteers and refused to discuss it further. Instead, Joanito suggested asking retirees from the local senior living community.

Much to Deirdre's surprise, however, Joanito totally changed her position in a later meeting with the president of their civic organization. In this meeting, Joanito suggested using the Boy Scouts and did not acknowledge that Deirdre suggested it nor did she comment on her about-face. Deirdre decided to be the bigger person and say nothing about being the source of the idea. She even went a step further to remind Joanito of her idea about asking the seniors. She wanted to demonstrate support for Joanito's idea to use seniors. Deirdre said, "Yes, and Joanito and I both agree that asking the seniors from Sunray Retirement Village is an option as well."

Very caustically, Joanito said, "I disagree. With doctors' appointments, driving issues, and travel, I think it would be difficult to find reliable volunteers among the seniors there."

Deirdre was baffled that Joanito seemed to disagree with her no matter what. She realized that Joanito was just difficult.

Justin and David's Story

Justin's co-worker David could be a great guy—sometimes. When Justin came into work each day, he didn't know if he would find "Good Buddy David" or "Difficult David." For absolutely no reason, some days David was moody, snappish, and uncooperative about work assignments. David and Justin had to work together every day, and when Difficult David appeared, Justin had become almost hesitant to ask for the reports he needed. David would say loudly, "I will have them ready when I have them ready" or "Alright already! Can't you wait just a minute?" Justin was mystified, and he had recently missed a deadline because he was waiting for David.

Alyssa and Candace's Story

Alyssa and Candace have both been members of the same neighborhood book club for six years and attend monthly meetings. When Alyssa walks her dog, she also sees Candace at least once a week. Alyssa has tried to be friendly to Candace and always speaks and smiles; Candace may or may not return the greeting and never returns the smile. Candace has even given Alyssa an eye roll and other demeaning looks when they are with their neighborhood friends. Alyssa feels that Candace is just difficult.

Ellery and Jason's Story

Ellery and Jason have been best friends for years. They enjoy trout fishing and water skiing, so they spend much of their free time on a local lake. Over the years, when Ellery has forgotten to bring the lunches or buy gas or some other necessary supply in advance, Jason hits the roof. He has an agenda in his head, and Ellery's occasional forgetfulness makes him crazy. Jason never has the attitude that they can just stop at a local convenience store and pick something up. He goes nuclear.

The good thing is that Jason doesn't stay angry for long. After he blows up, he has it out of his system and usually apologizes. Unfortunately, these emotional outbursts are taking their toll on Ellery.

Responding to Your Dragon

Some business people make an analogy about the various approaches to dealing with difficult people as similar to the ways you can approach a fire-breathing dragon. The first impulse you have is to slay your dragon. Translated into people terms, that means proving you are right and winning the point you are trying to make. You may go even beyond that to trying to manipulate people or make them respond in the way you think is appropriate.

Other people succeed by taming their dragons. This effective approach means winning the dragon over so that the dragon is not a barrier to your goals. In fact, you may find taming the dragon to be sufficient for your needs.

COMMUNICATION TIP

You can respond to a challenge with a win-win approach or a win-lose approach:

- **Win-win approach:** You find a solution that is considerate of and productive for your challenger and you. You let her win a point or a concession and are generous.
- **Win-lose approach:** You believe there is a winner and a loser in each negotiation, so you need to make the other person lose in order for you to win it all.

Sometimes, when you take the win-lose approach, you lose as much as your partner. Therefore, consider going with the win-win approach as much as possible.

The highest level of people skills, however, is to learn to dance with your dragon. Surprisingly, your dragon can be one of the most valuable people in your life if you learn to adjust to one another's quirky attributes and moves. For example, if you're working together on a project, your dragon will help you by pointing out problems and weaknesses. This is valuable information, because your friends will not be nearly as candid and critical as your dragon, making your dragon's feedback that much more helpful. Everyone needs a dragon on the team to point out potential land mines.

For example, one of the first things my former employer, management consulting company APC Skills, would encourage us to do was to find our dragons and give them key spots on our focus groups and committees. The result was threefold:

- First, we would find out much more quickly what was working and what was not because our dragons would critique us vigorously.
- Second, the dragon would become invested in our success since she was now part of the team.
- Finally, when other employees saw the usually complaining dragon working cooperatively with our team, we would gain credibility in their eyes.

This approach to valuing our dragon and learning to work in tandem with her was immensely valuable in finding solutions to problems. After we invested in the relationship for a while, our dragons were working for us and not against us.

Most of the time, we learned to appreciate one another. The dragon would turn out to be a conscientious professional whose fire-breathing tactics at the beginning were to protect his co-workers and to ensure that we were not going to reduce the quality of the work done at the company. Usually, our best and most creative ideas came from the dragon. Often, the initial crankiness at the outset of a project had been largely due to the dragon's having had great ideas for years that had been ignored. Once the dragon realized we were listening and were open to learning from her, she was more like a lamb. As we learned to follow her lead sometimes and she learned to follow ours on other matters, we found ourselves in step and doing a dance that resulted in productive changes in the work, the employees, and in the dragon himself.

Other Types of Difficult People

Not all difficult people are fire-breathers. They may be stealthy like Joanito, killing your spirits with a look. Sometimes they are uncooperative and mostly cause you problems through nonaction, the way David would often fail to give Justin the reports he needed.

Let's identify some of the specific types of difficult people and strategies for building more enjoyable, productive relationships with them.

The Zigzagger

In the story of Joanito and Deirdre, Joanito is a Zigzagger. This type of difficult person shows contradictory behavior, so she is hard to work or communicate with. The first thing you need to understand about this type, as with all the difficult personalities discussed in this chapter, is that their behavior probably has nothing to do with you. The Zigzagger is not contradicting what she told you last week just to make your life difficult; this is just her personality style. She probably skips from one idea to the next and may not even remember what she said originally. She may be an idea-a-minute person and would be bewildered why it bothers you that she has no ownership or memory of her previous idea.

Of course, there is the small chance that Joanito is being duplicitous and is glomming onto Deirdre's idea. You may never know whether Joanito is being unconsciously contradictory or if she has an ulterior motive. Either way, your approach to a Zigzagger like Joanito is similar.

First, using an email or text is a great way to deal with the Zigzagger. For example, if one existed, Deirdre could reforward Joanito's previous email recommending using retirees and objecting to the Boy Scouts to put an end to the confusion. Deirdre could have begun her email with something like the following:

> "Joanito, I want to make sure I give credit where credit is due. Your idea for using retirees was such a good one that I am passing it along to management."

COMMUNICATION TIP

You need to be extremely careful with the email reminder tactic. Don't take an "I'm right and you're wrong and here is the evidence" approach. If you forward the email, be sure to be positive and complimentary toward the Zigzagger.

Graciously reminding the Zigzaggers of the previous conversation can also be effective. For example, when Joanito rejected using retirees in the second conversation, Deirdre could have said something like this:

> "I'm surprised you changed your mind about using the retirees. Of course, I'm delighted that asking the Boy Scouts is back on the table. What changed your mind?"

The statements should not be punitive or self-serving. You should, however, acknowledge the about-face.

If the behavior is causing serious problems, sitting down with the Zigzagger to improve future collaborations may be in order. With a combination of empathy and assertiveness, this problem can be solved.

If you do approach a Zigzagger about her constant contradictions, be sure not to sound accusatory. Allow for the misunderstanding to be something you both can work on. In Deirdre's case, she might begin with something like this:

> "Joanito, I have misunderstood your intentions on several situations lately and would really like your help in improving our communications. You have many very good ideas, and I want to make sure I understand clearly what you intend in the future. Do you mind if we discuss a couple of situations that confused me recently and help me understand the changes that took place a bit better?"

The Prickly Pear

Some people are just prickly. They are vaguely annoyed by sounds, suggestions, minor changes, or pretty much anything. It is as if they have sensory nerves sticking out of every part of their bodies and sensors attached to all of their work and property. The slightest motion sets off these sensors and causes a complaint or comment. The complaint may be inarticulate and may even be just a *hmmph,* a groan, or a long sigh—just a little message to you that the Prickly Pear is not happy.

First, be aware that you cannot make the Prickly Pear happy. Her nature is to stay inflamed over something all the time. You should put forth every effort to avoid things you know are annoying to her. With that said, you cannot allow her dissatisfaction to rule your emotions and choices. Do the best you can, and ignore the groans and whines as best you can. She may not even realize she is sending you such negative feedback. At times, you may want to let her know the small and considerate things you are doing in an effort not to annoy her. For example, you may say things such as the following:

- "I know that when we study together, my phone vibrating bothers you. Have you noticed that I have powered it off lately?"
- "I know you are not a fan of fast food. I spent some time online and found a white tablecloth restaurant near us that is really quite reasonable. I hope you will like it."

Making an effort to meet the Prickly Pear halfway is a good idea. Responding to her every complaint and letting yourself be negatively affected is not. Use good judgment here.

The Critic

The Critic is more vocal and direct than the Prickly Pear because she believes she is helping you. She does not view herself as negative or difficult; she just wants to be helpful. She is compelled to share with you her observations, recommendations, and constructive criticism constantly. Even if you are wishing only to brainstorm with the Critic, she feels she owes it to you to let you know where you are wrong and what could have been better, in her opinion. Nothing you present to her will ever be accepted as is; she will always make some adjustment.

COMMUNICATION TIP

Analytical ... Evaluative ... Judgmental

This continuum shows three degrees of thinking critically. Critical thinking is a strength when you use it to build people up and make a contribution. Don't, however, feel you need to evaluate everything said to you. People don't appreciate that. You can easily cross the line and be perceived as judgmental.

The Critic probably does have some helpful ideas and insights, but she is far too impressed with her own credentials, superior knowledge, or contributions. She may even feel that when she is offering her criticism, that you are collaborating. It may feel that way her, but it surely does not feel that way to you.

Dealing with this difficult person is easier if you start with the realization that we all have a little bit of the Critic in us. We are all picture-straighteners. If we walk into a room hung with paintings, our minds go straight to the one painting that is hanging just a little crookedly. Most of us have filters that keep us from feeling compelled to voice every detail we might critique in someone else's ideas or actions. The Critic either has no filter or hers is askew. Looking at the Critic as having a filter problem is helpful. We all have thoughts of what we would have said or done differently. You can come to realize that the Critic may just be voicing what anyone else might have been thinking. Once you accept that the Critic may be a fan of your ideas and work yet still offer a suggestion, you can begin to be more comfortable. Even a compliment will be accompanied by a suggestion from the Critic, but don't let that make you miss the compliment.

At times, you may have to set the ground rules with the Critic. You may say something like the following:

> "Today, I just want to brainstorm. As you know, in the early stages of the brainstorming process, we just let the ideas flow. We don't edit or critique or evaluate the ideas. We just generate ideas. Later, we will get to the stage of refining the ideas. Would that work for you in our discussion today?"

If the behavior persists, use an assertiveness statement (see Chapter 11) to try to change the dynamic between the two of you.

"I feel less confident when you offer suggestions for changes and corrections when I am sharing my ideas in their earliest stages. I realize I don't have the details worked out yet. I really enjoy talking to you but would feel more confident if you could wait until we start talking about details before you offer constructive criticism or alternative ideas."

The Critic may feel rebuffed or even hurt by your suggestion because her view of herself as a valued helper will take a blow. Be gentle in how you say the words and be sure to express your appreciation for the Critic's time. And reinforce with thanks and compliments when the Critic is genuinely helpful.

COMMUNICATION TIP

If you don't ask your partner clearly for what you want, you probably won't get it. For example, if you need your partner to give you more attention, time, or consideration, ask for it using an action verb that tells her what you want her to do. You may not be able to change how people feel, but you can influence what they do and how they treat you. Asking is a start.

The Passive-Aggressive Atomic Submarine

The Passive-Aggressive Atomic Submarine personality may seem very quiet and peaceful, but lurking right under the surface is the potential for trouble. She may be as critical as the Critic, but she is more difficult to deal with because she will not say openly what she thinks is wrong. A simple passive-aggressive personality may be someone like Candace, telling you she is critical with a look or by withholding friendship or approval. A Passive-Aggressive Atomic Submarine may also be like Difficult Dave, bottling things up but periodically exploding. Either type can leave you feeling rejected and depleted. It is hard to be at your best when you are constantly walking on eggshells with a personality like this.

You cannot ignore the Passive-Aggressive Atomic Submarine for as long as you can the Prickly Pear. Although you should not use the word *abusive* to describe the explosive reactions, habitual blow-ups like this can be detrimental to your confidence, sense of calm, and stress level. Certainly, accepting someone's anger being dumped on you on a regular basis is an unhealthy relationship.

The best way to approach the passive-aggressive person is in a nonaggressive manner. Ask her for something so reasonable she cannot refuse you. Examples are the following:

- "Would you be open to considering a different way to do this?"
- "In a perfect world, we would both be able to design the solution our own way. Is there any part of mine you can accept as a compromise?"

- "What are your must-haves and what can we collaborate on?"
- "If we were to compromise a bit, how might that look?"

You can also follow the advice in Chapters 8 and 10 for having a difficult conversation and set some firm boundaries. No one has the right to make a habit of torpedoing your ideas, so it may be time to have a difficult but needed conversation. Everything from physical symptoms (such as high blood pressure and stomach acid) to emotional symptoms (such as depression or nervousness) could result if you don't acknowledge and address the problem. Any type of passive-aggressive behavior is more difficult to get a handle on, so you may not be able to get the cooperation of your partner. If you cannot resolve the problem, remember that one option is to move on from this relationship. Count the cost to you of maintaining the relationship and make a decision.

The Walking Encyclopedia

Closely related to the Critic is the Walking Encyclopedia. This difficult person buries you with details and information. She can't give you a synopsis; she has to give you all the background and context leading up to the point she is making. And she has facts; boy, does she have facts—lots of information. Young conversationalists have a code for this and it is not flattering; they simply say, "TMI—Too Much Information!"

One of the problems you run into with the Walking Encyclopedia is that she slows down the progress of any decision-making. Secondly, all that information just sucks the life out of a conversation or get-together. *Boring!* Finally, you can get so much information that you get sidetracked onto topics of lesser importance and never talk about the important things.

What can you do with these well-meaning folks who block you from getting what you need to get done because they must use up all the air time available for their minutia?

First, speak in concrete facts, especially numbers. Say things such as, "Henry, I have three points I need to make fairly quickly here." Second, put time limits on the conversation by saying you have a meeting in 10 minutes or that you must finish by noon. Also, speak in a staccato tone of voice. Finally, ask closed questions, not open ones. Closed questions encourage short, one-word answers: "How much was that?" "What time does it start?"

As you change the pace and the rhythm of the conversation, you may influence the Walking Encyclopedia to pick up the pace. Like any difficult person, however, this one may require a compassionate but assertive conversation about how you feel.

The Emotional Wreck

Have you ever had a friend who was a drama queen or made every minor problem into a Greek tragedy? Who could make a hangnail seem like a problem requiring major surgery? The Emotional Wreck cannot be that helpful because when a problem arises, she gets a form of hysteria. The hysteria may result in shrieking panic, depression, anger, or tears. Whatever the reaction, it is over the top and counterproductive to good communication.

Dealing with the Emotional Wreck requires assertiveness. If you recall the earlier example of Ellery and Jason, Jason is the Emotional Wreck. To combat the overreactions, Ellery first needs to tell Jason how he feels using an assertiveness statement:

> "When you unload on me like that, even when I deserve it, it leaves me feeling drained. I will try to make checklists and do better, but I would enjoy our trips more if I weren't so worried that I'm going to make a mistake."

Sometimes the emotion is not anger. Sometimes a relationship can wear out because one person is a constant emotional drain on the other person's time or energy. If your friend or colleague always seems to be sad, pathetic, or needy about a difficult situation in her life, you must have that conversation and be assertive about what you need. Allowing someone to stay stuck in self-pity is not being an authentic friend to them.

The Leapfrog or Joker

One person who is difficult to have a productive conversation with is the Leapfrog. The Leapfrog jumps from one conversation topic to the next; she is very hard to follow. Instead of engaging in a conversation you both can participate in, the Leapfrog follows her own path of the conversation and does not consider what you have to say on the subject. She grabs the reins of a conversation and drags it wherever she wants to go. You try to interject your side of the conversation, but by the time it's your turn, she has changed the topic. Her style of conversation is very distracting and may cause you to lose your train of thought or forget details. This style may be especially difficult if you are a very organized person.

A subset of the Leapfrog is the Joker. When you seem to be making serious progress in a dialogue, the Joker will interrupt the flow of the conversation with a joke or random, silly comment. When the choppiness of the conversation reaches a certain point, you realize that your partner is not that interested in a two-way exchange of ideas—she is just popping off comments.

HOLD THAT THOUGHT

A sense of humor is a gift. Using humor to avoid giving a straightforward answer or to communicate transparently is a detriment. Some people use humor because a topic makes them uncomfortable or they are trying to skirt an issue. Enjoy humor with your friends, but if you sense that the humor is too frequent or is a substitute for clear communication, it is time for a more serious conversation.

For decision making, you have to ask yourself if conversation is the best way to collaborate with the Leapfrog. You may be able to get your points across more effectively in a text or email prior to the conversation and bring a copy when you see your friend. Number the main points you want to make and ask the Leapfrog to address them. As she diverges from the topic, say, "What is your decision about #3? Would you be interested in what I found?" Bringing the Leapfrog back on task is best if you use very short, closed questions.

Once again, you can use the tactic of telling the Leapfrog at the beginning of the conversation the two or three topics it is important to you to cover. Because she has no focus, you will have to bring the focus to the conversation.

Identifying the Difficult People in Your Life—and Yourself

Who are the difficult people in your life? Identify someone who is difficult for you to communicate with or to build a relationship with. Now, review the types of difficult people in this chapter. Does your difficult person share any of the characteristics of one of these types? Will you try one of the suggestions in the chapter?

Here is the hard part. Do you share any of the characteristics of any of the difficult people described? Though it is hard to admit, we all have areas where we need to improve. Now visualize your difficult person. Would she think you resembled one of the difficult people described? You may find a spot or two for improvement yourself.

As you can see, the approaches to the various types of difficult people will require you to use the communication and people skills in all the previous chapters. The reality is that all people are difficult at times, and learning to work through the difficulties will broaden your friendship base and strengthen your relationships with the people you invest in this way.

The Least You Need to Know

- Each difficult person is difficult in her own unique way. Identify the type before trying to solve the problem.
- Don't try to slay your communication dragons; learn to dance with them!
- A combination of empathy statements and assertiveness statements can be very effective in dealing with many difficult people.
- Exploring your role in the difficulty can be helpful. When you talk to the difficult person about what you want from her, take ownership of the areas you need to work on as well.
- Some difficult people will not change and are not worth the negativity they bring into your life. Count the costs of keeping the negative person as a friend.

PART

4

Building Strong, Rewarding Relationships

Parts 1 through 3 dealt with meeting people and connecting with them in a positive and productive way. Part 4 starts an exciting phase: taking friendship to the next level as you build strong, rewarding relationships.

Chapter 13 shows you how take an acquaintance and turn that person into a friend. Chapter 14 shows you how to maintain a friendship after you have it. Chapter 15 gives you tips on how to be influential and persuasive with the people in your life. Chapter 16 teaches you how to make yourself clear in conversations, how to share information, and how to tell a great story, while Chapter 17 gives you the skills to collaborate with others and to build support for your ideas and goals. The last skill discussed in this part is the art of silence. Chapter 18 teaches you how powerful silence can be when used in a constructive way.

CHAPTER

13

From Acquaintance to Friend

Everyone wants a friend. Most of us want many friends. However, most of the people we know are acquaintances, colleagues, and neighbors. The opportunities for making friends are endless, but the opportunities are even greater to lose those opportunities.

This chapter will help you discover the sources for finding friends who are well-suited to your lifestyle, values, and interests. Even more importantly, you will learn how to take those relationships and build them into great friendships.

In This Chapter

- How to find a friend and start a friendship
- New beginnings starting with communication "touches"
- How to avoid overlooking the best candidates for friendship
- Best friends: complements, not clones
- Being the type of friend you are looking for

How Does a Friendship Start?

You can find best friends in many places. Some of the places people meet their friends are the following:

- Sports activities, such as a regular pick-up game at the local Y or the neighborhood adult soccer league
- Hobby clubs, such as knitting or book clubs
- A diner or small restaurant where you are a regular
- Work and work-related functions
- Professional organizations

- Civic clubs, such as Kiwanis
- Service projects, such as Habitat for Humanity
- Races and runs for charities
- Fundraising events, such as parties, casino nights, and fashion shows
- Homeowner's meetings and events
- Political events
- Cooking or wine classes
- Business conferences
- Religious gatherings
- College alumni events
- Concerts, plays, and lectures

All of the preceding events give you an opening to exchange remarks about the event you are there for. These events bring other people into your life who are interested in at least one thing that interests you.

Other Strategies for Meeting People

Other strategies for getting to know the types of people who would make friends who are well-suited to you include the following:

Volunteer. The hands-down best strategy for making friends is volunteering. When you work alongside a total stranger to register race participants, make sandwiches, sort donated clothes, or do any other task, you have an immediate connection. Find places you can volunteer and that you enjoy. The first place you try may not be a fit, but you will find your spot. A friend of mine was in an area that had so many people who wanted to volunteer for Habitat for Humanity that they had a wait list. My friend went to the Humane Society and found a group of the most interesting people he had ever met.

Ask a friend. Your current friends are the model for what works well for you as a friend. Ask your friends to connect you with their friends and see if there is a particular friend of theirs who would have a lot in common with you. You can then set up a lunch or dinner for the three of you so you can get to know the new acquaintance better.

Throw a networking party. Networking is not just for work! Invite some friends over and ask each one to bring someone you don't know. Everyone increases their circle of acquaintances this way. Maybe one will become a friend.

HOLD THAT THOUGHT

Use social networking sites, but take safety precautions. Never meet a stranger alone or give out your address or home phone number.

Use your kid's schedule as a social opportunity. If you have children, you have an instant group of acquaintances with shared interests. Be conversational with the other parents as you wait at carpool, sit at T-ball practice, or watch ballet practice. Offer to help the room mother, the teacher, the school secretary, and the librarian or to drive on field trips. Get to PTA 15 minutes early and chat with another early bird.

In short, you can find friends anyplace you go if you are aware, friendly, and intentional about introducing yourself.

Living with Expectation and Openness

An exciting way to live life is to live with the expectation that there are many people out there who would want to be your friend and who have talents and experiences that would equip them to be a valued friend to you. If you live with that expectation, your behavior will change. Normally, if you enter a doctor's waiting room or enter an office for any kind of appointment, you might come in, not establish eye contact with anyone, and look down at a magazine for the entire wait. If, instead, you think, "I may be about to meet the best friend I ever had here," you will put on an air of openness that may make someone want to strike up a conversation with you. You will enter the room, show a connection to someone by eye contact, and smile. You will become a magnet for opportunities. Some people look very shut down, but you will not be that person if you live with the openness that a new friend may be out there in your day-to-day activities.

That doesn't mean you're desperately looking all the time. It doesn't mean that you're disappointed if you don't meet someone new every day. You just live your life in such an inviting way that when that person crosses your path, you look open for business!

Don't Fish in Empty Ponds

If you read the previous section with great interest, it probably means that you have not been finding the kinds of friends you desire or you are not finding enough of them. Maybe you've been fishing in empty ponds. This simply means that sometimes you have exhausted the potential of a community or an area for finding friends. The activities you participate in and the places you frequent just do not offer an ample stock of potential friends for you to choose from. How can you make friends with people with common interests if you never run into them?

COMMUNICATION TIP

If you do what you've always done, you'll get what you've always gotten.

Change what you're doing. Change your routine, your memberships in organizations, and your geographic location if necessary. If you are looking for a change in friends, other changes may be necessary. Join some new clubs or athletic groups. Attend concerts or artistic events if that is your area of interest.

For example, Dina was a 30-ish professional who felt her life was unsatisfying on several counts. Not only had she been hurt by several of her female friends in recent years, she also had a string of failed dating relationships. A friend told her she was fishing in the wrong ponds. Dina's after-work activities consisted of going to the bars and singles-only events that attracted the same old crowd she had been running into for years. She needed to find some new ponds with different fish.

She began taking cooking classes at a local gourmet shop where she met many new female friends. These women were married and had an entirely different set of friends from Dina. Some of the married women began to set Dina up with friends and co-workers of their husbands. These men never went to singles events or the types of bars Dina had been hanging out in. Not only was this a new pond, it was a better pond.

Dina also decided to start attending a singles group at her local church. This was a type of singles event she had not tried. Again, she met new friends, male and female.

Over the next year, Dina found the kind of quality and mutual respect in her new friendships she had never found in her old friendships. She had just needed to try some new activities.

Like Dina, you may also need to change up some patterns or ways you spend your free time. You attract what you put out there. Be sure you're living a lifestyle and going to places where you will meet the kinds of friends who will bring you joy and support for the long term.

Beginnings and "Touches"

Friendships start when one person goes out on a limb to show more than casual interest in the other person. Sometimes, the catalyst between staying acquaintances and becoming friends is to ask if you can contact a person. This is known as a *touch*.

DEFINITION

A **touch** is contact made between people. Touches include conversations, phone calls, texts, emails, and so on. Relationships are built on touches.

For example, you are just chatting with someone you have never met at a mutual friend's wedding. You find out that you both love frozen yogurt. Instead of walking away with "It was great to meet you," say, "Would you like to get yogurt sometime?" or "If you give me a contact email address or phone number, I'll send you the address of that yogurt shop I told you about." Either way, you have a second touch.

Some touches are less risky or intrusive than others. Asking if you can email someone is less intrusive than asking for their phone number. Asking for a phone number is less intrusive than inviting the person to dinner. Similarly, asking someone to coffee is less intrusive than asking him to lunch. At first, it is best to ask for the least intrusive contacts so the person can take time to get to know you slowly.

Friendships also develop when you take a greater interest in an acquaintance's problem, project, or pride and joy. If you have an acquaintance you would like to become a friend to, use the listening skills from Chapter 2 to show great interest in something they are telling you. You can empathize with a problem, or you can show your interest in a project they are working on or a trip they are planning. When you demonstrate to someone that you find their issues interesting, that is very appealing. Generally, people like to be around others who find them fascinating, and you have to demonstrate your interest with your active listening skills.

Because friendships usually develop from the number of connections you have, sometimes certain friendships may take longer. You may find yourself seeing the same person at the gym over and over. Eventually, you might want to approach the person and say, "We must keep the same work schedule. I usually see you working out here at the same time I do." Don't pursue beyond that on the first touch or you may be perceived as the creepy stranger. The other person may also have wished to get to know someone at the gym, and this may be the start of at least an acquaintanceship.

Remember that cultural differences prevent some people from being too friendly in the first or second encounter. They feel they are impolite to be too personal too soon. Don't jump to the conclusion you are being rejected. Give the person some space and look for cues they may be welcome to another conversation.

HOLD THAT THOUGHT

Usually, a slow start to a friendship is better than a fast start. Many people like someone at first, but if the person wants too much contact at first, the new friend can become uncomfortable or feel cornered, even if he really likes the initiator.

You May Not Recognize a Friend at First

Many friendships start very gradually. In fact, you may not even like a person who later becomes one of your best friends. Take these examples and see if any apply to you.

Lucy and CeCe's Story

Neighbors Lucy and CeCe had been introduced by a mutual friend, but the chemistry was just not there for a friendship at first. Both attended some of the same parties given by the young professional crowd of singles they were a part of. After a year of just saying "hello," they both went to a party thrown by their apartment complex. They found themselves standing together and began making small talk about the people they had been dating. CeCe's ears perked up when Lucy described a man from out of state who came to Dallas occasionally just to see her. Everything Lucy said about the man sounded like CeCe's out-of-state boyfriend who had said he was coming to Dallas just to see her! CeCe told Lucy about this coincidence and the two decided to drop the young man for his deceptive ways. They laughed at this coincidence and found they had many similar tastes. In one conversation, they went from being acquaintances to starting a friendship that is still going on three decades later!

These two women who did not even particularly like each other at first have held each other up through marriages, divorces, difficult children, and financial disasters. They would both tell you that this friendship has been one of the most valuable parts of their lives.

Trish and Debra's Story

Trish and Debra were both friends of Susan but only acquaintances to each other. Debra felt Trish was conceited and not very friendly or down-to-earth. Trish's designer clothes and her solemn facial expressions when the three had dinner made Debra feel that Trish did not like her. She wished Susan would not invite her to come along because Debra felt self-conscious around the sedate, dignified Trish. Debra did not feel she could be as playful and casual as she and Susan normally were.

These sporadic dinners went on for about two years. Strangely enough, the three became closer because of food! They began to meet almost every Sunday night for an early dinner. Each one had trouble deciding what to order as everything on the menu looked good. Slowly, a tradition evolved. Trish would order the fried mushrooms, Susan would order the artichoke dip, and Debra would order a salad, and they would all share. It became fun to look forward to the comfort of a cozy ritual, and sharing food from plate to plate broke down some of the formality between Trish and Debra.

HOLD THAT THOUGHT

One reason some people clash when they first meet is they are too much alike! For some reason, seeing some of our strongest qualities in someone else makes us uncomfortable or even competitive. Give people time. First impressions are largely based on chemistry and are very unreliable.

One evening, Susan was out of town on business and Trish called Debra to go to dinner just with her. At dinner, Debra said, "I was really surprised when you called. I always thought you just accepted me because I was a friend of Susan's." To Debra's surprise, Trish said, "I've always wanted to get to know you better. I so admire how comfortable you are in any setting. I wish I could be more like that. To be honest, I didn't think you liked me."

Two lessons can be learned here. First, you should never make assumptions based on someone's facial expressions, their clothes, or other external clues. Second, if Trish had not risked rejection to break down the barriers between them by calling, this friendship never would have happened. The two became like sisters and are still having dinner together whenever they can. They rarely see their charming friend Susan, but the two acquaintances are now best friends.

Bobby and Sam's Story

Bobby and Sam had an adversarial relationship from the time they were in preschool—they had gotten into a wrestling match on the playground! Later, they attended different private high schools and both played football. They were fierce competitors against each other on the field. After high school was over, the two happened to run into each other and found that time had done an interesting thing. The two young men could laugh about those rolling-in-the-dirt fights in preschool. They relished talking about every play in the games they played against each other in school. They realized they had a rich shared history, including their early mutual friendships, football, and the private-school experience. They remain great friends and are more intentional about staying in touch now.

The takeaway here is that you may find yourself at odds with someone who is too much like you! If you can get past the initial friction, you may discover a wealth of things in common that you can enjoy.

These examples demonstrate what a loss it can be to hold on to first impressions that can be keeping you from a valued friend. Reconsider some of the people who have not made a good impression on you in the past. Is there something about one of them that makes them worth a second chance?

Overlooking the Small Stuff

Don't allow small, inconsequential things to make you lose a truly great friendship. In order to find friends who are enduring and who will be a meaningful and positive part of your life, you must first define what is important to you.

Start by writing down what you would consider your top five values and what you think your values are based on. Next, write down three to five activities that are important to you and that you would want to share with a friend. Continue to make lists of things that are important to you. Now pick out the two or three things on these lists that are must-haves in a friend.

COMMUNICATION TIP

Not everyone has a written list, but everyone has a subconscious list—a model of a great friend and the characteristics he should have. Now that you have a list, you pick up on clues more quickly that a certain person may be compatible with your values or lifestyle.

Next, have a sobering talk with yourself. Face the fact that you can't have everything in one person. That's why you have more than one friend. You may greatly enjoy sports yet have a friend who is not athletic. That friend may be great to chat with, travel with, cook with, or attend concerts with. After all, you can't do athletics every hour of the day. Decide what must-haves are deal breakers. Often the deal breakers relate to values, so be sure you have clarified yours before starting this exercise.

As you go about looking for new friendships, notice people who have several of the characteristics on your lists. Don't be put off if they clearly don't have all of the items on your list. You won't have all the items on their lists either!

Looking for Complements, Not Clones

When looking for new friends, look beyond superficial aspects, such as looks, wealth, or fashion tastes. It isn't wrong to be a fashionista, but not all your friends need to be fashionistas. Enjoy your fashion with some friends, but perhaps your new friend has more in common with you professionally or artistically. Or your friend may just be a great listener who loves to hear you talk about your fashion finds and the ups and downs of your day. That also has value to you. You can have different friends for different needs and facets of your life. Look for a *complementary friend.*

DEFINITION

To complement means to complete someone or something. A **complementary friend** completes you in some way. We all have areas of strength and weakness. Your complementary friend will be different from you and may have strengths that you need to develop. Your friend will also be lacking in some areas where you can make a contribution. Different is good. Find friends who complement you and do not just compliment you.

Think of yourself as a puzzle with many pieces. You have many colors and shapes that make up the person you are today. But you, like everyone else, have missing puzzle pieces. You may not have developed certain social skills, such as listening, or you may not be well read. A complementary friend may be very strong in these areas. He will build you up just by being around him.

Jane and Kia's Story

Jane and Kia were good friends and both highly educated. They were also very different. Jane was a voracious reader of nonfiction. She loved to read biographies and bestsellers about business and the economy. Kia was an English major and preferred novels and short stories to nonfiction. When they first met, Kia almost rejected Jane as a friend because she was annoyed at Jane's insistence on talking about the most recent nonfiction books she had read. At first, Kia refused to even consider reading nonfiction books. She loved the fun and the thrill of romantic stories of heroes and heroines. But Kia knew that Jane was a good complement to her and decided to give the friendship some time. After all, Jane shared all the important values Kia felt strongly about, and that meant a lot. Also, Kia often felt at a disadvantage when she was in business conversations. She knew there were gaps in her knowledge that a steady diet of fiction had not filled. Almost like taking her medicine, Kia continued listening to Jane's accounting of what she had read recently.

Jane continued to buy Kia the best of the nonfiction she had read for birthday gifts. Jane was careful to give her the books that read more like novels. To her surprise, Kia actually enjoyed some of these. And even when she did not read the books, Kia began to realize how lucky she was to have Jane give her entertaining synopses of the latest bestsellers.

Although Kia never developed the love of nonfiction her friend had, her willingness to stay in the friendship paid off. Kia came to realize that in Jane she had a friend of stellar character, great compassion, and similar values. They were very congenial, whether traveling together or sharing a pizza. And Jane admired Kia's outgoing personality, her sense of humor, and her wry observations about people. Kia is glad she did not lose all of that because of one area they did not have in common.

COMMUNICATION TIP

Develop friends who will help you grow. Don't look for a clone of yourself. Look for someone who completes you and rounds out your life.

Don't Focus on Differences

When you begin to be friends with someone, don't let a minor difference or annoying habit make you lose someone who will enhance your life in important ways. Focus on the things you do have in common. You can enjoy the things you don't have in common with someone else.

That doesn't mean that annoying habits are inconsequential. Even the smallest things can make some people want to run. Common annoying habits that wear on people include the following:

- Chewing gum and making associated noises
- Making other noises with the mouth or breathing
- Cleaning teeth or ears in public
- Repeating certain phrases, such as "you know" and "like"
- Boasting because of insecurities
- Continually being late

Your pet peeves may not be on this list, but you probably have some. You can adjust, or you can have a thoughtful conversation with someone who becomes a true friend. Just don't let this peeve defeat a friendship before it begins. Major on the majors; don't major on the minors!

Being the Friend You Want Others to Be to You

Whether you realize it or not, you have a mental wish list of what you wish your friends would do and say and be. No matter your good intentions, you go into relationships with expectations.

No matter how wonderful and loyal a friend is, he will not meet all your expectations consistently for all time. Life intervenes, and he may not have the time or energy at a certain moment to respond the way you want. Going into a friendship knowing that even your best friend can't possibly meet every expectation takes a lot of pressure off of him and protects you from disappointment. Showing your friend the mercy and latitude he needs is part of maintaining a deep, long-lasting friendship.

Like other people, you also have different preferences in how you want friendship to be expressed. Some people call these *love languages*. You may be a person who wants friends to send you thoughtful cards or small gifts to tangibly demonstrate their caring for you. Or you may prefer your friends to tell you verbally how much you are cared about or admired. You may, on the other hand, measure a friendship by actions, such as helping you move or helping with other tasks. There are many ways people evaluate friendship.

Your friend, on the other hand, may be geared in a totally different way. Take Jim and Rohit, for example.

Jim was a gregarious, outgoing guy, and very verbal. He was always telling his friend Rohit how much he appreciated his friendship. Jim often told Rohit many of the things he valued about Rohit and their relationship. Rohit would smile appreciatively and say, "Thank you."

This began to bother Jim. He wondered if the friendship meant as much to Rohit as it did to him. He disregarded that Rohit had been there for him in many ways. Rohit gladly drove Jim to work each day when Jim's car became unreliable. Rohit offered to loan Jim money when Jim was concerned he could not afford the new car he needed. Rohit was also very flexible and would enthusiastically agree with any plans Jim wanted to make when the two of them got together. All the evidence of friendship was there—but not the words. These two men just had different ways of expressing their caring and loyalty. Jim came to realize that Rohit's depth of caring was equal to his, but he would have loved to have heard it expressed at some point.

COMMUNICATION TIP

Often, old sayings are popular because there is great truth in them. Here is some conventional wisdom about friendship:

> To have a friend, you need to be a friend.
>
> Friendship isn't a big thing—it's a million little things.
>
> A friend is someone who knows all about you and loves you anyway.

What is your love language? Think of a friend who made you feel cared for. How did he express this caring?

If you want to make your friend know you care, try to do so in his love language. Not usually a gift giver? Make a note in your Outlook calendar to remind you to buy and send a gift if your friend likes that type of thing.

How do you know what your friend's love language is? Often, you can tell by watching what he does. If he sends you cards, they probably like cards. If they are quick to say, "I'll help," he probably feels that actions speak louder than words. Whatever your friend's preference, try to accommodate it occasionally. A good friend is worth the effort.

The Least You Need to Know

- Sources for finding friends are endless, including sports events, your neighborhood, children's activities, classes, and religious organizations.
- Strategies for making friends include volunteering, asking friends to make connections for you, attending networking events, and using social networking.
- If you are not meeting people in your current social activities or routine, change!
- Look for friends who complement who you are rather than ones who are exactly like you.
- Be the friend you want others to be to you.

CHAPTER

14

Building and Maintaining Special Friendships

In This Chapter

- Building rewarding friendships that bring you joy
- Friendship-ending mistakes
- Avoiding common hurdles when building a friendship
- How regular maintenance of your friendship can pay off

Many people long for deeper, deeper long-lasting friendships. But finding someone who has the potential to be a really good friend is just the starting point. When you think someone might be a valuable part of your life as a friend, you want to be sure you continue to build the relationship. Often, friendships die or never flourish because of neglect or a few common mistakes. This chapter shows you how to build on and maintain a budding relationship and to achieve a healthy friendship that brings enjoyment and satisfaction to both friends.

How to Build Friendships That Bring You Joy

Why do some relationships develop into lifelong friendships while others don't? Long-term relationships need a strong infrastructure if they are to stand the test of time. The building blocks of a relationship are mutual respect, genuine caring, flexibility, time, common interests, and similar values. To build a good relationship, you should be able to tick these boxes, or it will be challenging to take your friendship to the next level.

Mutual respect. Sometimes all of the elements of a friendship are there except this one, and that is a fatal flaw. Neither party should feel superior in the relationship. You can have different skills and talents, but each should appreciate the gifts of the other person. Some people mistakenly think that their befriending another will better the other person; this type of condescension leads to an unhealthy relationship. Both partners should feel they make valuable contributions to one another's development while not trying to "change" each other.

COMMUNICATION TIP

Strong friendships require balance. Learn to be flexible without being taken advantage of. Learn to be honest without being insensitive. Learn to be caring without smothering.

Genuine caring. If your friend suffers a financial or personal loss, does it tug at your heart as if it were your own? If not, ask yourself why. An unwritten clause in the understanding between friends is that you care about them, their family, and all that concerns them. If you don't care for anyone in this way, consider discussing the topic with a counselor. Not only is it a wonderful experience to be cared for, it is equally as rewarding to care about another person this way. You will never mine the richest and most rewarding parts of your humanity until you learn to care about someone as much as you care about yourself.

Flexibility. This is a biggie. If you want friends, you have to be flexible. Friends don't always want to do what you want to do. They aren't always available when you want them to be. In order to have friends, you will have to compromise over and over. Of course, your friends should compromise, too. Don't be matchy-matchy and try to make everything perfectly equal; however, there should be give and take on both sides of a friendship. You will need to accommodate her preferences and idiosyncrasies sometimes, and she will need to accommodate yours at other times. And yes, you have some.

Time. Friendship will cost you. The main thing it will cost you is time. You will have to invest time in doing some of the things your friend wants to do that are beyond your common interests. You will have to be there for your friend at times that require sacrifice on your part. You will need to take time to be thoughtful of her and to do favors for her. Count the cost, because a good friendship is well worth it.

Common interests. Just liking each other is not enough. To sustain a relationship, you should enjoy doing some of the same things, even if it is just discussing good fiction or the history of golf. You really need only one common interest—a sport, a hobby, a religion, a love for travel, passion for the environment, and so on. Spending time together is more fun and interesting if you have an activity you can both look forward to occasionally. Your friend does not have to share every one of your interests, but she should share at least one.

Similar values. You may not have all the same beliefs as your friend, but your values should be similar. If you see right and wrong through vastly different lenses, you will eventually have a breach. You should know what people's basic beliefs are about diversity, honesty, and other key issues before you invest in a friendship. If your friend feels it is okay to engage in small acts of dishonesty and you are uncomfortable with that, you will be increasingly uncomfortable through the years. Or if your friend has prejudices or strong opinions on ethical issues that differ from yours, they could eventually diminish the friendship or end it.

Consider all of these aspects as you build a friendship.

Building a Friendship

A few of the steps for building a friendship based on these principles are as follows:

- **Let your friend set the pace at first; err on the side of starting too slowly.** Don't overwhelm your friend with attention, texts, and plans. Depending on how introverted or extroverted a person she is, she may not like as much contact with others as you do. You can't tell by outward signs if a person has introverted tendencies. No matter how much an introvert likes you, being around people saps her strength. She needs space. Give people space until you know how much "touch" they want.
- **Take cues from your friend about what she would like to do when you do get together.** Be considerate of her hints that she does not like spicy food or that she prefers not to see R-rated movies.
- **However, don't expect your friend to always be the one who chooses the activity or restaurant.** Have some good suggestions of your own. Strike a balance.
- **Demonstrate active listening skills.** This is how you learn more and grow your friendship. Chapter 2 offers wonderful coaching in how to be a great listener.
- **Be considerate of your friend's budget.** If she can't afford expensive restaurants, eat in or find a diner you both enjoy.
- **Do something thoughtful occasionally.** Don't buy gifts at first, as that could be awkward, but send a congratulatory text or email when she closes a big sale, signs the lease on a new apartment, or has a birthday or anniversary. Never fail to acknowledge the death of a family member with a card or flowers. Many friendships have ended over this omission.
- **Always, always tell the truth.** Real friendships are rooted in honesty. You may have to skirt certain topics or be diplomatic when she asks, "Do these pants make me look fat?" Still, be sure what you do say is the truth. A Sicilian proverb says that "A friend is someone who will tell you that you have dirt on your face." Do tell your friend she has dirt on her face, but tell her she wears it well!

Money, Time, and People

As you build on your friendship and the areas I just listed, keep in mind that you have to be considerate of your friend's limitations. Many relationships end because one friend does not realize the limitations of her partner in the areas of money, time, and people.

Your friend may really enjoy going out with you, but her budget may force her to say no to dining out or attending events as much as you would like. Even if your friend earns a good salary, student loan debt, credit card debt, or other obligations you are not aware of may not allow her to participate in all the activities she would like. If you sense that money may be the reason your friend is saying no to going out as frequently, try suggesting no-cost or low-cost alternatives. Coffee dates are less costly than dinner dates, and some outdoor music events are free. Look for civic and cultural events in your city that are great for people-watching but that do not charge admission. Festivals and holiday celebrations that are free to the public are excellent options for walking and talking with a friend.

Time can also be point of difference in a growing relationship. Your friend's job or family situation or many other factors may limit her time. Also, some people who are detail oriented and very health conscious take longer to just do everyday tasks, such as cooking, caring for their bodies, and maintaining their home. If your friend needs more "me" time than you do, give her that time and more. If you try to win more of her time than she is comfortable giving, she will probably need to back off from this friendship because she does not want to disappoint you. Learn what your friends are willing to give and what they are not.

COMMUNICATION TIP

Every friendship needs three kinds of time: time together, time with friends, and time apart. Where do you need to make more time in your existing friendships?

The final category where friends experience divisiveness is over people. It may shock you to find that, although you love your friend and all about her, you cannot say the same about her friends. Sometimes the nicest people attract people who are very different from them. You must be able to coexist with her friends and even like one or two of them. Your socializing should not always be alone or with your friends only; she should be able to build some events around her circle of friends. Try to engage these people and find what value is hidden there that your friend has discovered. Looking critically at her friends will feel like a judgment of your friend to her and will discourage her from including you in group activities. No friendship can grow through the years without the inclusion of others.

Friendship Fizzlers

Why do some friendships start out like a rocket and then fizzle? Keeping and maintaining friendships is hard, as you'll see in the following examples.

Linda and Eve's Story

Linda and Eve were best friends and as close as they could be. They had raised their young children together and lived at playgrounds, pools, and one another's houses for four years. When their children started school, Linda took a job as a teacher. Eve was comfortable with Linda's making new friends and knew they would see less of each other. They remained very close for the first year of Linda's new job and still got together with and without their children as often as they could. In the second year of Linda's teaching, she became friends with a younger group of teachers who liked to party hard and whose values were very different from hers and Eve's. Eve respected Linda's right to change and even adapt her values, but the excessive drinking and cavalier attitude to marital infidelity concerned her for her friend's sake.

When they were together, Eve tried to steer the conversation to their shared interests so she would not seem judgmental. Even though Eve said nothing, Linda began to be uncomfortable sharing what was going on in her life with Eve. Her own guilty conscience over an extramarital flirtation made her want to avoid her discerning friends as much as possible. Eventually, Linda stopped returning Eve's phone calls. That lasted for two years, until Linda almost lost her husband and family due to some unwise choices she had made. Linda had been going through a phase. She had married young and had never sowed her wild oats, so she had allowed the younger crowd to influence her to compromise her values.

When the phase was over, Linda wanted very much to resume her friendship with Eve, whose values she shared. Linda was fortunate that Eve believed in loyalty to friends, even when they disappoint you. They resumed their friendship, but Eve had made other good friends in those two years. The two were never again as close as before, but at least the friendship survived the breach. Most do not.

Jesse and Darius's Story

Jesse and Darius had been close friends for five years. They enjoyed going out for wings and beer after work, playing street hockey, and going to an occasional Giants game. Jesse was Darius's best man at his wedding and really liked Darius's wife Tina. But after the wedding, Jesse began to feel that Darius did not enjoy time with him as much. Whereas they had gone out for wings at least once a week when Tina and Darius were engaged, now that they were married, Jesse was lucky to get Darius to say "yes" once a month. The last time Jesse asked Darius to take in a ball game with him, Darius suggested that they take dates. The guys had never done that in the past.

Jesse began to feel that Tina disapproved of him and that she was discouraging Darius from seeing him. In reality, this was just a lifestyle change. Though Tina did want her husband to come home more often than when they were dating, she had nothing against Jesse. Still, Jesse's resentment of Tina made it hard for him to have conversations with Darius about his new life. Darius was uncomfortable knowing there was tension between Darius and his bride. He started avoiding those conversations, and unintentionally, avoiding Darius. No big conflict happened; life happened, and these two guys did not know how to communicate through it. This friendship fizzled.

How to Keep a Friendship from Fizzling

If you could see a problem coming in one of your friendships and could prevent it, would you? Of course you would. Knowing some of the common problems that lead to friendships falling apart could give you some prior warning about some hazards to watch for. The following table lists some all-too-frequent ways friendships die or become weaker. The descriptions of each pitfall may give you a heads-up about some landmines that may be possible in one of your current friendships.

As you read, note anything that sounds familiar. Perhaps these conditions don't exist now, but is there potential for any of them to happen in the future? Please read thoughtfully and consider how to prevent any of these friendship fizzlers from happening to you and your friend.

Friendship Fizzlers	How to Avoid
Going through a phase	All friendships have the ebb and flow of intensity and intimacy. You will go through good times and bad times in a long-term friendship. Sometimes, life just happens and you take a break from each other. A strong friendship can take a break from time to time and be richer for it when time or circumstances allow you to spend more time with one another again.
Clash of values	At some point in your friendship, talk about your values. Agree to be honest with each other when those values are compromised. This is a deeply emotional area with ties to parents and one's own self-worth, so be careful what you say. Emphasize different, not better or worse. If you value a friend, be willing to take her back after the clash is over.
Diverging interests; outgrowing a friend	As your friend learns and grows, keep up. You don't need to have all the same interests, but show an interest in what your friend cares about. Be open to new things. If you haven't learned something new in the last year, you need a serious lifestyle change. Stay engaged. Stay interesting.

Friendship Fizzlers	How to Avoid
Betrayal	You may not bounce back from this one. Support your friends as much as possible. Don't do anything that seems to be taking someone else's side against her; abstain and avoid. Never share her confidences, even if you think it's for her own good.
Jealousy	Even the best of friends can feel jealousy at times. You can be honest about your wishes for a new house or your desire to have traits your friend has. The fact that you chose each other as friends indicates she has qualities you admire. Be glad for your friend as she would be glad for you. Don't compare. She did not get your share of the pie.
Taking each other for granted	When people are first getting to know each other, they are very accommodating and thoughtful. Don't stop just because you know your friend will like you anyway. An old friend is worth more time than a new friend. When was the last time you invested some creativity and thoughtfulness into a long-term friendship? Surprise your friend by treating her as if she is someone special and exciting—because she is!

Friendship Maintenance Can Be Fun

What are some fun and exciting ways to keep things fresh and fun in your friendship? You put your best self out there with new friends, and you often plan interesting things to do. The maintenance of a long-term friendship can be equally exciting.

Girls' Nights Out

Many friends make a commitment to having a girls' night out at least monthly. They put it on the calendar well in advance and honor that commitment. They don't leave February's girls' night out before they get a date on the calendar for March. Calendars are required. These commitments to a girls' night out can be with the two of you or they can be with a small group of friends. Good friends can be guilty of taking time together for granted, so a girls' night out is a remedy for that problem. This is a lighthearted evening, usually very casual, and allows friends to refresh themselves and escape the stresses of the usual routine.

And guys, a girls' night out can easily become a boys' night out with one obvious change.

Grooming Dates

Similarly, grooming dates are a solution for many busy professionals. For example, Kris and Ashley had been best friends in college and had both taken jobs in Boston upon graduation. Both were busy young career women. Kris worked for a consulting firm and Ashley was in her first year as an associate at a law firm. Their companies had reputations for working their younger employees long hours. These friends found that when Ashley had the chance to leave the office at a decent hour that it rarely coincided with a time Kris could get away. On the Saturdays they did not work, their time was consumed with running errands and squeezing in grooming appointments for things like manicures and eyebrow waxing.

One day, Ashley became discouraged over how little time she got to spend with her old friend and was determined to figure out a solution. She began to compare their calendars and their patterns over the last few months. She thought about her biweekly manicure appointments that gave her a full hour or two of downtime with no one to talk to. She knew Kris did the same thing. She called Kris and asked if they could go together to get their nails done on Saturday. Taking care of this errand together gave them at least an hour to catch up and talk face to face. When time permitted, they grabbed lunch or a yogurt afterward and continued the get-together.

COMMUNICATION TIP

Some friends have found that going to the Laundromat together or even grocery shopping at the same time has given them a few extra minutes of face time. Other friends have started dinner cooperatives that actually save them time. Each person in the cooperative cooks a meal and makes enough for four to seven people. Everyone freezes the meals and then they meet once a week to distribute the meals to each other. For one night of cooking, they accomplish the cooking for the entire week—and the get-together when they trade meals is a bonus.

Conferences

Conferences can also be a chance to connect with friends, especially ones who aren't in the same area. For example, Jake and Ivan had a different method of maintaining their friendship. They had begun work when both worked for the same information technology company in Pittsburgh. They were both married with children, so most of their time together had been spent at the office. After three years of steadily going to lunch together and cutting up together in meetings, Jake was abruptly hired away to work for a Silicon Valley company. Now on opposite coasts, they were concerned that their friendship could not be maintained. Ivan did not want to accept that and began brainstorming a solution. He called Jake and said, "You know, our company encourages us to go to one professional conference a year to stay up-to-date on our industry. I'll bet your company does the same. Which conference will you be going to in the coming year? If it works for my boss, I'll try to attend the same one."

The dynamics of their relationship changed, but these two stayed in touch through the years by attending conferences. Being creative in how you find time to maintain friendships is a must since most people are far too busy today.

Texting

Texting is also a quick and easy way to remain connected to friends. For example, Houston, Adam, Hagan, Carl, Erskine, and Kevin were high school friends. They saw each other fairly frequently during their college years because they traveled to parties and sporting events at one another's universities. They also returned home regularly for Christmas and for spring and summer breaks. They then graduated and faced the reality of full-time jobs.

They were scattered in six different cities and had few vacation days to travel. These once close friends actually became closer, and the force that brought them together was fantasy football! They developed a fiercely competitive fantasy football group and kept in frequent touch by texting. They shared news and stats and all sorts of football-related information throughout their days. As time went on, they shared the day's frustrations with projects, kudos and wins they experienced, observations on their new cities, and all kinds of professional and person information.

Although they had little time off as they were busy building their careers, these friends' fast electronic conversations were the perfect solution for keeping in touch. Even more important, these conversations with close friends became part of the fabric of their days and kept them from being so lonely. They were constantly in touch with friends who knew them well and with whom they shared a history. The continuous online conversation has lasted many years, and the guys have grown even closer despite the geographic distance that separates them.

COMMUNICATION TIP

Celebrating milestones in the lives of your close friends is another way to enhance your friendships. Be sure to get together in some way to celebrate birthdays, promotions, babies, weddings, and housewarmings. You should know these things about your friends, and special occasions are a good excuse to reinforce your friendship.

Communication Audits

Finally, not all get-togethers are purely for fun. Some can be for constructive purposes. Some friends meet yearly to do a sort of communication audit. They agree to listen equally and supportively to one another for 30 minutes each. They discuss what has gone well in the last year and anything they would like to adjust for the following year. Both partners use great care to bring up constructive criticism in the kindest way possible that conveys deep respect and appreciation for their partner. This type of meeting may have an annual date (such as New Year's) or may happen informally. It is not for all communication styles. But a communication audit prevents small things that are bugging one partner from becoming big things.

A simple grid like the following (with Partner A and Partner B taking 30 minutes each to answer the questions before collaborating on answers for another 30 minutes) can be used to record differences, but my preference is to just talk through the issues. Not documenting the audit with the form has a more intimate and more supportive feel; nevertheless, first-timers may need a format to get them stated.

Annual Communication Audit Questions

	Partner A	Partner B	Partner Collaboration
What has gone well?			
What could have gone better?			
What adjustments or new ventures do you hope for next year?			

All of these ideas are just a starting point for your friend and you to think of ways to build and strengthen your friendship. What are your ideas for that unique friendship in your life?

The Least You Need to Know

- The building blocks of friendships include similar values, common interests, mutual respect, genuine caring, flexibility, and time.
- Even great friendships face hurdles. Be willing to work through obstacles and even rebound from temporary breaks in the friendship.
- Some of the obstacles friendships may face are going through phases, diverging interests, betrayal, growing pains, jealousy, clashes of values, and taking each other for granted.
- Every friendship needs time together, time with friends, and time apart.
- Friendship maintenance also requires a balance of fun activities and serious steps, such as communication audits and time set aside to talk about changes.

CHAPTER

15

Being Influential and Persuasive

To truly understand people, you must understand their wants and needs—two very separate things. And to learn to influence, persuade, or motivate people, you must understand your own wants and needs. Perhaps this sounds simple, but there is more to self-understanding than you may realize.

This chapter introduces you to common human motivators that will aid you in touching people's hearts, convincing them to do the right thing, and getting their help and support. You learn a model for conducting a persuasive conversation that will increase your chances of getting what you want. You also learn the effective ways to ask for help, as opposed to the ineffective way most people ask. In short, you will be empowered in this chapter to be a highly influential person with the skills to persuade others to say "yes" when you need them most.

In This Chapter

- The basic motivators all human beings share
- How to persuade anyone using the tactics of influence
- A proven model for a persuasive conversation
- How to ask for what you want–and get it

Basic Human Motivators

What makes people do the things they do? What can you say or do to make them want to do what you want them to do? Psychologist Abraham Maslow set out to define these wants and needs. Maslow's Hierarchy of Needs has become the widely accepted starting point for learning about human motivation and how to tap into it in order to be more influential.

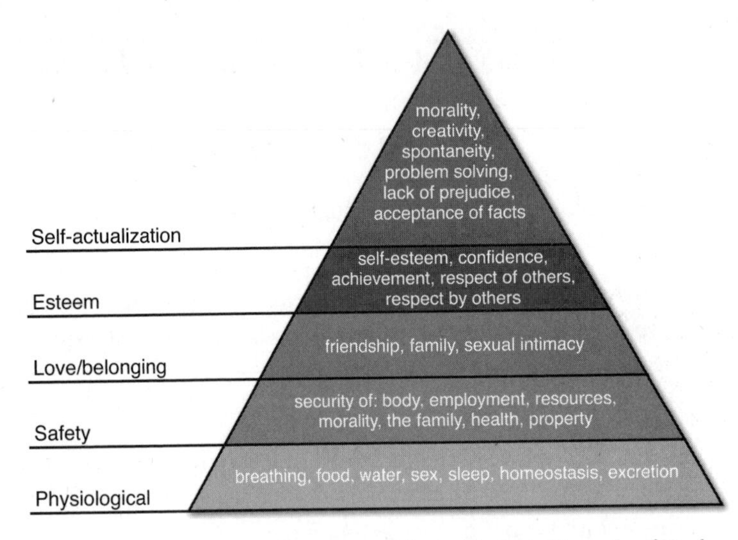

Every human want or need is accounted for in Maslow's Hierarchy of Needs.

First, Maslow broke down human needs into five broad categories. He said that every person has needs in these areas: physiological, safety, love and belonging, esteem, and self-actualization.

Within these areas are some specific motivators you can address in order to persuade people to respond as you wish them to. These motivators have been used by sales professionals for years to convince people to buy products and services. Counselors use these needs to help influence behavior. Motivational speakers often use a combination of these triggers or motivators to move people to do whatever their goal is—from helping them to quit smoking to convincing them to improve their lives in other ways.

COMMUNICATION TIP

Use your knowledge of your partner's motivators in your approach to persuading him. What needs does he have? Is there anything lacking that you can help fulfill? Is there any reward or desire he has that you can help him gain? Fulfilling your partner's needs increases the chances that he will be willing to fulfill yours.

To explore human motivation, let's start at the most basic level.

Physiological

At the most basic level, humans, like all animals, must meet their physiological needs. These needs include breathing, food, water, sex, sleep, and bodily systems that work efficiently. You simply cannot live without most of these, and the human race needs all of them to survive. You really cannot begin to think of the other needs until your most basic physiological needs are met.

For example, Tara was on an airplane heading to Pittsburgh to conduct a meeting for her company. She was pregnant and was pushing the boundaries of when her obstetrician said she could travel by air. She was stressed about many things. She was worried about her image as a pregnant woman presenting to a room full of mostly male executives. She was worried that her ego might suffer a blow because she was not sure of some of the research she had received from her teams. She was fearful she might be embarrassed by not knowing the answers to some of the more detailed questions. All of that changed in seconds, however.

Pittsburgh is not prone to having tornadoes, yet as Tara's plane approached the airport, a tornado began to pass through, moving slowly across the Pennsylvania landscape. The pilot was clearly unconcerned and even seemed to find the situation interesting as he announced, "We're actually passing over the tornado. It should be away from the airport soon. We have about an hour's worth of extra fuel, so we're going to circle 'till the tornado passes through."

But it didn't. Twenty minutes, 30 minutes, and then almost 40 minutes passed. When the pilot came back on the public address system, he told the passengers that the tornado was no longer directly over the airport, but that it was close enough to be causing high winds and that, despite this, he would need to begin the descent to the airport. In a few minutes, the passengers felt the familiar sensation of the descent, but the air was rough and the plane shook and vibrated. The cabin lights then went out and the plane's oxygen flow stopped. Normally, the oxygen masks would have deployed, but there was nothing normal about this trip. People were gasping for breath or trying unsuccessfully to hold their breath. Panic was setting in.

Tara was in shock and disbelief that her life had changed in a moment. She would have traded all she owned in that moment for a deep breath of oxygen for herself and the baby she was carrying. All worries about her presentation, self-esteem, or career were gone. All she could think of was her desperate need for oxygen. Finally, the masks dropped and she was able to take a lifesaving breath of that vital commodity she had never fully appreciated before.

If you are motivating people, consider whether their basic needs are being met. Rarely are people deprived of oxygen, but hunger may be an issue. Clean drinking water or a good night's rest may be motivating for some listeners and some causes you are trying to get someone to support. Before you consider appealing to more sophisticated needs, be sure you address the physiological needs.

HOLD THAT THOUGHT

Politicians who make speeches appealing to high-level needs will be at best misunderstood and perhaps even vilified if they are addressing a group where hunger or clean water are problems. People need the basics, so consider these first when you want to motivate people.

Safety

Closely related to these basic needs is the need for safety. People have a deep need to know that their bodies, jobs, health, property, and families are safe. They want to feel that their morality and resources are not threatened in any way. When you're trying to convince someone of something, ask yourself whether your listener is threatened in any of these areas. Will what you're asking the listener to do help improve safety in any of these areas of the listener's life?

Love and Belonging

The next need in the hierarchy is a more emotional need than any I have discussed so far. We all have a need to be loved. We all have a need to belong to a group, a community, or a family. We are not healthy or productive if we are devoid of this type of human touch. Think about what you are trying to persuade the other person to do. Will it enhance his ability to make or keep friends? Will it allow him to be a better and more valued family member? Will it enhance his ability to grow closer to his friends or be understood and loved more by his family?

Television commercials exploit this need shamelessly. Parents are shown who earn their family's love by buying a bucket of chicken, taking them on trips to amusement parks, and purchasing them new phones with more features. Who knew love had such a clear-cut price?

But it is not unethical to encourage people to do the right thing if it will simultaneously improve family ties. For example, in Atlanta, the Hosea Williams Feed the Hungry event feeds hundreds of homeless and poor people every Thanksgiving. Many years ago, organizers had problems finding enough volunteers to serve such a massive crowd. The media started sharing stories about the families who opted to spend Thanksgiving serving lunch to those less fortunate rather than enjoying their own Thanksgiving in the privacy and luxury of their homes.

Clips were shown of families saying how participating in this annual tradition had drawn them closer. More than one family mentioned that it ended the petty bickering about whose house would be chosen for the meal or whether the stuffing would be cornbread or white bread. The unity and joy of the families interviewed were a strong motivator for many families to decide that their family would sign up to volunteer the next year.

Being aware of these motivators is not a bad thing if you use them wisely and ethically.

COMMUNICATION TIP

Being part of a community will enhance your people skills. Communities come in many forms: families, school classes, social clubs, sports teams, religious organizations, military units, work teams, or cliques of friends. If you are not currently a part of a community, look for a group that needs someone with your qualities and personality and where you feel comfortable. Being part of a community helps you understand and respond to all people more effectively.

Esteem

Next on the list of motivators is the need for esteem—both the esteem of others and self-esteem. This need for esteem may take the form of seeking to be more confident or it may be more of a quest for achievement.

The self-improvement industry would not exist if people didn't desire so earnestly to be respected and admired by others. We are living in the era of career coaches and life coaches, all of whom offer the underlying motivation that you will be more attractive, confident, and admired if you follow their advice and pay their fees. Self-help books regularly make the bestseller list because they promise to enhance the Self (with a capital "S").

People are so preoccupied with self that their search for making themselves more skilled, attractive, and esteemed can actually lead to self-doubt. Too much introspection will inevitably reveal imperfections. We all have them. People go to extreme measures to try to measure up to impossible standards. Some men are even getting beard transplants if they are unable to grow the full beards they see their friends sporting. Some women are getting breast implants, while others are getting breast reductions.

One of the strongest motivators today is the offer of greater self-esteem or the regard and respect of others. Marketers seem to have a subliminal message that the world is a huge popularity contest and that you must use their products and services or be voted least popular.

Appealing to this motivator is not all bad, but you must be careful. A good use of this motivator is to encourage students to achieve the best grade they can by accomplishing schoolwork to the best of their abilities. The improper use of this motivator is the setting of unrealistic goals or the same goals for all students. Many students are experiencing stress and depression, and some have even committed suicide from the pursuit of a high GPA or SAT score.

Friends can motivate each other appropriately. Some work teams are banding together to get healthier and are encouraging each other through group weight loss. They encourage, compliment and, yes, esteem one another and it helps them stick to a healthy regimen.

An occasional note to a friend telling them that you notice something nice or skilled that they did or that you are celebrating some minor accomplishment is very motivating and boosts your friend's self-esteem.

Self-Actualization

At the highest level of motivation is *self-actualization*. Maslow includes the following motivators in this group: morality, creativity, spontaneity, problem-solving, lack of prejudice, and acceptance of facts. Clearly, these motivators represent the best in us that we strive to incorporate into our lives every day. These more refined motivators prompt us to help our fellow man, pursue art and not just commerce, understand ourselves and others better, and make exciting discoveries and inventions. Self-actualization is well worth studying and investing time in.

DEFINITION

Self-actualization is the achievement of one's full potential through creativity, independence, spontaneity, and a grasp of the real world.

You can sometimes see this level of need achieved in the lives of famous entertainers. When many entertainers start out, they are literally starving artists—they sing for their supper. As they get a start in the business, all they want is steady employment and to feel safe. As the need for safety becomes fully satisfied, motivations become more sophisticated. You see many entertainers begin to hunger for the respect and recognition of their peers or lobby for awards that are testimonies to their achievements such as Grammys or Oscars. They may even pursue humanitarian efforts.

We pass through all of these levels of need whether we are the average person or a rock star. Knowing that your partner is motivated by these needs is extremely helpful in preparing you to persuade him.

Sadly, unethical people can use these motivators in not-so-altruistic ways. They can persuade people to give them money or make commitments. Cults have been known to manipulate people using basic human motivators. The leaders of these cults may become masters at convincing people that their needs can only be fully met through the cult or even through the leader himself. Perhaps the most famous cult leader was Jim Jones, who convinced over 900 followers to commit suicide in 1978.

Although the cult is an extreme example, it does demonstrate how intelligent people who seem to have a stable background can be persuaded to do uncharacteristic things when someone appeals strongly to their basic human motivations. Understanding human motivation can make you a better friend and co-worker and broaden your understanding of people greatly. Used for those purposes, understanding motivators is a positive force for good.

The Tactics of Persuasion

Ironically, effective persuasion requires you to first think of the other person in order to get what you want. What are his strongest needs at this time? From your experience, what type of information does he find most motivating and appealing? Before you begin to speak or write in order to persuade someone, first develop a profile of the person.

COMMUNICATION TIP

People can't be talked into doing anything and you can't change people. People can, however, change themselves if they choose. All you can do is present information that will make them want to change or agree with you. Presenting information that appeals to their strongest motivators can influence someone to make the choice you want.

What are his likes, dislikes, and fears? Beginning sales representatives are told they should try to profile their customers by asking themselves what would keep him up at night with worry. Would it be safety? Security? Fear of lack of respect? Tailoring your persuasive efforts to your partner's wants and needs greatly enhances your effectiveness.

Talk to your partner about the benefits to him of granting what you are asking. If he is more likely to give what you ask if there is a humanitarian benefit, don't leave that out. If doing what you ask will make him more employable and that is a present need, approach him from that angle.

Persuasive Conversation Model

A simple model exists for a persuasive conversation. No one can guarantee that you will win your point every time—there are no magic words. However, the following nine steps have proven quite successful:

1. Engage. For this, engage your partner in a conversation that is general and pleasant and related to a topic he enjoys. Don't bring up the topic related to your request.

2. Ask questions. You should ask questions that are distantly related to your topic. For example, if you need to ask your brother for a loan to pay for your child's class trip to the Smithsonian, you might begin by asking your brother to remember what fun you had on a trip in his youth. Saying, "Do you remember when we were ten and went to 4-H camp?"

3. Motivate. Bring up a motivator that might appeal to him. In this example, the brother has a strong need for respect. You might say to him, "You know we all look up to you as a great provider for your family."

4. Describe the situation. This requires you to give details on the issue. "Janel wants to go to Washington on her class trip to the Smithsonian in March. As you know, I've been unemployed since December."

5. Ask for what you want. This is a direct statement of your want—for example, "Would you loan me the $300 dollars so Janel will not miss this trip?

6. State the benefits. Tie positive outcomes to your partner's motivators: "She will always remember that it was Uncle Jim who made this memory possible" or "You've always done so much for the family and we have appreciated all you've done. This is a favor I will never forget."

7. Offer to do something. If appropriate, this gives you an opportunity to say what you will do. "I will pay you back with 7 percent interest as soon as I land a job" or "I will clear that garden area you've been wanting cleared for so long, and I will finish by the time Janel returns from her trip."

8. Thank your partner. Whether the answer is "yes" or "no," thank your partner. Thank him for his time or for previous favors. Reiterate that you mean any positive things you may have said earlier.

9. Follow up a few days later and thank your partner again. Many people don't expect this follow-up. Don't ask for the favor again; just say what you appreciate about your partner. Even if your partner never says "yes," this step eases tensions and strengthens your relationship. If your partner has assets, power, or a relationship you value, you should nurture that relationship with this unexpected thank you.

Try this model the next time you want to persuade someone to say "yes." Experiment with it. You can't script your partner, so it may not go exactly as you plan, but having a plan that includes motivators, benefits, and thank yous increases your chances of success.

Asking for Exactly What You Want

Asking for what you want is one of the most critical parts of the persuasive conversation. Perhaps that is why people dread that part. Some people feel they need to take a big gulp before putting that request out there. It is important that the asking be done correctly and effectively.

An "ask for what you want" statement has two parts. The first part is a strong action verb that tells the listener exactly what action you want him to take. You might say, "email me," "sign the form," "ask your class," or "decide." Naturally, these verbs sound a lot better and will be received much more positively if you use "please" before them.

The second part of the "ask for what you want" statement is that the action must be something your partner will do. In other parts of your persuasive conversation, you tell what you will do, but in this one sentence, you must very clearly state what it is that you want.

Often, the asker wimps out and states what he wants in a vague, passive way. Passive is not persuasive. Note the passive way of stating this request:

> "We will need to collect that information by the end of the reporting period."

A strong "ask for what you want" statement with an action verb and clear directions is better:

> "Please send me your trip report by February 26 so I can to get your expense money to you by the end of the month."

Politely but strongly and clearly asking for what you want has been proven to be effective by insurance companies requesting information on forms, by the U.S. Postal Service in asking people to follow directions, and in dozens of sales surveys. Be conscious of this the next time you take that big gulp and ask for what you want.

People call it the art of persuasion, but it is really more of a science. Try the formulas and recommendations in this chapter and watch how much more successful you will be in getting the results you want.

The Least You Need to Know

- Abraham Maslow says that every person has needs in these areas: physiological, safety, love and belonging, esteem, and self-actualization.
- People go through an evolution in what needs are a priority to them, starting with the most basic physical needs and evolving into a need for self-actualization at the highest point.
- Use your knowledge of basic human motivators for ethical purposes and not for manipulation.
- To persuade your partner, you must engage him in a pleasant conversation, ask questions before bringing up one of his motivators, describe the situation and benefits, ask for what you want, and thank him—and then thank him again a day or two later.
- Never forget the basics: please and thank you.
- "Ask for what you want" statements must have a strong verb that your partner will do and a clear description of exactly what you want from your partner.

CHAPTER

16

Giving Clear Information

How skilled are you at passing along information? The ability to inform others in a clear and descriptive way is a necessary people skill. You may need to explain how to do something, such as how to cook a dish or write a résumé. You may want to talk informatively about the trips you've taken or the events you've attended. Another reason for building your skills to inform others is simply to be more interesting. The bulk of all conversations include some sharing of information. Shouldn't this be a priority for you as you develop your people skills?

This chapter will give you steps to take to be an interesting and informative speaker who can explain anything clearly. You will find value in these skills every day, whether you are learning these skills for your personal or professional development.

In This Chapter

- Achieving clarity in your communication
- How to organize your information
- How to prepare and deliver your information
- Concluding your information in a memorable way
- How to tell a great story

How to Be Clear

The first priority in informative speaking is to be clear. This may sound obvious, but clarity is a challenge. You have to take the steps needed to make sure your message is as clear to your audience as it is to you. We all have a style of communication that is natural to us. The information comes to your mind and flows in a certain way that seems natural to you. However, the way your mind works may be quite different from how another person's mind works. You may perceive and envision information quite differently. So what we say may seem clear to you, but your partner may not understand it at all.

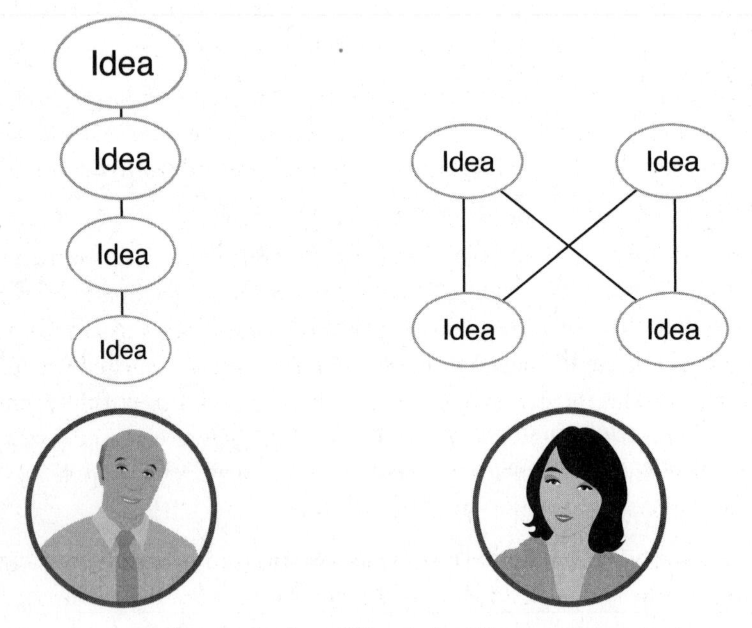

Conversation flows differently for different people.

Seven simple steps will help you achieve clarity no matter what your partner's communication style:

1. Assess what your reader knows and tailor your message.
2. Break your message into small, manageable parts.
3. Preview your message.
4. Deliver your information concisely using easy words.
5. Tell your story two ways (such as orally, visually, or kinesthetically).

6. Summarize your key points.
7. Follow up.

Let's go over each one in detail.

Assess What Your Reader Knows and Tailor Your Message

The first step in giving information is to assess what your listener already knows and then tailor your communication. Does she fully understand the terminology and background information that you understand? Is her knowledge as sophisticated as yours, or do you need to explain some basic terminology or facts before you deliver your message?

Most of us have had the experience of calling a technology support line and having the technician progress too quickly. Especially if your equipment or software is new, the technician may assume that you understand where certain apps or icons are and what they do. If the technician moves ahead of you even one step, you're lost.

Technology isn't the only area where people can communicate in confusing ways. Travel directions are notoriously difficult for some people to understand. Most people feel that they are great at giving directions. If they're communicating with someone who thinks the same way they do, their directions may be clear. But if they're communicating with someone who processes information in a different way, the communication may break down. For example, some people think in terms of direction and will say, "Go east on I-75." Other people think in terms of landmarks: "When you see a Kroger store, turn at the next left." The best directions are a combination of facts, directions, and landmarks.

Just as you can talk faster than your receiver can process, you can also hinder communication by talking too slowly. If you're explaining something to someone but start at far too basic a level, she will tune out and may not tune back in to the parts she needs to hear. Giving people information in the way they best receive it is the key to delivering information effectively.

Break Your Message into Small, Manageable Parts

To communicate clearly, it's important to break information down into bite-size pieces, especially if it is lengthy or complex.

For example, Candace teaches business communication to college students. One of the assignments she gives requires the students to come up with a creative idea for a business meeting and to then hold the meeting in a role-play fashion. The assignment is complicated and has multiple requirements. Candace found that students were overwhelmed to hear the entire assignment in one class. Now she tells them to come up with a creative idea in one class and gives them the directions for brainstorming. Candace waits until the next class to tell the students about the role-play they will do to actually hold a business meeting. In that second class, she goes over the requirements, such as creating an agenda and taking minutes. Previously, these items were often missed by the students. They were suffering from information overload.

But because Candace has separated the bulk of the information into two manageable classes, the students understand and retain far more.

HOLD THAT THOUGHT

Information overload is a common malady today. People are receiving information via their phones, computers, and the media. You may feel your message isn't hard to understand, but if you consider that it's part of a ton of other information coming at your partner, you may see why she misses some things you thought you made clear.

People like to have a clear list of items or facts when you deliver complex information. Just as this section is broken down into seven steps, you can often break your information into steps or topics.

Preview Your Message

To accomplish this step, you need to give the reader a preview of what she's about to learn. The second paragraph of this section told the reader what she could expect. It said, "Seven simple steps will help you achieve clarity no matter what your partner's communication style." Now the reader will be listening and watching for the seven steps and knows that the goal is to clearly deliver information to diverse receivers.

Deliver Your Information Concisely Using Familiar Words

This step is about telling the information in as concise a manner as possible. Most people think that lengthy descriptions may keep the listener from missing important information. The truth is that too much detail obscures the important facts. If you crowd the listener's mind with too much information, she will subconsciously filter some out. You never know what the receiver will miss, but it may be something very important to you.

Use extremely short, easy words if you want to create vivid word pictures. If you tell someone you're going to "show" them something, they get a much clearer picture in their minds than if you use a larger word such as "illustrate." Television and texting are just two of the factors that make today's receivers prefer short, easy words.

COMMUNICATION TIP

Many popular sayings indicate that people prefer brevity:

"If I ask you the time, don't tell me how to build a watch."

"The strong, silent type."

"He was a man of few words."

"Be sincere, be brief, be seated." (Franklin D. Roosevelt originated this saying.)

Tell Your Story Two Ways

Studies show that receiving information in more than one medium can vastly increase understanding. Some people are visually oriented and need to see a concept illustrated to understand it. Others are more auditory and need to hear an explanation. So if you have told your listener your story orally, consider drawing a diagram, map, or other visual to reinforce what you just said.

Some people are just "hands on," or kinesthetic. For this type of person, it's highly effective to allow her to work through the steps of a process. For example, letting her operate the equipment or participate in cooking the new recipe will make your explanation more memorable. Using props is also helpful. If you're trying to explain to your teenage daughter why she should add oil to her car, take the lesson into the garage. Point to what you're talking about as you teach her the consequences of failing to add oil and remind her of the advantages of maintaining her vehicle.

Also, adapt your style to the personality of your listener. Some people like to know interesting details as you pass along information. Other people do not want to get sidetracked with fluff.

For example, Ann, Caroline, and Cara were planning a surprise birthday party for their friend Anita. Cara was the organizer, and she knew they needed to assemble their guest list quickly. She knew her call to Caroline would be fast. Caroline was a woman of few words and wanted her friends to be the same. She was a doer and not a talker. Cara called her and simply said, "Caroline, I've put together a list of the people I think we should invite. Would you like for me to email it to you so you can add or delete as you see fit?" Caroline agreed and appreciated the economy of Cara's communication.

If Cara had been that straight to the point with Ann, Ann would have been hurt. She would have missed the fun of discussing each name on the list and reminiscing about good times with each one. Cara knew that when she called Ann, she needed to allow time to enjoy talking about the shared history the women had with each invitee. They would talk about each friend, share updates on her life and family, remember funny stories, and make observations. Cara adapted her communication style to the way each friend enjoyed receiving information.

Summarize Your Key Points

This step involves briefly summarizing the two to four key steps or points you've just delivered. This helps your listener pull it all together and strengthens memory retention.

For example, at the end of the conversation with Caroline, she could have summarized this way:

> "So you will be sending me the list of your invitees, and I am to call Cara to get hers. Then we are meeting on Thursday to plan the food and the decorations."

Follow Up

This final step is often overlooked. In this step, you follow up with your receiver. Depending on the situation, you check back in a day or up to one week later and ask if she has questions. You encourage her if she is learning a process and offer help and some brief reminders. This type of support is invaluable to some learners and reinforces their commitment to follow your directions well and thoroughly.

Organizing Your Information

When you have a great deal of information to deliver, take some time to decide how you will organize the information. Some topics just naturally flow if you talk about them in chronological order—you simply tell what happened first, second, and third. Stories and jokes are told this way. In the workplace, procedures and reports on events that have occurred are also organized chronologically.

HOLD THAT THOUGHT

If you're asked to give a sequence or history, take a moment to ask yourself where it all started. Often, people begin to tell about the events and continue to have to "back up" to include some omitted information that the listener needs to know. Taking a moment to be sure you're starting from the very beginning will give your story a smoother, more logical flow that your listener will appreciate.

Showing the comparisons and contrasts between two choices or products or services is a more complex but often very helpful way to communicate information. For example, if your sister asks you for your opinion about what phone she should buy, this method would be the most helpful. You could narrow the choices down to two and first tell what they both have in common by comparing them. Next, you could tell her the contrasting advantages and disadvantages of each. This is the best way to deliver information when a choice has to be made.

Probably the most common way to organize your information is topically. For this, you choose the three main topics or themes of your message and then organize all your facts around those.

When you're trying to be persuasive, you may choose to organize by order of importance. Today, people have such short attention spans that I recommend you start with the most important point you have first and then tell your second most important point, and so on. At one time, starting with your least important point and ending with your kill shot was considered equally effective. But in the era of the preview pane in email and speed dating, you are safer leading with your most sizzling point.

There are many approaches to organization, but the main thing is to have a plan. Don't count on the hope that your words will just fall into place and be organized naturally. Analytical listeners, in particular, will try to figure out your organization from your first words, so be sure to have an approach.

How to Prepare

Sometimes, you will have no advance warning that you will be asked for information. You will need to do the best you can on the spur of the moment. This impromptu speaking still must sound as if you have it together. When someone suddenly asks you to say a few words and you are not expecting it, keep three things in mind:

- Don't forget to say something gracious as your opening line, as if you are delighted this bomb just dropped in your lap. You might say, "I am always happy to talk about this wonderful nonprofit."
- Ask yourself, "What is the one important fact I should get across?" This is a fact that you or another stakeholder would feel is valuable for others to know.
- Ask yourself, "Where do I want to end? What is my final line, point, or event as I tell this?" If the event is in chronological order, what is your final event? That is your target. Now find a way to get there.

However, at other times you may have some clues that you will be asked to talk about your vacation, your project, or some other topic. When you have time to prepare, take advantage of it. Ask yourself if bringing pictures or slides would be helpful. If you will be telling people about your new home generator and how it was fantastic during the recent ice storm and you think your neighbors will probably want one as well, write down the contact information of your vendor on cards in advance. Always bring your own cards, also, that have your contact information so people can contact you.

COMMUNICATION TIP

Ask yourself whether you need to add some facts or support from the experts. Expert information is easily accessible online for most topics.

Talk through what you plan to say. Decide ahead of time what side stories you can eliminate. People enjoy succinct stories and information. Also, decide in advance what your three to four main points should be. Don't forget to cover these main points. You can omit some details, but these are your facts that you will make sure to cover. Don't memorize, but be very clear in your mind about what your opening remarks will be. The delivery of a good story depends on a great opening.

More formal presentations will be covered in Chapter 19, but even for an informal conversation where a friend is depending on you for information, ask yourself if you need to do some quick research. For example, would your friend find it helpful if you told her about the generator manufacturer's leading competitor? Keep in mind what you think your listener wants to know. Tell everything she wants but not one fact more.

How to Start

I discussed briefly in step 3 of the seven steps of providing clear and informative communication that you should preview your main points. That is the most basic building block of informative communication, but you want to move beyond the basics. You want to capture your listener's attention. Some people call the first line of a good story "the grabber." You want to have a sentence at the beginning that reaches out and grabs people. Here are some examples:

- If a college student were sharing information with his peers on how to conduct an informational interview, he might say, "I learned something the other day that will help increase my chances of getting a job even before I graduate." His listeners will not be able to resist hearing the details, as this information is in their best interests and rather timely.
- If the mom who leads the neighborhood playgroup wanted to share information about replacing the local playground equipment, she might start with, "I learned the other day about a leading cause of broken bones in children, and we have that cause right here in our neighborhood."
- If you're talking to your neighbor about a new weed killer you discovered, you might say, "I just discovered something that has saved me hours of backbreaking work in the yard."

After the grabber, state your topic or purpose. You can then cover the main points as concisely as possible and move toward your conclusion.

Telling a Great Story

Great storytellers are always in great demand. People love to listen to stories if they are told well. What are some tips for telling your stories in a way that will enthrall your listeners?

When you tell a story, you want to be more stimulating than when you pass along other types of information. The best way to stimulate your listener's mind and create word pictures is by appealing to her senses.

When you begin your story, your reader needs to know where she is and what the surroundings look like. Use vivid colors and words to make your listener feel she is there. Make her see what you see when you recollect this story. If food is involved, be sure you describe the various flavors and colors of the food.

As you name the people in your story, describe each one briefly but clearly. Pretend you're reporting a crime to the police. How would you describe these characters? How short, tall, pale, dark, fidgety, dignified, fragrant, or smelly would they be? How would they be dressed? When you try to describe each one, what is the first word that comes to mind?

Now tell the actions that took place. When you talk about action, use action verbs. Avoid using too many "being" verbs, such as *am, is, are, was, were, be, being,* and *been.* Instead, tell what you did and what the people in your story did. If you were trying to describe how someone walked across the room, you could conjure up a much more vivid picture if you used words like *sauntered, ambled, sprinted, galumphed, prissed, minced, hopped, struggled, strode,* or *glided.*

COMMUNICATION TIP

Action verbs may be visible actions or invisible actions. If your character is at work, he may be performing invisible actions such as *analyzing, deciding, choosing, thinking,* or *providing.*

Be sure to get the sequence of your actions right. You may need to practice your stories in advance or even write them out the first time you tell them. This way, you can edit and get the sequence and wording the way you want them before you try them on an audience. You should know in advance what the high point or climax of your story is going to be. After that funny, thrilling, or interesting moment, will there be a conclusion as well? Sometimes the climax is the conclusion. At other times, you add a moral to the story or a poignant comment or a challenge as your concluding statement.

Like most people skills, your storytelling becomes better as you practice it. Do you have a friend who will help you try out your stories? As you tell her your story, what does she feel is missing? What were her questions? What could she not visualize? Is there part of your story she feels you could have left out?

How to Conclude Memorably

The main requirement of a conclusion to a good story is to *have* a conclusion. Many people just trail off at the end. You need a strong, emphatic conclusion. Your listener should know that's the end. Often, you end with what you've learned or with an idea for going forward. You also can simply summarize what the point of the information is.

The best endings have a punch. Some of the ways you can end a story include the following:

- A memorable or funny line that one of the characters said
- A surprise
- A circling back to the beginning to show the listener how the story or character has gone full circle
- A moral or lesson learned

Whatever your ending, deliver it in a punchy and energetic style. Emphasize key words. For example, Paul Harvey was a famed storyteller on the radio. His voice would vary from soft to loud and his word emphasis kept audiences enthralled. He often used surprise endings. At the end of each broadcast, he would end with, "And *that's* the rest of the story." His primary emphasis would be on *that's* and his secondary emphasis was on *rest*. His delivery made the end very emphatic and compelling.

COMMUNICATION TIP

The formula for a great story? Have a vivid setting; appeal to the senses; include memorable characters and lots of action; and end with an unforgettable climax, thoughtful comment, or challenge.

Have you paid much attention to the key words you're emphasizing in the stories you tell? Pick out the words that are the most important or most dramatic. Say those words a bit louder and with more emphasis and breath behind them. This emphasis prevents you telling your stories in a monotone. You can have a thrilling story, but if you tell it as if you're about to go to sleep, your audience may doze off! At appropriate times, sound thrilled, frightened, concerned, or affectionate. Your voice is an important accessory to your well-crafted story.

Whether you're telling a story, telling someone how to do something, or passing along any other information, you owe it to your listeners to be prepared and interesting. Taking a moment to think through the advice in this chapter as you prepare what you will say is well worth the time. When your listeners enjoy your story more and respond with appreciation, you will begin to enjoy telling your stories even more. An interesting thing will then take place. Your stories will improve with each telling, and you will become more skilled at passing along information. You will improve in this important area of people skills.

The Least You Need to Know

- The first step in delivering information effectively is to assess what your reader knows and tailor your message accordingly.
- Prepare ahead of time any information, handouts, or pictures that will enhance your information.
- Open with a statement that grabs your listener's attention.
- Be sure to have an ending to your story that is so emphatic that your listener knows it is the end.
- Keep interest high with action and action verbs; descriptions of characters, places, and objects that appeal to the senses; and a few unexpected twists.

CHAPTER

17

Collaborating with Partners

There are many, many reasons to choose to partner with someone, and learning to be an effective and appreciated partner is an important life skill. Perhaps the most important reason for learning the skills of partnering with others is that you cannot escape partnering in life. At some point, you will have to work with someone to get what you want or to fix a problem. Even if you're an individualist, you will at some point have to depend on someone else—or someone else will depend on you. Even Howard Hughes, who was obsessed with avoiding human contact and had millions of dollars to help him do it, found himself forced to depend on people toward the end of his life.

Families are a partnership, as are neighborhoods, work groups, Sunday School classes, and health-care teams that see you through illnesses. Whatever partners are in your future, this chapter will help you make any partnership more productive and enjoyable for both of you.

In This Chapter

- Developing the "you" attitude
- Making your partner's goal your own
- How to build consensus
- How to ensure everyone does his fair share
- Communicating more effectively by delivering news sooner rather than later
- Effective partnerships and how they work

The "You" Attitude

The first principle of being a good partner is to develop the "you" attitude. This attitude is countercultural and counterintuitive. Today, everyone thinks of "me, me, me." We are all about our convenience, our needs, and our interests. The "you" attitude requires you to look at a task from the viewpoint of your partner. What would he like to do? What possible problems could this cause him? What could you do to make this task appeal to his interests and talents? What could you help him gain from it? Putting your partner's needs and wants first revolutionizes the partnering process.

COMMUNICATION TIP

The benefits of collaboration are many. Partners help you gain ideas and a different perspective, stimulate your thinking, hold you accountable, provide a second set of eyes to review your work, help you reduce errors, and add creativity and excitement to any project.

Start by asking yourself how your partner's goals and needs may differ from your own. For example, are there generational differences? Is your partner younger and would prefer to rely more on technology for communication? Or is your partner older, with a preference for face-to-face meetings at a more leisurely pace? Are there needs that are gender-specific? Does your partner have an artistic bent you don't have that may help him visualize things differently from you? Is he left-brained and analytical? Are you going to need to be patient while he processes a great deal of information that may or may not prove helpful?

People are truly as different as snowflakes, so your partner may differ from you in a thousand ways. Before you begin a partnership, spend some time assessing the many ways your partner differs from you. This process will take some time if you do it right. Think deeply about the following things you have observed in your partner:

- The conversation style he prefers
- Whether he is more of a thinker or a doer
- His patience level and work pace
- Quirks and habits
- Typical ways of interacting with others
- Areas of interest and strength
- Turn-offs and pet peeves

This is just a short list to get you started. Let your mind roam to past conversations and experiences with your partner. What are his likes and dislikes?

Next, look at the task you have ahead of you. How do you think your partner will see the task? What do you think he will want the approach to be? What are some of his strengths and weaknesses that might relate to this task? As you assign roles and plan your project, what parts can you suggest your partner take that he will enjoy?

One of the most charming partnerships I have ever seen is that of Dell and Ann. They have been managing estate sales together for over 40 years! Both are in their eighties now but are still working full-time as a highly sought-after team behind Dell & Ann Exclusively 10 to 4. No two people could be more different.

Dell was an academic prodigy and is extremely well read. She has a highly analytical mind and a gift for numbers and finance. When they hold an estate sale, Dell prices the books and can immediately spot first editions and other valuable books among the less expensive items. She serves as cashier and processes the money transactions quickly and accurately at the door of the sale. She handles the taxes and other bookkeeping tasks as well.

Ann, on the other hand, is a social butterfly and a born salesperson. She floats throughout the sale chatting up the crowd and encouraging them to buy, buy, buy! She knows what certain regular customers like and will lead them to just the right items and tell them how good it looks on them or would suit their home décor. It's hard to say "no" to this charming octogenarian. She is also wonderful at meeting potential clients and building an instant connection with them. As they compete against other similar companies in their area, Ann is a secret weapon. Many people have chosen Dell & Ann Exclusively 10 to 4 because they wanted to work with such an endearing woman.

These two women have found that being polar opposites is not a reason for conflict but a real asset. They are complementary halves of a very successful small business. They understand that they are going to look at their business from totally different perspectives and have come to an agreement on how to run it. They respect each other's abilities and know their partner's strengths and preferences. They can talk frankly about dividing up the tasks and knowing which partner does not have the ability to handle certain people or certain tasks. They have come to let the other partner work more in the area of their gift and do not get frustrated if one or the other does not work as effectively in some roles.

Dell is thoughtful of Ann, and Ann is thoughtful of Dell. This is the "you" attitude working like a well-oiled machine.

Your Goal Is My Goal

In the best partnerships, both partners have the same goal. Making your project appealing and valuable to your partner greatly increases his interest in and commitment to your goals.

For example, start-up technology companies often split as a company grows. Two friends start off as compatible partners to design a software or hardware solution. The two partners may be highly compatible for this creative stage of the business. With growth and success, however, different types of decisions need to be made. If the company is successful, should they sell it? Should they sell to a larger company or go public? What role should the original partners play? This may be a case of no longer having the same goals.

The partners may both have started out with two goals: make money and create crazy-good technology. Later in the partnership, though, each partner may prefer one of those goals over the other. As the company grows, mass-producing the technology may mean some minor sacrifices on quality. Or one partner may realize they need a cash infusion from a mergers and acquisitions fund in order to take the business global. The other partner may want to keep the business closely held and not give any equity to a third partner. Their goals are evolving and how they view those goals is changing. Vigorous dialogue and a commitment to a process for objective decision making are required if the partnership is to survive. Many partners cannot survive growing pains as a partnership evolves. They split or buy one partner out, and they lose the benefits of a proven collaborative partner.

Therefore, trying to understand your partner's goal and attempting to help him achieve that goal can help save the partnership. Continue to talk and collaborate from time to time. Goals and needs can change. An ongoing dialogue allows you to be on top of those changes and protects both partners from being blindsided.

Building Consensus

Some partnerships consist of more than two people. Whenever you grow to three or more people, the process of coming to agreements gets more complex. Now you have to build *consensus* among more people with diverse views and needs. Building consensus helps you build a broad base of support that will provide a stronger foundation for what you're trying to accomplish.

DEFINITION

To build **consensus** means coming to an agreement that is the best combination of a group's ideas and opinions. It's about building a blended solution from all factions and ideas in a group.

You build consensus one person at a time. Going to each person and asking their viewpoint and sharing your ideas is worth the extra time it takes.

Merrill Johnson is a great example. She learned that the county was planning a road extension that involved the main street in her neighborhood. The county wanted to clear some acreage at the back of her neighborhood to connect the neighborhood's main street to a major road a few miles away. This extension would link separate neighborhoods and provide another option for commuters wanting to access the interstate and speed up morning commutes.

But Merrill realized that turning their neighborhood street into a connecting road to the interstate would bring commuters driving at high speeds through their neighborhood. As it stood now, children could safely ride their bikes through the neighborhood. Those days would be over. The neighbors knew each other and could spot strangers. That, too, would end, as many strangers would use this shortcut. Finally, Merrill knew that the homes on the route to the interstate were in a lower price range and in less attractive neighborhoods. The new road would link and almost merge their neighborhoods, bringing down property values. Merrill knew she had to find some strong allies to help her convince her neighbors to protest the new road. She needed partners.

Merrill first went to Sherry. Sherry was a banker and good with numbers. She had been that kid in your class who always did more research on term papers than the teacher required. Sherry had a young son whom she doted on. Merrill told her that by the time her son would be able to ride a two-wheeler, the days of safely riding a bike in Big Oaks would be over. This was the right approach to Sherry and she committed to help.

Merrill then asked Sherry if she would like to do some research to demonstrate that extensions like this hurt neighborhoods and property values. She asked if Sherry could find any similar situations that had resulted in safety issues.

Merrill then approached Bill and asked him to help. Bill was an attorney and an eloquent speaker. Merrill asked him to be the pitch person to present their findings at the next homeowner's meeting. When Merrill told him that his property value could be affected, he was in.

Finally, Merrill asked Garron to join her partnership. Garron was an extremely well-liked person who had devoted many hours to making the neighborhood a better place to live. She had worked on every committee, from play group to landscaping. People knew that neither money nor selfish interest were ever Garron's motivators. Merrill convinced Garron that stopping the road was the right thing to do. Merrill then told Garron that she really did not have to do anything official. Instead, Merrill asked Garron to just begin to mention to the people she was chatting with the reasons she would be backing the protest against the road. This grass-roots approach would help build support before the next homeowner's meeting.

> **COMMUNICATION TIP**
>
> Most great accomplishments happen through partnerships. Race drivers will tell you that the pit crew does the most critical work in a race. Babe Ruth always gave credit for his success to the team. The most successful coaches—such as Vince Lombardi, John Wooden, and others—never worked toward developing breakout individual stars but on teamwork every day. Whether you are partnering with a friend, your family, or your boss, working in partnership can make you both come out as winners.

The night of the meeting, Bill delivered a persuasive and well-received presentation about the reasons for opposing the extension. It was fully supported by case studies, charts, and statistics put together by Sherry. Much of the crowd was already receptive because they knew Garron thought the protest was the right choice. All the partners used their diverse gifts and the homeowners voted unanimously to protest the extension. When the county planner received a letter of protest signed by 140 taxpayers, she decided to back off. This partnership was a success.

What Is Your Role as a Partner?

When you join someone as a partner, you both should be clear about what your role is. In the previous example, all partners were equal. All Merrill had was an idea. She did not have the skills to execute her idea and she knew it. Some homeowners might have viewed Bill as the leader, but the partners knew he just presented what the others had come up with. A short-term push toward a goal can work without a leader, and the story is a good example of that.

In most partnerships, however, one partner usually emerges as the leader. If that happens, the partners need to be especially clear about who has responsibility for what. Also, if one person perceives he is the leader, he should verify with other partners that they are comfortable with this. Partners need to communicate about many things, including the following:

- Who can speak for the team, and what are the limitations?
- What are the areas of responsibility for each partner?
- How much time do the partners expect each person to devote each week?

If one or more partners are not happy with the agreement on any of the preceding, the partners need to continue to make adjustments and sacrifices to come to a compromise. When both or multiple partners use the "you" attitude, finding a solution that works best for everyone is possible.

Everyone Doing a Fair Share

One of the most difficult aspects of partnership is that there is sometimes an imbalance of workload or initiative or investment. Part of the reason for this imbalance is poor planning. When there is no plan in place, no one visualizes in advance all that needs to happen. If one partner doesn't know all that the other partner is doing, it isn't his fault if the imbalance occurs. Only after you have a detailed description of all that needs to take place can you begin a discussion of who does what and how to make sure everyone does his fair share.

For example, when Carl married Ashley, he imagined having the same type of marriage his parents had had. His mother had not worked outside the home, so she had taken care of all the cooking, cleaning, and household chores. His dad had done the lawn maintenance, car detailing, and other services that now were done for Carl and Ashley by others. Carl happily left all of the household chores to his new bride, without considering that Ashley worked 40 hours a week outside the home. He had a great deal of leisure time; Ashley worked for hours each day after work.

One Saturday, Carl asked Ashley if she would prepare breakfast for them. She wanted to say, "Fix it yourself," but she had been told that the first year of marriage was difficult and was trying to be flexible. She knew that no partnership is ever 50/50, and she did not mind giving more than her share. But on that Saturday, the imbalance got out of hand. When she put the breakfast on the table, Carl looked at his grapefruit half and frowned.

"What's the matter?" asked Ashley, already sounding as if her patience were wearing thin.

"It's okay," said Carl. "You just forgot to cut around the grapefruit wedges."

With that, Ashley unloaded all the frustration and resentment she had felt for the first four months of their marriage. She accused Carl of even more than he was guilty of and called him some colorful names. He was shocked, as this was the first time he had been given a clue that Ashley's vision of being a partner in marriage was different from his antiquated vision of marriage.

They had never sat down and really made a list of all that needed to be done to run their home and take care of themselves. When Ashley eventually was able to talk to Carl without anger, they made such a list. They found the things on the list that Carl could do best, such as laundry and grocery shopping. When the responsibilities were more equitably distributed, both partners enjoyed their time together more.

Communicating Sooner Rather Than Later

Carl and Ashley's situation illustrates some important advice for partners. When a problem arises, communicate it quickly and without judgment or hostility. During the first week of the marriage, Ashley could have said, "I'm sure you did your own laundry before we married. How about putting in a load of clothes while I cook dinner?" But Ashley was trying to be nice and stuffed all her resentment back until she exploded. She said many things she regretted that day. If she had started to make a few suggestions to her husband early on, the conversations may have been a bit uncomfortable, but the problem never would have escalated into the serious problem and regrettable remarks that resulted. Whereas Carl's mistake was that he never considered things from Ashley's perspective, Ashley helped perpetuate the problem by not communicating.

This couple resolved their differences, but many partnerships of various kinds dissolve over the issue of one partner not doing his fair share. Imbalance can hurt partners who volunteer, work, or play together. The imbalance is not always about workload. Imbalance can occur when one partner feels he is investing more money or other resources than his partner.

For example, Evan and Austin had been college roommates. Evan came from a wealthy family and never thought about money. He was so thoughtless, in fact, that he often forgot his wallet or neglected to bring enough cash. He had been brought up in circles where no one ever had to worry about such things, as it was no hardship for friends to pick up the check. Austin, on the other hand, was from a lower-income family. He had no financial help from anyone. He did, however, make sure he paid his own way and did not expect his wealthier friends to help him. He conscientiously went to the ATM before trips and dinners and made sure he had plenty of cash.

Ironically, the poorer of these friends began to pay more and more frequently for their evenings out and for expenses on road trips. Evan was not even aware of the situation. Austin, on the other hand, was painfully aware, as he was spending money he hadn't budgeted for. Austin was embarrassed to tell Evan that he couldn't afford to continue covering checks for him. Instead, Austin began to say he was busy when Evan wanted to hit the bars or go to a nearby beach for the weekend. Because they never discussed the real reason Austin was saying "no," this friendship slowly ended.

COMMUNICATION TIP

If you have an imbalance in your partnership, don't walk away—do an audit. Ask your partner to help. Make two lists. List all the resources (including money) you invest in the partnership on one page. Your contributions will be in a column on the left and your partner's will be on the right. For the second page, use two columns to list the time you spend and the time your partner spends on the partnership. These lists are the start of a discussion that should not be accusatory. Instead, ask your partner for his suggestions for bringing your partnership back into balance. Once you see his list, you may be surprised to see that he is investing in ways you didn't realize.

Communication early on would have solved this problem. All Austin had to do was communicate with Evan that he couldn't afford to pay both bills. If they arrived at the movies and Evan was short a few dollars, Austin could honestly say he didn't have enough money for two tickets and offer to drive Evan to the ATM. Or, on the way to the beach, Austin could have said, "I'm a little short on cash this weekend. If I run out, you may have to front me some money." This would let Evan know that he needed to go to the ATM because Austin would not be bailing him out.

Evidence That Partnerships Work

When Kinko's and FedEx combined to offer both copying and office services along with delivery of mail, people had twice as many reasons to visit these popular stores. This is a partnership that just made sense and increased store traffic.

Similarly, the Dunkin' Donuts brand began partnering with Baskin Robbins ice cream, offering something for everyone in the family and enticing more people to come into their stores.

In the entertainment world, George Burns and Gracie Allen are considered a classic comedy team and are studied by comedians today as a brilliant example of timing. For most comedy teams, success lies in each partner consistently fulfilling his role. One person is usually the conventionally intelligent and suave partner, while the other is the wacky but hilarious jokester. An exception to this is the pairing of Tina Fey and Amy Poehler hosting the Golden Globe Awards. In this case, you have two zany but brilliant comedians who work flawlessly together.

Often, car dealerships increase their profitability greatly by partnering with a similar company. If the company sells luxury cars, such as Mercedes, they may also partner with the Rolls Royce manufacturer to appeal to more buyers.

Starbucks expanded their number of partnerships explosively in the last few years. You will find this franchise in hotel lobbies, university cafeterias, and all kinds of places that once sold their own coffee. This organization has been creative in finding a way to add value to what their partners are already doing and to make a profit for themselves at the same time. After all, isn't enriching both parties what partnerships are all about?

What about you? Make a list of all the people you partner with. Which are working really productively and creatively? Would your partner say he is as pleased with the balance in the partnership as you are? Do any require a conversation that should take place sooner rather than later? Consider asking your partner to read this chapter and then make some lists and have some conversations. Great partnerships are worth maintaining.

The Least You Need to Know

- The benefits of collaborating include stimulating your thinking, coming up with more diverse ideas, holding each other accountable, catching errors, and inspiring creativity.
- Instead of a "me" attitude, adopt a "you" attitude and consider your partner's preferences, interests, and pet peeves.
- Approaching your project with attentiveness to making it appealing and valuable to your partner greatly increases his interest in and commitment to your goals.
- Building consensus helps you build a broad base of support that will provide a stronger foundation for what you're trying to accomplish.
- Know your role as a partner. If there is a hierarchy, clearly establish who is the leader.
- A person who feels he is investing far more time, money, or other resources than his partner can develop resentment and the relationship can be permanently damaged.

CHAPTER

18

When to Stay Silent

Knowing the power of silence is a great asset for a person who wants to deal effectively with people in all kinds of circumstances. Intentional, thoughtful silence can be the perfect response to the needs of some people. Silence can be profound, caring, and comforting to people who need a good listener and someone who will think deeply about others. Silence can also display strength when applied correctly in a situation that requires firmness.

In this chapter, you learn the art of silence and how to apply it when dealing with people and the situations they present. You will learn how to be silent, when to be silent, and why to be silent at selected times.

In This Chapter

- When to stay silent and when to speak
- Silence: the greatest negotiating strategy
- Sensitive subjects that sometimes require silence
- The art of intentional silence
- How not to use silence

Key Times to Stay Silent

People experiencing grief often talk about how horrified they are at what people say to them. The bereft person may react badly when people say things such as the following:

- "She is better off."
- "At least her suffering is over."
- "There is a purpose in this death."
- "You have to move on."

Although there may be truth in any one of those statements, sometimes the words can be jarring or insensitive. Any words might be rejected by some people experiencing deep grief. This is a situation that might call for silence.

It might also call for "announced silence." Sometimes you need to announce that you're going silent so that the other person can be comfortable with what you're doing. Sometimes it's better just to say a simple, "I am so sorry. I am just going to be here with you if you need me. You can talk or just be. I am comfortable either way. Don't feel you need to make conversation."

COMMUNICATION TIP

It is a tremendous relief to be given permission not to talk. Telling your friend that you are comfortable with silence introduces her to the idea of experiencing your companionship with no obligations for making small talk. Great intimacy can be developed in these times of companionable silence.

Use the following table to help you learn to use silence in two entirely different ways: to enjoy silence with a companion or to wield silence to apply pressure.

Companionable Silence	Silent Pressure
Feels supportive to your partner	Does not support what your partner is saying; may be intimidating
Offers companionship when words are insufficient, such as during grief	Offers no relief from an awkward silence and can lead to an apology or a better offer
Should be announced in advance so your partner understands the reason for your silence	Does not announce in advance

Ed and William's Story

Ed and William were brothers who attended different colleges in the Boston area. Ed was a year older and had immediately made many friends at his college, joined a fraternity, and was fully enjoying college life.

When William started to attend college 40 miles away, he seemed to be following in his brother's footsteps. He did enjoy the excesses offered through fraternity life, however, and his grades slipped. He entered his sophomore year under great stress because he was on probation. He then experienced a tragedy that threw him into a depression. His roommate and fraternity brother accidentally mixed alcohol and prescription drugs and died in the fraternity house after a party.

William was unprepared to deal with the intense grief he felt. He tried to drown his sorrows and got a ticket for driving under the influence. Although the school's discipline committee took pity on him and did not expel him, he was under more scrutiny than ever because he was still on academic probation. He felt stressed, depressed, and unfocused, and could not concentrate. William was a macho guy, however, and could not articulate these feelings to anyone. Ed sensed something was wrong, but William continued to say he was fine and to go about his daily routine.

Before the accident, William visited his brother and stayed in the spare room at his apartment about once a semester. They planned the visit in advance and it was usually to attend a concert or other event at Ed's college. One Friday night, William's pain over his friend's death overwhelmed him. He was filled with so much despair that he felt he could not bear it. He was afraid of what he might do. He called Ed and said, "I think I'll come up and spend the weekend."

Ed had the sensitivity to not ask questions. He said, "Sure, come up." He led William to think he had nothing to do that weekend, when in fact he had to break an important date to be there for his brother. When William arrived, they talked about nothing. William told him about a lecture he had heard in a history class. Ed was mostly silent, as he hoped William would get to the real reason for his visit, but he never did for the rest of that night. After about an hour, William went into the spare room, closed the door, and slept for 12 hours. The next day, he stayed in his room most of the day, coming out in the late afternoon to eat a sandwich and to sit with Ed for about an hour. Somehow Ed knew not to ask questions. He let William have his alone time, but stayed close and was available for the few times William emerged.

That pattern was repeated for the next six weekends. On the final weekend of this odyssey, William and Ed were sitting in the living room on Friday night. William, as usual, was talking about nothing—the traffic and the rain. There was an unusually long silence and then he said, "I guess you've noticed I've been coming here a lot." Ed almost laughed but just said, "Yes." William went on to tell him that he had been in a very bad place, but that he had begun to feel he was going to be alright. He thanked Ed for being there and told him he probably would not be back for several weeks, as he needed to get his life back in order at his own college.

William had needed time to heal, and Ed had sensed that he just needed Ed to be there. Ed did not counsel or offer wise words. He was just present. Sometimes people need us to be there, but they don't need us to be chatty. This was one of those times. William was able to slowly recover from his grief and depression thanks to his brother's wise use of silence.

Conversational Space

Not all uses of companionable silence are this dramatic. Often, our friends just need a space in the conversation where no one is talking. For most conversations, a volley of words going back and forth is a good thing. It feels like a lively conversation. At other times, your silence can be just what your friend needs.

Suppose your friend has something difficult to say to you. It is hard for her to bring it up, so she is just prattling away. If you continue prattling away as well, she may never have the space to say what is really on her mind. A long silence may be just the prompting she needs to say to you, "There's something I've been meaning to say to you."

You may also need to give space if your friend is not as quick as you are to think of what she wants to say next. We all have different paces. She may be slower at processing what you say. When she does not respond immediately to what you say because she is deeply processing your meaning, you should not pop back into the conversation with more explanations or questions. Always pause after you say the last word in your sentence. Give your friend a moment of silence so she can respond at her own pace. That pause will result in a more leisurely but much more enjoyable and revealing conversation.

COMMUNICATION TIP

The phenomenon of the power of silence has been around a long time. Have you heard the term "pregnant pause" or the phrase "silence is golden"? A pregnant pause is bursting with meaning though not a word is said. And the value placed on silence is equal to gold.

Silent Pressure

Not all silence is companionable. There are times that silence can be intimidating. Or it can simply place pressure on your conversation partner to amend what she said, offer an apology, or come up with a solution. When you don't jump in to take the pressure off your partner by making small talk, you indirectly apply pressure to her. Sometimes you do need to take this extra step to be sure people do the right thing.

The following two scenarios demonstrate the use of applied pressure through silence.

George started a printing business 10 years ago and, partly due to the efforts of his first employee, Patrick, the business was successful for a long time. For the first two years, Patrick handled customers and did most of the printing and copying, working long hours almost every weekend. Patrick was always friendly and customers loved to talk to him. A new competitor in town hurt the business tremendously, however. George decided to cut back to one full-time employee. Unfortunately, it wasn't Patrick.

When they sat down for this difficult conversation, George was prepared to give Patrick the same offer of part-time employment he gave everyone else. Silence changed his mind.

George said to Patrick, "Unfortunately, I'm forced to cut back all the employees to part-time except Evan. I need his computer and technology skills here full-time. You will work thirty hours per week and that means you will officially be a part-time employee."

Patrick was in shock. His usual response to disappointing news in the past had been, "That's all right. I understand."

This time, he offered George nothing but silence. The uncomfortable pause while Patrick did nothing to let George off the hook was palpable. In those seconds, George had time to feel the full weight of what he was doing. His lack of appreciation for 10 years of loyal service and Patrick's contributions hit him as never before. He sensed he was making a big mistake. Still, he had to make some changes. He cast about in his mind for what he could do for Patrick. He then broke the silence with an offer.

George said, "Patrick, I'm going to give you a different package from the other part-time employees. Although your hours will be fewer, I will pay you a higher hourly wage based on your current salary. And I will continue to pay your health insurance for six months. It is my hope that business will pick up by then and you can return to full-time. If that happens, there will be no disruption in your insurance benefits."

At that point, Patrick thanked him and they were able to continue to work together.

In another situation, silence led to a much-needed apology.

The marketing department of a large university specialized in analytics. One day, they were told that the communications department would be merged with their department. The numbers-oriented experts in analytics were horrified to be associated with professors who represented soft skills. Their lack of respect for the communications professionals was evident from the beginning, but they were always civil.

One day the committee who made decisions about hiring new faculty met to discuss the hiring that needed to be done for the upcoming school year. The committee was all marketing analytics folks except one communications person. The committee leader said, "We have a lot of work ahead of us because we have three open marketing positions and candidates who meet our standards will be hard to find. We also have one communications position to fill."

For a moment, a committee member had a memory lapse and forgot there was a communications person in the room. He said, "Yeah, anyone with a pulse."

The insult was shocking. The communications professor did not use her extensive skills to articulate a rebuke or a challenge to what he had said. She simply looked at him calmly and as if she was very interested in what he would say next. And she waited for a long time. Everyone expected a snappy response from her, so they did not feel the void of silence either. They just watched her watch him. Finally, he broke the silence with a profuse apology.

Several things happened in that minute of silence. First, the communications professor looked more powerful than the marketing professor who had misspoken. She achieved her goal of a deserved apology without saying anything accusatory or obvious. Second, she gained the respect and appreciation of everyone on the committee. It took courage to be able to sit there calmly and look the man in the eye as he squirmed. She was the only one from her department there, but she represented her group with dignity. There was no whining or complaining, just silence.

Sometimes, you say more with silence than with predictable words. If an apology is deserved after someone blurts out an inappropriate statement, letting him stew in embarrassment for a minute or two and come to the realization that she is just wrong can be more effective than pointing out the obvious mistake.

Silence When Negotiating

The classic use of silence as a communication tool is also used in negotiations. When your partner is trying to give less than you want her to give or to make you pay more than you think fair, sometimes wordiness isn't the solution. Sitting there in stony silence can sometimes make the other person back down when explanations and wheedling are not gaining you any respect.

Some car salesmen have used this technique for years. At first, they may talk incessantly. They try to entrap you to express an interest in buying the car. For every objection, they have a solution or they reframe the information. They will then go to their manager one or more times in a display of advocating for a better deal for you. They will probably even lower the price. At some point, though, the salesman may go on the offensive and apply a different type of pressure. He will summarize all he has advocated for you and put the deal in writing on the table. He will say, "I've given you everything you said you wanted. There is no reason left not to sign this contract." Then the silence begins. He stares you in the eye while you sit uncomfortably in a small office.

If you say something like, "Well, I'm still not sure that is the best decision for me right now," he will not respond. You continue to get silence.

Some customers do not know how to end a conversation like that. They were fine when the salesman was arguing with them. They do not know how to respond to the silent stare. More than one customer has been intimidated into signing a contract just to end this negotiation and get out of there.

Silence When You Don't Return a Call or Email

Not all silence takes place live. You can also use silence when you don't return a phone call, text, or email.

Teri really wanted the job that was about to be posted at the call center where she worked. Her boss Sandi had told her and her co-worker Lena that she was about to resign in order to go back to school full-time to get an MBA. Teri and Lena were friends as well as co-workers. Sandi had always trusted Lena and clearly valued her opinion more than anyone else's on the team. Lena, however, didn't want Sandi's job. She preferred the less pressured position of being a customer service representative.

COMMUNICATION TIP

What is your response pattern? Your friends and colleagues will learn your patterns of response. Do you only check email once a day or every few days? People will not expect an immediate response from you. But if you are one of those people who is on the ready at all times answering texts, emails, and calls in real time, people will expect a timely response. When you don't answer for a few days, you have already sent a message to the receiver—and not a positive one.

Knowing Lena didn't want the job, Teri went to her with great confidence to ask for her support for the position. She knew that having Lena's stamp of approval would carry a lot of weight with the selection committee. Lena had worked in the call center for 12 years and understood the needs better than anyone. Teri figured that since they were friends, Lena would naturally support her.

When Teri met with Lena, she spent a few minutes on small talk before she said, "Lena, I'm going to apply for the manager's position."

Lena's pause at this news should have told Teri that Lena had reservations, but Teri was so excited and sure of herself that she plowed on. When Lena didn't jump in with an enthusiastic response, Teri said, "And I want your endorsement. If you say something to Sandi and the selection committee in my favor it will really help my chances."

Lena searched her mind for something neutral to say to extricate herself from this situation. Lena thought Teri was a great friend and great on the phones, but she knew that Teri did not have the organizational or people management skills for this job. She did not want to see her friend get in over her head. Teri could even be fired if she mismanaged the department. Lena knew this was not the right choice for the company or Teri. She finally said, "When did you decide this?"

While Teri continued to talk, Lena came up with a few neutral responses to buy herself some time. She tried to come up with a way to respond to her friend that was completely honest but not hurtful. Finally, she said, "Teri, are you sure? Have you thought about all the evenings Sandi takes work home and the hundreds of details she has to keep track of? This job requires dealing with very difficult people all day long. I wouldn't want that for myself, and I'm surprised that it appeals to you. Please tell me you'll think about it and let's talk about it when you have more time to consider how this will change your life and impact your leisure time." Lena expected that Teri would get back to her after thinking about it.

Teri was hurt, but she agreed to do some thinking about it. The more she thought about it, though, the more she resented Lena. Lena was supposed to support her no matter what because they were friends. Teri became angrier and angrier at Lena but didn't say anything to her. Teri decided to let Lena think about what she had said. She expected an apology or a show of support. She waited for Lena to call. Lena didn't.

In Teri's mind, Lena was the one who should break the silence by communicating first. Teri really thought that eventually Lena would realize how wrong she had been and come to her and offer her support. That never happened. Lena's silence told Teri the truth: Lena did not feel she was the person for the job. They never discussed it, but the message was loud and clear. Eventually, an experienced manager was hired, but the damage to the women's friendship had been done.

In this case, Lena should have gone to Teri after the manager was hired to see if the friendship could be mended. Lena was not wrong for her initial silence, as Teri was the one who was supposed to get back to her. But staying silent when you know there is tension between your friend and you is usually not a good use of silence.

Staying Silent on Sensitive Subjects

Certain sensitive subjects should be avoided in polite conversations. Even if someone else brings up these subjects, you should avoid participating in the discussion. Some of these include the following:

- Controversial or unpopular political stands or legislation
- Discussions about who is rich and how much money people make
- Gender issues, generalized comments about either sex, and homosexuality

- Sweeping generalizations about any group, such as northerners, teenagers, senior citizens, and so on
- Religion
- Discussions about drugs, alcohol, gambling, or other topics that are causes of addiction
- Humorous remarks that diminish the reputation and image of anyone

When you hear conversations start on these topics, gauge the relationship you have with the speaker. Naturally, with your family or a close friend, you may be able to make a generalized comment about teenagers, but saying the same thing in front of a stranger may cause her to think you are negative and down on a whole group.

HOLD THAT THOUGHT

We all hear people make funny remarks about people getting drunk or stoned. If you join in such a conversation or even agree, you may tarnish your image in front of someone who has experienced pain and loss due to a family member's addiction. If you want people who take these topics seriously to see you in a negative light, participate. If not, choose the option of silence when these topics come up. It is safer and far more sensitive.

You also have to be careful with humor. Clean humor that doesn't make anyone the butt of the joke is rare. If the humor in any way crosses the line to teasing or diminishment of a person, your response to the comment or joke should be silence. Not laughing or responding sends the message that you are not agreeing with the jokester about the people ridiculed.

The Art of Intentional Silence

Being intentionally silent is an art form. People are silent in different ways. You can vary your facial expressions, the way you frame your silence, and the degree of your silence.

First, you can alter how you look at people when you are companionably silent versus when you want to register silent pressure or disapproval. When you're being companionably silent, be sure to look at your partner with great kindness and start with a warm smile. The smile should not be broad and toothy, but affirming and pleasant. When you're trying to apply silent pressure, on the other hand, don't smile. Don't glare either, as that diminishes your power. Look at your partner with a level gaze and no hint of approval or support for what she has said. Blink only when necessary, as too much blinking makes you appear to be uncomfortable. Because you are in the position of power, you want to show no discomfort in waiting as long as you need to in silence.

Next, frame your silence. As described earlier in this chapter, announce that you're being silent. You might say something such as the following:

> "I'm here for you, but don't feel you need to say anything."
>
> "If I am quiet, it's because I'm trying to be sensitive to the fact that you may need some quiet moments. Let me know if I can do anything."

Silent pressure does not require any prefacing remarks. You just go silent very abruptly after your partner speaks. Again, it's critical that your silence follows something your partner says.

Finally, there are different degrees of silence. Total silence is used for silent pressure. Companionable silence allows for sounds such as "ah" or "oh" that are not words. These listening noises prove you are responsive and listening, yet they are not intrusive. As your partner talks, these noises simply affirm to her that you understand and care. You still are not contributing your words and opinions to the conversations. You're just being comforting.

The Ineffective Use of Silence

Not all silences are good. When you're silent because your mind is blank or because you're in a bad mood, you aren't using silence correctly.

One time that people feel ineffective with their silence is in job interviews or other times someone in authority is asking them for information in a direct way. Being put on the spot can make your mind go blank. Instead of getting that deer-in-headlights look and coming up with nothing, assure the questioner that you're about to answer her question.

In a job interview, you might say something like the following:

- "I'm just taking a moment to give you the best answer to this question."
- "I agree that that is an important question. Let me give you an example of how I've handled that in the past."

If your boss asks you a question, you might say something such as the following:

- "For me to answer that question fully, do you mind if I check on something and get back to you?"
- "I'm working on that. Would you mind if I gave you a more complete answer when I call you back in a few minutes?"

If you're put on the spot in a social situation, you can use one of the following:

- "Would you mind if I give this some thought?"
- "That's a great question. If you don't mind, I'd like a moment to really think this through."

HOLD THAT THOUGHT

If you waste your silences by blanking out over questions asked of you, you lose the power and authority of the intentional silences that can pressure your partner into giving you the response you desire.

In short, silence is a powerful communication tool, but you want to use it intentionally and with a great deal of skill. Silence can be an eloquent response to a friend in need, or it can establish you as the most powerful person in the room in a negotiation. Practice the art of silence to improve your effectiveness with friends and adversaries.

The Least You Need to Know

- A companionable silence can comfort a grieving friend if you let him know in advance the reason you're being quiet.
- Some people process information more slowly, so a moment of silence at the end of your sentence gives them the time they need to respond.
- Silence can apply pressure that will lead to your partner's offer of help or an apology.
- Silence can be intimidating and increase the personal power of the silent partner.
- Your lack of response to a call, text, or email is a type of silence that can convey your unspoken opinion or stand on an issue.
- Avoid responding to controversial topics, such as politics, money, social issues, people groups, religion, addiction, or demeaning humor.

PART

5

Dealing with Differences in Communication

Part 5 teaches you to enjoy and work effectively with all kinds of people in our multicultural and multigenerational culture. You will learn not just to deal with differences but to benefit from them and use them to enhance your life. Part 5 presents a very forward-looking and positive approach to finding increased opportunities to build your people skills with new and interesting people in a variety of ways.

Chapter 19 helps you explore your personal borders so you can expand them. You will learn more about cross-cultural relationships and how to invite more diverse people into your life. Chapter 20 gives you new insights into your own unique gifts and your signature style. Chapter 21 gives a panoramic view of our multigenerational society and what each generation can offer you as a friend or a colleague. You will learn to adapt to the four primary generations and learn tips for creating mutually beneficial relationships.

CHAPTER

19

Embracing Differences in Culture

In This Chapter

- Causes of communication breakdowns
- Excelling at cross-cultural communication
- The value cross-cultural relationships can bring you
- Letting people into your life and broadening your horizons

What a boring world it would be if we all grew up in the same kinds of neighborhoods, were brought up with the same beliefs and traditions, had voices and accents that sounded just the same, and were not varied in age or appearance. The world is more stimulating, exciting, and interesting because we encounter such diverse people every day.

Yet the very things that make people interesting are the same things that can cause communication breakdowns if not handled properly. We sometimes fail to connect with people or build relationships with them because we don't know how to acknowledge our differences and make them work for us and not against us.

This chapter explores the value of having differences and focuses on how to make diversity a force for good in your relationships with others. You will learn approaches for being more effective in the cross-cultural world we live in.

Differences That Cause Communication Breakdowns

It is unwise to say, "I don't see any differences in people," because the differences do exist. Suppose you were in charge of planning a two-day conference for 500 employees. If you disregard the fact that some people's religious beliefs require they eat no meat and are not allowed to eat foods prepared with animal products, you might leave a number of your attendees hungry for 48 hours.

Being informed about differences and respecting people who have different backgrounds from you is necessary for living in our global world. Our neighborhoods are multicultural, our schools are multicultural, and our workplaces are multicultural. Seeing the differences is not the challenge; handling differences with sensitivity is.

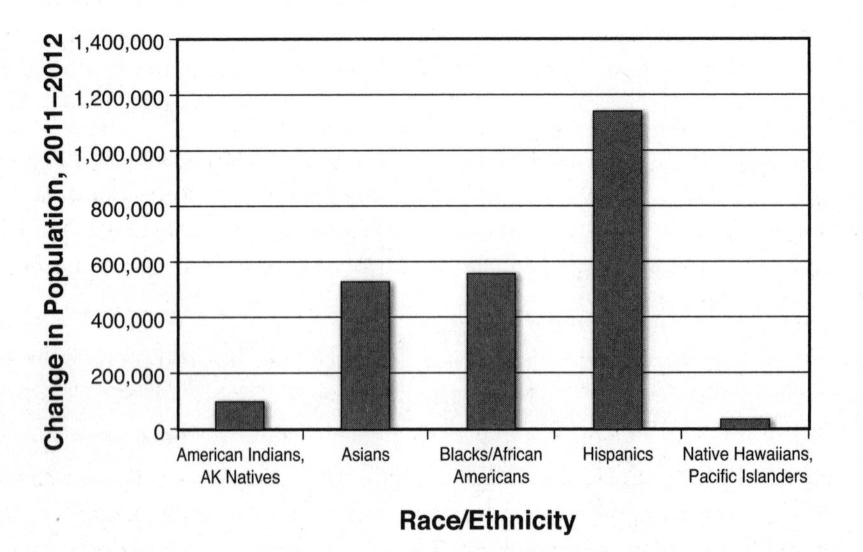

The latest data from the Census Bureau show that America's demographic look continues to change, becoming older and more racially diverse.

(Source: Diane Kurtzleben, *U.S. News & World Report,* June 13, 2013)

Diversity isn't just a matter of ethnicity, age, and gender. Two American-born citizens can be very different from one another if one is from an urban area and the other is from the farmlands; if one was brought up in great poverty and the other in great affluence; or if one is from a conservative community in the east and the other is from a liberal community in the west.

COMMUNICATION TIP

Career counselors and recruiters agree: One of the most valuable things you can do for your career is to become fluent in a second language. In today's multicultural society, you need at least two. It is not unusual for Asian and Eastern European young people to know three or more languages. This increases both their job and social opportunities.

So how do you fully embrace diversity and enjoy all the relationships and advantages it offers? You must be honest about your differences with others. The major differences in people from different cultures derive from five major areas: low- versus high-context culture, time orientation, space and distance, gender differences, and age issues.

Low- versus high-context culture. A low-context culture is one that is very tied to the literal words that are said. These cultures want exact statements and focus on the facts in a conversation. These persons are very direct and will ask plainly and swiftly for what they want and say more bluntly what they do not like. They prefer you to state the bottom line than to frame what you're saying in an attempt to be gracious. The words are more important than the context.

A high-context culture is one that is not focused on exactly what was said but the way it was said. What were the feelings and implications behind the words? What was the demeanor of the person talking? A high-context person is very concerned about the manners and customs; being polite is a high priority. In other words, they are more influenced by the context or whatever is going on around the words than the words themselves.

If you're selling a high-context person your car, he will be more interested in sizing you up and sensing if he can trust you. On the other hand, the low-context person will want an inspection report and then get everything in writing.

You can offend high-context people if you try to pin them down to facts or contracts too soon. They need you to invest in the relationship more and to spend time on pleasantries before getting around to asking for what you want. They want the first part of the conversation to be spent in getting to know one another before any activity starts.

Time orientation. Time orientation is closely connected to low- and high-context issues. Some cultures are known for precision in scheduling and a commitment to punctuality. Other cultures are more relaxed about time; if you're invited for dinner, showing up 30 minutes late may not be a big problem. In a low-context culture like the United States, your host might be insulted at your lack of respect for their time and effort—if you were supposed to arrive at 7:30, you should be there at exactly 7:30.

Space and distance. Some people need a great deal of personal space around them to be comfortable. A foot and a half of distance between them and a conversation partner is a minimum. Others like to be very close to someone while talking in order to feel connected For example, a friend who "gets in your face" to talk may feel most connected to you when only inches separate you, while you may be distracted by such close proximity. The space needed can vary depending on circumstances, too. On a crowded train, you may feel perfectly comfortable being an inch from someone. On the other hand, if you are the only two people on a long elevator ride and your companion is almost touching shoulders with you, you may feel awkward. Gauging the amount of personal space needed by others is a people skill you must develop by observation. You can tell someone needs more space if he's backing up or leaning slightly backward as you speak to him.

Gender differences. Many cultures have different rules for women than for men. This stems from early beliefs that women had to be cared for and protected by men. Now that women are often the primary or sole wage earners for their families, this protective care is no longer welcomed by many women. Still, some cultures continue to have rules for women about modest dress and communication that are different from the rules for men, and you should be aware of remaining differences.

HOLD THAT THOUGHT

Sexual attraction can definitely affect a conversation. An underlying attraction on the part of either party can block communication and understanding and distract from the topic under discussion.

Age issues. The world is changing its views about age differences, but some biases remain. At one time, most people retired at 65, but now that people are living longer, healthier lives, some people are starting second careers at that age. Similarly, at one time we didn't take 20-somethings seriously in the workplace. But technology has leveled the playing field for workplace success. Younger people are some of our most successful entrepreneurs and can often manage tasks faster through technology than some of their older peers. Still, a big gap in age can change the dynamics of a conversation. Ironically, people may have a bias about a very young or a very old person. In truth, both age groups bring unique value to any discussion or effort.

So now that I have identified the major areas of difference, how can you use the differences to enhance your communication and not block it? You want to have friendships and relationships with people of all ages, all genders, and all cultures. Life will be richer, projects will be more successful, and people will be happier through inclusion rather than exclusion.

How to Approach Cross-Cultural Communication

The best approach to living happily and effectively in a multicultural community is to learn all you can about your neighbors and associates. Reading books and online articles is a start, but engaging people in conversations is an even better way to make them and you more comfortable.

At first, you should steer conversations to safe, noncontroversial territory. If your heritage is Mexican and you want to get to know your Pakistani neighbor, your conversation should start with topics such as the neighborhood and the community. That is what you have in common. Initially, focus on your similarities and not your differences. If you have children at the same school or you attended the same party recently, talk about those commonalities.

COMMUNICATION TIP

Your success in engaging with people from diverse cultures and backgrounds means striking a delicate balance. On one hand, you must not focus on the differences to the point that you are uncomfortable or make the other person uncomfortable. On the other hand, you must acknowledge differences so you can be sensitive to the needs other people may have.

Ideally, your neighbor will bring up traveling to Pakistan or mention that he has no local relatives or talk about a dish he is preparing that is endemic to Pakistan—something that will allow you to ask open questions that will encourage him to share more. You can say things such as, "Tell me about your trip," "How often are you able to see your relatives?," or "Where did you hear about that dish? I'm unfamiliar with it." As he talks, you can encourage him by eventually saying, "I really don't know much about Pakistan, but I have always been fascinated by your country. I would like to learn more about it."

Most people enjoy talking about their cultural or ethnic heritage if they can tell about it when they want and on their own terms. Be open and encouraging, but try to allow your partner to bring up the cultural difference first. Also, don't stay focused continuously on the difference. As much as you want to talk about Pakistan, the next time you see your neighbor, talk about other interests as well. Just as you would with your other friends, ask him if he saw the Athletics game last night or what he thinks of a local news story. Don't let your differences be the focal point of your relationship, even if you are being very supportive.

In addition to becoming more informed and engaging in honest conversations, you always want to be sensitive and honest simultaneously—quite a challenging combination. If you're having your Pakistani neighbor over for the first time, ask him in the context of a conversation what his needs are. For example, you can say, "We are so pleased you are coming for dinner on Friday. The menu is wide open at this point. We are usually gluten free, ourselves. Do you have any health restrictions or dietary preferences we should take into consideration?"

Having honest dialogues with people broadens your views but also advances relationships. Most people will enthusiastically begin to share their history and culture. And by the way, you may think your history and culture are very mainstream, but you have traditions, foods, and rituals that may seem just as exotic to others!

The following are some different ways you can enhance your world through cross-cultural experiences:

- Travel at every opportunity, whether it's vacations, visiting friends, studying abroad, and so on.
- Volunteer to work on events or in nonprofits for another people group, such as Greek festivals or refugee tutoring services.
- Participate in blogs hosted by people from other countries or develop an email or text relationship.
- Learn about various cultures through courses at local colleges and community schools. For example, Black, Asian, and Hispanic studies are popular now.
- Join an organization that supports a culture other than your own.
- Learn a second language.
- Make cultural diversity part of your social life—concerts, games from other cultures, and meeting with new friends with different backgrounds.
- Invite culturally diverse people to join your family in different ways, whether it's hosting exchange students, visitors, or newcomers trying to get to know your community.

What's in It for You?

Diversity is rewarding in many ways. Diversity offers you the most interesting friendships and relationships of your life. Any product or service benefits from broadening the need for new products and services because of a more diverse population. Looking at issues from unique and creative viewpoints of diverse people stirs innovation, which is much needed today. Marketing professionals are finding explosive growth in sales by learning more about various *people groups* and targeting their ads and other media to address differences and preferences. Recent groups that have been targeted for marketing campaigns have been Baby Boomers and Latinos, and the increases in sales have affirmed the wisdom of this target-marketing effort.

DEFINITION

A **people group** identifies a group of people who have something in common, such as culture, ethnicity, a common physical trait, or other unique attribute. For example, Hispanics, people with disabilities, and homosexuals are different types of people groups.

Inclusion yields more ideas, more contributions, more richness, more resources, and more choices. Exclusion stifles and limits all of those things, so consciously work toward finding ways to participate more frequently with people from other cultures and backgrounds. You can't easily see things from a different perspective than the one that has been created by your life experiences and your heredity. You can, however, make a friend who has different life experiences and a different heritage. Looking at products, services, society, and life through his eyes will broaden your mind and your way of thinking.

Reaching out to make friends in other age groups and from other cultures broadens your interests and makes your life more colorful and exciting. You may be better prepared for travel or work experiences because of your diverse relationships.

For example, Maryanne realizes that her life has been greatly changed for the better in the last 10 years because of her many friendships with people from other cultures. She had been brought up in a farming community in the Midwest where she rarely met anyone who was not a U.S. citizen of European descent. All that changed when she arrived at her dorm on the first day of college and met her roommate, an 18-year-old Iranian named Amira.

Amira was a devout Muslim whose family had faced religious persecution in Iran under the Ayatollah Ali Khamenei. Maryanne developed great respect for Amira as she watched her practice her religion as devoutly as Maryanne practiced her Protestant faith. Their religions were very different, but their commitment to preserve their faith while in college was the same. Likewise, both faiths required the young women to abstain from alcohol and premarital sex. Maryanne and Amira became strong allies and helped stave off the loneliness they might have otherwise felt.

As their discussions continued and became more candid, Maryanne learned that the quest for religious freedom Amira's family had made was very much like that of the founding fathers in America. Although Maryanne continued to invite Amira to Protestant church services to understand her beliefs, she did it with extreme sensitivity and respect, knowing the price Amira's family had paid to worship as they wanted to.

Jose was another friend of Maryanne's. Maryanne never really danced until she met Jose. He introduced her to salsa dancing and the Macarena. She learned that these rhythms made it easy for her to fall into the moves of the dancing and that she loved it. She had also been a serious meat eater. As Jose cooked for her, she realized that the tastiest dishes he made had no meat. She began to enjoy cooking meatless meals and experimenting with cilantro, cumin, and chili pepper.

The greatest change in Maryanne's worldview, however, happened when she became best friends with Rita, a fellow political science major. Rita was Indian, though she had lived in the United States since she was 3. Though Rita was Americanized, her family still honored their culture. Maryanne observed how the family worked together to develop the best gifts of each child in the family and to support them in getting a good start in life. She learned about sustainability first hand by watching how much less wasteful the family was than her family. She attended Rita's cousin's wedding and believed that it was the most beautiful ceremony she had ever witnessed. She loved the bright colors and the pageantry that contrasted to the black-and-white backdrop and the staid ritual of the typical American wedding.

COMMUNICATION TIP

Today's multicultural society is no longer thought of as a melting pot where we all merge and try to be alike. Instead, it is more like a mosaic. We retain our colors and brilliance from our differences, but we find ways to fit together to create a whole that works beautifully together.

The high point of her friendship with Rita was their graduation trip to India. Visiting the workplace of Rita's cousin and seeing their appreciation for the limited space of their living quarters increased Maryanne's respect for Rita's people.

Perhaps Maryanne's best education in college came from her friends. Now when she meets a coworker or someone she is thinking about hiring for her department, she considers the potential for fresh ideas and diversity that someone from another culture can bring.

No one has to send Maryanne to a diversity class. Her life has become so much richer and better through her friends from other cultures. She has been able to offer many excellent suggestions to her boss about marketing to various people groups and she knows the polite way to interview Indian, Mexican, and Iranian job candidates. Maryanne understands the global marketplace because she knows the preferences and life experiences of her multicultural group of friends.

Broadening your base of friends may introduce you to new marketplaces, new music, new foods, and new forms of entertainment. This is something you can share with them equally from your culture.

Expanding Your Personal Borders

Countries have borders, but people do, too. Are you missing opportunities to form wonderful relationships because of personal "borders"? Ask yourself the following 10 questions:

1. Out of the five best friends in your life, are most of them similar to you culturally and ethnically?
2. If you look at the top 20 acquaintances or colleagues you see most frequently, are most of them similar to you culturally and ethnically?
3. Are all of your best friends within 10 years of your age?
4. When you travel, do you prefer to stay in the same hemisphere?
5. When you travel, do you seek out American foods and go to places where Americans congregate?
6. Of the writers, artists, and musicians that you like most, are the majority American?
7. Do you have routines that keep you going to the same parties, frequenting the same bars and restaurants, doing the same activities, and meeting the same people all the time?
8. Would your friends be surprised if you suddenly became best friends with someone whose culture and ethnicity were radically different from yours?
9. With your friends from different cultures, do you spend more time doing things you were brought up doing than things they were brought up doing?
10. Are you satisfied with the knowledge you currently have of other cultures and other people groups?

Each "yes" to a question is an indicator that you should consider broadening and relaxing your personal borders. Be intentional about meeting and developing deeper friendships with people you might feel are very different from you. You may be missing the friendship of a lifetime because you are unknowingly looking for someone who shares your background or culture. In reality, someone from a different background or culture could prove to be far more interesting and have more to offer on many levels.

The Least You Need to Know

- Handling cultural differences with respect and sensitivity is a rewarding challenge.
- Assess whether you're dealing with someone from a low-context culture who is more literal or someone from a high-context culture who takes communication cues from demeanor and nonverbal signs.
- Most people enjoy sharing their history and culture, so learn all you can about them.
- A multicultural group of friends can introduce you to new marketplaces, new music, new foods, and new forms of entertainment.
- Expanding your personal borders will improve your people skills and provide you with more friends or allies. Diversity is the ultimate win-win situation.

CHAPTER

20

Identifying and Adapting Your Unique Gifts and Style

What's your style? Are you creative and intuitive? Straightforward and direct? Analytical and cautious? Sensitive and caring?

Sometimes the way we give and receive information and connect with people is called a *learning style;* others may call it our *personality style* or *communication style.* Whatever you call it, you have style. Each person you meet or befriend has her own style. To have amazing people skills, you have to learn to understand your own style and how it affects others. Similarly, you have to learn how to approach people with styles that are vastly different from yours. This chapter shows you exactly how to do that.

In This Chapter

- What is your communication style?
- How to adapt your style to others
- Emotional intelligence—how to use it
- Valuing and applying the differences between introverts and extroverts
- What are your unique gifts?

Identifying Your Style

Kendra Cherry discusses the various components of personality or communication style in her article "Learning Styles Based on Jung's Theory of Personality for Ask.com." She lists psychiatrist Carl Jung's description of the basic components or motivators of our style. Note that Jung shows both ends of the spectrum for each personality component:

- Extraversion (extroversion) vs. Introversion
- Sensation vs. Intuition
- Thinking vs. Feeling
- Judging vs. Perceiving

No one relies on just one style. We all operate as thinkers, feelers, intuitors, and judgers at different times of the day and during different tasks. Over a lifetime, however, we learn that certain styles work better for us than others. You may have found that you are more successful in connecting with people if you listen for feelings rather than facts. Or you may have found that, based on your early training or difficult experiences, you had better get all the facts first and not be so dependent on feelings. As you develop a sense of what will be the most rewarding style for you, you tend to make that your "go-to" style and operate from it more than from the other styles.

Let's take a look at a very general overview of the four major styles most people identify with: Sensor, Intuitor, Analytical, and Emotive. Which one is the style you lead with most often? What is your backup style? Which style do you tend to rely on least? You must come to a deep understanding of your style in order to comprehend the impact you have on those whose styles are different.

Once you understand your style, the next step is to try to identify the style of the person you're dealing with. Learning to make adjustments to your words and actions in order to work well with others is sometimes called *style flexing*. The following descriptions of the four major styles will help you understand your style and develop your style-flexing skills so that you can connect with others successfully.

DEFINITION

Style flexing means adjusting your words and actions to connect with another's style.

The Sensor

Push, push, push. Rush, rush, rush. A Sensor has the Nike attitude: Just do it! A Sensor wants the bottom line, just the facts, and to cut to the chase.

Sensors are often viewed as leaders because they can synthesize information fast and make quick decisions. They can understand the scope of a problem quickly and come up with an efficient solution faster than most of their peers. Other styles often like to rely on Sensors to be the courageous souls who can be counted on to go first and to act when action is needed.

When a Sensor starts a project, she wants to do it in the most efficient way, taking the shortest distance between point A and point B, and it's a pity if any poor soul gets in her way. Lee Iacocca was a Sensor. A plaque on his desk summed up the Sensor style. It read, "Lead, follow, or get out of the way."

A Sensor is very honest and straightforward, occasionally blunt. She's ethical and means well, but her tunnel vision to get a task done causes her to occasionally overlook others' input, agendas, or even feelings. She gets impatient with too much time spent deliberating or engaging in group decision-making activities such as meetings, focus groups, and extensive interviews. She will even at times prefer to take the whole project on individually in order to finish it and be done with it. She'd rather do it herself than continue what she considers endless conversations or meetings trying to gain consensus about what to do next.

Time orientation: The Sensor's time orientation is definitely in the here and now. She doesn't care to spend much time pondering the future or dwelling on the past.

People Skills Sensors Need to Develop

In a Sensor's eagerness to finish first, early, or even on time, she may appear pushy and aggressive to some people. Very sensitive people want their input considered thoughtfully and responsively, but a Sensor gets her fill of that toward the end of a project and skips all that "junk" (in her opinion). She scares more cautious people who prefer things to be done meticulously rather than quickly. She is just more willing to risk mistakes.

Sensors need to develop the people skills of listening and empathy; otherwise, they can develop tunnel vision and tune out what others are saying in their haste to accomplish goals quickly. They also need to adapt their fast tempo to the slower tempo of some of their colleagues.

The Value of Sensors

If I want a person to move a mountain, I'll call a Sensor first. They're great to have on your team—especially if you are not a Sensor. It's not just that she will mobilize herself and others to action; it's that she has many wonderful qualities:

- She is loyal.
- She is dead honest (even if it's not in her best interest).
- She is a leader.
- She quickly implements change once change is inevitable (and we are in continual change these days).

COMMUNICATION TIP

If you're a Sensor, be aware of your strengths but be equally aware of how you can come on a bit strong for other styles. The secret to great people skills is style flexing–adapting your style to the style of the person you're dealing with.

The Intuitor

Intuitors can be visionary and have insights into people, projects, and trends long before some of the other styles. They get "vibes" and may see a trend coming early on. They seem to be on the cutting edge in their thinking and like new things. They are one of the few styles well-adapted to a society that is in constant flux and change as ours is. Some companies are even hiring "futurists" today to help predict the changes that can affect their products and services, and Intuitors are excellent in roles like this.

The Intuitor is a far-out thinker, the original "think outside the box" person. The conversation of a group may be going along in a straight line and suddenly the Intuitor may pipe in with an idea that is completely new and unrelated to anything said up to that point. She makes these mental leaps to creative or different ideas, and not everyone will follow her logic. Her leaping ahead to different and new ideas may feel like second-guessing to you at times, which can be uncomfortable. During conversations, you may find her saying things like the following:

"But what about …?"

"Or you could …."

"I don't know, what if …?"

"What about doing it this way instead?"

"Have you ever thought what might happen if . . .?"

Some people call her a dreamer or someone who "marches to the beat of a different drummer." Some may find her downright flaky or weird.

Time orientation: The Intuitor's time orientation is in the future—always thinking about what's over the horizon.

People Skills Intuitors Need to Develop

An Intuitor thinks of things not as others see them but in her own unique way. She creatively visualizes how processes or events might change and appear tomorrow or a decade from now. Because of this, she's often out of step with her neighbors and co-workers. Because she's coming from a unique viewpoint, sometimes people can't figure where she's coming from with all the seemingly off-the-wall stuff she thinks up. She enters a room and ultra-conservative people start humming the tune to *The Twilight Zone.*

She may appear critical instead of weird. She bores easily. Because Intuitors like to play with ideas, they rarely accept anyone's idea quickly and at face value. They question; they look at other alternatives; they twist and contort your idea until it's not exactly what you meant. This doesn't feel like team spirit, so the Intuitor doesn't appear to be a team player.

Intuitors need to develop the skills of finishing well through perseverance and attention to detail. They are great starters but not so much on completing projects. Investing in their teamwork skills and their time management skills can make these people excellent employees or partners in any arena.

The absolute worst combination of styles is getting two Intuitors on the same team. Why? Because each will have a unique and innovative idea that differs from the other Intuitor's idea. All Intuitors hear different drummers. And each really believes that her idea is the best and that the other person just doesn't have the vision to see it. Two Intuitors butt heads like goats. Find a different combination for a successful team project or partnership.

The Value of Intuitors

Still, if I wanted a mountain moved, I would call this gal even before I called the Sensor. Why? Because she would look at alternatives and possibly come up with a solution that we "normal" thinkers would never have come up with. She might say you don't have to move the mountain at all; instead, she might say to build a monorail through the mountain. In short, Intuitors are great assets to a family and friends for the qualities they usually demonstrate:

- They are innovative and creative.
- They embrace new technology.
- They adapt well to change.
- They see what others miss.

The Analytical

The Analytical looks at everything carefully and is a real thinker. She loves to study things before making a move, and her steps are carefully thought out in advance. She makes fewer mistakes and takes fewer risks. She will probably be the best-informed person in the room, and if she isn't, she will be working on it.

She loves to gather and organize information. If you give an Analytical an outline or a survey, she'll tell you a better way you could have organized it. She sees things others do not because she is very thorough and skilled at looking at things with a critical eye. She's often accused of having "analysis paralysis" because she feels she can never have too much information before she makes a decision. She wants her bases covered (as well as other parts of her anatomy).

If you want a mountain moved she's good to consult because she'll make sure you don't make mistakes (she's a stickler for corrections) and you'll have a plan for what you do with the mountain as you lift it, move it, and place it—all in charts, spreadsheets, tables, and outline form. Still, she might not get the mountain moved this year.

Time orientation: Her major orientation is in the past because she wants to see what she can learn from history, facts, and research. The time orientation of this type can also be said to be past, present, and future because she carefully considers all eventualities, historical data, and existing conditions.

People Skills Analyticals Need to Develop

If you have a deadline, the Analytical will drive you crazy. She'd rather study a problem to death than risk making even a small error. She wants reports and follow-up, and, in general, she creates a whole lot of work for others. She can also be critical. You can present a great project that solves a huge corporate problem, increases productivity, and puts millions back into the budget, but the Analytical may only comment that your report has a typo on page 24, paragraph two. She's trying to help you be more accurate, but you still want to dive over the table and choke her.

She may come across as formal or old-fashioned. And she can be boring when she gets bogged down in detail. Some feel she has trouble getting to the point.

To develop better people skills, Analyticals need to learn to more responsive to the person in front of them and less focused on the minutiae of the information they are hearing. But being responsive should not come in the form of grilling their partners about the information. They need to develop flexibility and openness to new ideas. In today's communities and workplaces, more risk-taking is expected and people do not devote extensive time to double-checking and verifying everything to the degree that makes an Analytical comfortable. Learning to let go and acceptance that they cannot control all outcomes are valuable lessons Analyticals can learn.

The Value of Analyticals

Ask an Analytical to partner with you because she will find flaws or weaknesses everyone else may overlook. She inspires confidence in your ideas and projects because she is so careful. She's a great balance for more impetuous types like the Sensor.

In short, her qualities include the following:

- She is thorough and well prepared.
- She is competent and accurate.
- She is organized.
- She is objective.

The Emotive

Emotives are ambassadors and often caretakers. They can be very caring and are excellent at helping diverse people come together and work toward a common goal. An Emotive may find things like birthdays, resignations, or pregnancies events to celebrate or acknowledge even on the job. She will be an excellent partner to help plan neighborhood events, family showers, or the company picnic.

Emotives are usually sensitive to the feelings of others and can help you be more sensitive as well. She will have radar to help you avoid social gaffes or insensitive remarks.

Not only is the Emotive sensitive to others, she is just plain sensitive. Before you start talking to her about the subject on your mind, you must spend five minutes asking her about how her weekend was or her tennis elbow, her new house, or something that has nothing to do with your topic but that is of great personal interest to her and her only.

She gets along well with everyone on a team and for good reason. When a project comes up, her first concerns are things like how all people will be affected, how outsiders will react, and other people issues. If you asked her to move a mountain, she might want to know if it's going to hurt anyone's feelings if we move it.

Time orientation: The Emotive's time orientation is definitely in the past. Your past shared timed together helps you build a successful relationship with an Emotive. Recalling previous conversations, calls, and appointments links you to the Emotive and helps you get her enthusiastic support when needed.

People Skills Emotives Need to Develop

Emotives can occasionally be too emotional in work or decision-making situations. Feelings, alliances, and personal ties may, in rare instances, get in the way of objective decision-making. An Emotive may perceive incorrectly that a teammate is cold or even hostile if that teammate doesn't schmooze enough. In return, an Emotive may be perceived as wasting time in conversations and meetings on personal issues, a behavior some still feel is socially unacceptable or unprofessional.

Emotives need to learn to step back, take a breath, and force themselves to be objective when they feel offended or dismayed at the insensitivity of others. Even when an Emotive is concerned that the insensitivity is directed at others, she needs to pause to decide if input or comment is really needed. Learning to let go of many of these emotional reactions will make the workplace much more relaxed and productive for the Emotive, as well as the people around her. Emotives also must learn to offer suggestions using the motivators of the other person. For example, if an Emotive wants the boss to teach the other employees to be more sensitive to diversity, she must consider the communication style of the boss. A Sensor will respond best if little description or back story is given, but the Emotive can say how much more productive the team will be and that they will work faster together. An Analytical boss will receive this better if the Emotive gathers some statistics to back up the point. The Emotive wants others to take action because it is the right thing to do, but to be effective, the style preference of the other person must be appealed to.

Three questions an Emotive should pause and ask before getting involved are the following:

- Is this an important issue for me to undertake at this time, and is it my responsibility to tackle it?
- What might be some positive outcomes of my getting involved, and is it possible these will be achieved without my involvement?
- What could be the downside or repercussions to myself and others if I become involved, and is it worthwhile?

Emotives also need to develop a safe person or two to vent to about issues of concern. These people should not be Emotives but people who can help show how other styles may perceive the same issues. This helps strengthen Emotives over time while still allowing them to talk out their feelings.

COMMUNICATION TIP

Many employers use personality or communication assessments to identify the style preference of potential employees, such as Meyers-Briggs (see mbti-test.com for a free version or mbticomplete.com/contents/learnmore.aspx for a fee-based version with certified professionals). These assessments can be extremely helpful in aiding a manager in helping the new hire adapt to teammates and management. These assessments are based on the work of Swiss psychiatrist Carl Jung.

The Value of Emotives

The Emotive is the premier team player. Not only will she build good relationships, but she will help the rest of the team bond. She is a great catalyst to help other styles work together. Although she invests a lot of time in people issues, let's face it: people *are* pretty important to any issue.

An Emotive is also very strong in reading nonverbal communication. Sometimes friends and coworkers send definite messages about their likes and dislikes without using words. An Emotive can pick up on these clues early and save you from going down a wrong path. Emotive qualities include the following:

- She is worthy of a high level of trust.
- She encourages teammates.
- She gives attention to others.
- She works well with all other types.

People Skills 101: Adapting Your Style to Other Styles

Knowing your style only has value if you learn the style-flexing skills to adapt to the styles of others. Here are some things to remember when you approach someone of a different style. You can style flex to be more successful in winning whatever you seek if you are considerate of the other person's preferences. Whether the outcome is friendship or the achievement of a common goal, take these steps to adapt to each of the following styles.

Sensors

Make your main points fast. Offer solutions, not problems, and offer your best piece of information in the first few sentences because you may lose the Sensor after that. Move fast, speak with energy, jump into critical issues quickly, mention time constraints, negotiate hard, and state the bottom line.

Don't be surprised if the Sensor doesn't want to partner or work as a team, as she often prefers to do things solo. If you have questions, make them specific and short. If you're teaching a Sensor something, let her try something early that she can succeed at or you may lose her.

To shorten your remarks, pretend you're filling out an online form that will only let you use a few words. How would you say it?

Always be scrupulously honest—even blunt—with a Sensor. Lay on the line the basic facts, the goal, the resources, the options, and the barriers—then just watch these incredibly productive people go.

Phrases a Sensor might respond to positively:

> "You have two great options for the entrée for your rehearsal dinner."
>
> "As your doctor, I see three steps you must take immediately to lower your blood pressure."
>
> "If you choose this heat pump, you can save almost $400 a year."

Intuitors

Be patient with Intuitors, who may seem unfocused or talk about subjects that seem unrelated to the agenda or something high-tech or cutting edge; they may have a style that seems a little argumentative or challenging at first. Prepare yourself for the other person's style being different.

As you speak, mention anything new or cutting edge. These folks bore easily, so don't describe ideas in length. If you need an answer or a resource, be sure to ask for a deadline, as Intuitors are not great at finishing what they start.

HOLD THAT THOUGHT

If you're concerned that an Intuitor is opposed to your idea, don't force your idea on her. Instead, involve her in brainstorming a problem to come up with the best idea. Keep the conversation moving and ask for her opinion often.

Start meetings or projects with them using wide-open questions. Let them start with their conceptualization of what's going on rather than forcing them into your preconceived mold. Suggested phrases include the following:

> "We're offering a new service to only a few of our customers at this time. I thought you would be a perfect candidate to use this service since it's tailored to your business."
>
> "Jim, you're having trouble with this last course in your MBA program and have never had problems before. Let's sit down with your academic advisor and the instructor. The four of us will then explore possible solutions so your GPA won't suffer."
>
> "This type of juicer is new. I hope we can buy one because I've never seen anyone we know use one before. We could be the first."
>
> "Do you have any ideas for changing the landscaping around our neighborhood clubhouse? What we have has no curb appeal and doesn't survive the summer heat well."

Collaboration is the key with Intuitors. Ask, don't tell.

Analyticals

For Analyticals, come across as a little formal or even academic. Be well-prepared with all necessary papers, notes, maybe even an agenda. Your opening remarks should have a very organized structure that summarizes your key points. Tell the Analytical your plan or idea in an organized, 1-2-3 way. Offer facts, research, and expert opinion to back you up. Give the Analytical time to think and consider; do not pressure.

For example, if you were trying to convince an Analytical to purchase a heat pump, you might word it this way:

> "A heat-pump water heater will be the most cost-effective choice for you based on the studies done by our energy experts, a comparison of two existing homes compared to yours, and my review of your last twelve months' bills."

If a son were trying to convince his Analytical father to send him to a private college instead of a state college, his approach might be more effective if he said something like the following:

> "Dad, I hope you'll allow me to attend the private college I mentioned instead of the state university as you suggested. I've put together a comparison of the two, and you may be surprised at how small the cost difference is. I've contacted both institutions and have a complete comparison of costs, from tuition to books to housing. More importantly, I've talked to the financial aid director at both and there are actually more scholarships available at the private college than at the state university."

The key to gaining the respect, friendship, or cooperation of the Analytical is preparing and being informed before you speak.

Emotives

Most of all, be friendly with Emotives. It's more important that they like you than your ideas. What was the last thing the Emotive talked to you about? Start the conversation with that topic.

If nothing comes to mind, start with other personal interests of Emotives. Comment on their photos or on hobbies or topics important to them. Be observant to see what's important to them. Be open and share your similar interests.

Be sure to offer praise and avoid criticism, as Emotives are easily hurt. They may be concerned about anything risky, yet they may make an impulsive decision if it feels right. They enjoy a more casual atmosphere and approach. Build history with them with more "touches," phone calls, texts, emails, or other contacts.

Sample phrases to kick off the conversation may include the following:

> "Did you finish up the United Way Campaign work you were doing?"
>
> "Are you still working on your vacation plans?"
>
> "Are your coaching duties over for the season? Did you have some good players?"
>
> "Is your daughter enjoying all the senior year activities?"

Emotives have a high degree of emotional intelligence, a characteristic all styles need to develop.

Emotional Intelligence

Just as IQ measures your ability to handle information and to analyze facts, emotional intelligence (EI) relates to your ability to understand and deal with emotions and the complexities of your own feelings and those of other people. Those with highly developed EI can read the emotions of others and respond more appropriately than those with less developed EI. Just as importantly, having mature EI skills means a person can identify and deal with her own feelings more proficiently. This insight gives people with great EI more control of their emotions. Another benefit of EI is the ability to "read" people and situations, helping to avoid conflict and to build better relationships.

Unfortunately, some people have never developed a high degree of EI, but it can be learned. Most of the skills this book, if practiced for 30 days, can lead to improvement in EI. Some personalities are so skilled at learning and remembering information that they are too focused on facts and not feelings. Recommendations in Part 1 of this book, in particular, will help you begin to focus on the underlying feelings behind the words in conversations, emails, and texts.

COMMUNICATION TIP

In "Emotional Intelligence," Peter Salovey and John D. Mayer proposed a model that identified four different factors of emotional intelligence: the perception of emotion, the ability to reason using emotions, the ability to understand emotion, and the ability to manage emotions.

Developing your people skills means developing your EI. The first part of that process is to learn to evaluate and manage your own emotions and how you react and are perceived by others. The second part is to be able to discern and respond appropriately to the emotions of others.

An infant or toddler may actually laugh when they see another child cry. They have no discernment and do not have the control to respond appropriately. As we mature and evolve, we are expected to respond to others in the way they would most like for us to respond instead of following our first reaction.

You may be tempted not to ask someone what is wrong when you see them looking sad or depressed, but a person with highly evolved people skills will usually express concern or interest. You may want to avoid an uncomfortable conversation, but forming strong, authentic relationships means you will occasionally have to experience these uncomfortable conversations.

People who never acknowledge the feelings of others are described as "shut off" or emotionally "shut down." Relationships never advance past a surface level. Open up. Express an interest when people send you cues that they are experiencing joy or sadness or concern.

Introverts and Extroverts

Have you ever described yourself as an extrovert or an introvert? Actually, we are all blends of the two with tendencies toward one or the other. Carl Jung said, "There is no such thing as a pure extravert or a pure introvert. Such a man would be in the lunatic asylum."

Extroverts draw energy from being with people, interacting with them, and having conversations. On the other hand, introverts are drained of energy from too much human interaction and activity. In a work environment, an extrovert will be more productive working with a team and collaborating constantly, while an introvert needs to retire to her cubicle or office to think from time to time.

As you approach new people, be aware of their introverted or extroverted personalities. We often feel people do not like us, so we are not friendly to them when in reality the person is just introverted. An introvert may enjoy your company very much but can only tolerate anyone's company for a while. An introvert then needs alone time to recharge her batteries. Don't feel rebuffed if an introvert retreats when you feel you are both enjoying a conversation very much. At some point, introverts just go on overload and need a break, even from their favorite people.

And don't let external appearances mislead you about who is an introvert and who is an extrovert. Johnny Carson was an introvert, as are many other famous comedians. Their interior thought life and observation of others makes them skilled at picking up on human foibles and things that are funny to the rest of us.

Conversely, the extrovert needs time with people and thrives on human interaction. If an extrovert has very much time alone, he will call someone or text someone or try to make something happen. They think better and are more productive when they are working with others.

Introverts, on the other hand, may barely be able to think after too much time in close quarters with others. They may need to separate for a time from a team or a partner in order to offer ideas or comments.

HOLD THAT THOUGHT

Be careful not to generalize about introverts and extroverts. For example, many think introverts are shy, while extroverts are shallow; in fact, introverts can be quite sociable, and extroverts can be very thoughtful. Don't let first impressions mislead you.

Tips for Dealing with Introverts

You can deal with introverts much more effectively if you follow some basic principles. At the first sign that the introvert wants to be alone, be sure to support her in taking a break—she will be more comfortable with you in the future. Don't "work on" introverts to try to make them more extroverted. There is nothing wrong with introversion; in fact, we need more introverts who can comfortably be quiet and listen. And let the introvert choose times and locations most comfortable for her for getting together. Finally, when planning activities with a mix of introverts and extroverts, plan ways to draw out the introverts so the extroverts don't drown them out.

Tips for Dealing with Extroverts

Naturally, extroverts require a completely different approach. Remember that they would prefer to do even simple tasks together. They will be rich in ideas and collaboration if you meet with them to brainstorm or discuss anything. And don't be misled if an extrovert is extremely friendly. They can't help themselves. Don't read too much into their behavior. An extrovert will be the life of the party and then come home and say, "I never want to do anything with that couple again!" Finally, extroverts need more praise and encouragement than most people. If you don't verbalize some of both, they may feel you don't like them.

Both introverts and extroverts offer value to your life and lend richness and texture to your world because of their unique gifts. Try to include some of both in your circle of friends.

You May Have Other Gifts

You may have gifts in the area of people skills that we haven't discussed here. Some people are fascinating because they are experts on a certain subject. Others have a great laugh or a musical voice that just draws people to them. People are drawn to others for quirky things like accents or kooky fashion.

Take an inventory of what gifts you have as a friend, conversation partner, or co-worker. What have people in the past found appealing about you? What did your parents, siblings, teachers, or mentors compliment about you? If you don't know what your gifts are, ask roommates, co-workers, neighbors, or others to help you identify your strengths.

Focusing only on your weaknesses and developing those is a mistake. It is equally important to develop your assets. These are the qualities and attributes that make you uniquely you, and there are people who will find your combination of gifts extremely appealing. Showcase them and share them with the people you meet.

The Least You Need to Know

- The Sensor is direct, moves fast, and is candid and decisive.
- The Intuitor style is creative, forward-thinking, likes to try new things, and bores easily.
- The Analytical wants to research, consider, organize, and review before making decisions or moves.
- The Emotive is very sensitive to the feelings of others—and her own.
- Emotional intelligence is a mark of maturity, as it demonstrates the ability to control one's emotions.
- The introvert gets energy from within, while the extrovert draws energy from being with others.

CHAPTER

21

Adapting to Generational Differences in Communication

To have truly great people skills, you need to connect with people of all ages. If you limit your friendships and circle to only the people in your age group, you miss out on some of the most talented and fascinating people you could ever know. The richness, value, and knowledge that people in the generations above and below you could bring you are vast. And you will never know what you're missing if you don't purpose to develop multigenerational friendships. This chapter will give you approaches for being extremely effective with people of every generation.

In This Chapter

- Thriving in a multigenerational world
- How to adapt to the four different generations
- Ways each generation can offer you benefits
- How the blended generations are changing the world

Adapting to Six Different Generations

Depending on the expert, we now have as many as six generations coexisting and communicating simultaneously, as you can see in the following table. Extended lifespans have increased our opportunities to learn and benefit from people who may even be in their 100s! At the other extreme, never have there been such great opportunities to learn from people much younger than our generation. Each generation seems to be more and more technologically savvy, so they are often the "experts" that older, more experienced generations turn to for help and answers. Their openness and adventurous way of embracing change are models for older generations who didn't grow up with a rapid rate of change.

HOLD THAT THOUGHT

What if everyone you know was exactly your age? What would you miss out on if there were no one older or younger than you? Each generation brings insights the other generations have not developed as thoroughly.

Today's Generations

Generation	Born	Age (in 2014)
GI Generation (sometimes grouped with "Matures")	1901–1924	90–113
Silent Generation (a.k.a. "Matures")	1925–1946	68–89
Baby Boom Generation	1946–1964	50–67
Generation X	1965–1979	35–49
Millennial Generation (a.k.a. Generation Y)	1980–1999	15–34
Generation Z	2000–	14 and under

Source: U.S. Chamber of Commerce Foundation (emerging.uschamber.com/MillennialsReport)

For these and many other reasons, honing the people skills to establish relationships with people of all generations is more important than ever.

The U.S. Chamber of Commerce Foundation's "Millennial Generation Research Review" (emerging.uschamber.com/MillennialsReport) gives this general description of the varied generations:

> "If each generation has a personality, you may say that the baby boomer is the idealist, shaped by Woodstock, JFK, RFK, and MLK. Generation X is the skeptical independent, shaped by latchkeys, Watergate, and the PC. Generation Y is the connected, diverse collaborator, shaped by 9/11, texting, and the recession.
>
> It is therefore understandable that the stereotypical ambitious boomer workaholic may be critical of one who does not share the same ethics and values. The independent Gen Xer may not appreciate the team orientation and desire for seemingly constant feedback. At the same time, the social-minded Millennial may not understand the priorities of other generations."

Of course, you can't generalize. Older people are fast becoming technologically savvy and find that handling everything from managing finances to making travel arrangements is easier using online resources. Some Millennials are punctual and engaged, defying their stereotype. So the first thing to remember is that you have to evaluate what each person wants in a conversation or relationship before rushing toward any generic approach. What are his preferences and interests? Yes, the decade in which we were born has an influence on our lives, but we should never assume that everyone in a generation will be the same.

Omar's Story

Omar was always a leader in his school and in his college. Socially he was very popular and he also was a strong student. Because of the way his peers valued and admired him, he felt he had mastered interpersonal relationships. His mother had told him several times that his lack of eye contact and his unresponsiveness in their conversations made conversations with him less enjoyable, but he felt she was wrong since his style appeared to work with everyone else around him.

What Omar didn't realize was that his mother was one of the few older adults he communicated with on a regular basis. Everyone else was in his age group. Of course, he dealt with professors, but they were usually lecturing. He really hadn't had to engage in dialogue outside his age group. All that changed when Omar graduated.

With his new degree, Omar moved from the East Coast to start a new job with a company in San Jose, California. Apartments were astronomically expensive, so he found a roommate on Craigslist. The roommate was a bit older, and suddenly, Omar's world changed. He had lived surrounded by 18- to 25-year-olds. Now, even though his co-workers were younger, his roommate and neighbors were mostly Boomers, as were his boss and his customers. Suddenly, his unresponsiveness and lack of eye contact was not just his mother's hang-up; it was a generational thing.

His first clue was when he went on a sales call with his boss Hyang. After a meeting they had with an important customer, Hyang said, "Omar, why didn't you respond when Dillon said he was considering revamping his internet security system?"

Omar's eyes widened. "I didn't hear a question in there," he said.

"No," said Hyang, "but he was opening up the topic for discussion. It's our job to express an interest in the customer's plans. You need to pick up on topics the customer is bringing up and especially on changes and problems he's hinting that he wants to address."

This was a revelation to Omar. He assured Hyang that he would be more attentive next time.

A few weeks later, Omar's roommate Wes asked if they could sit down and discuss a few things. Omar felt such a meeting was a bit formal but agreed. Wes started by saying, "I've tried to bring up two things that have bothered me several times, but I don't see you doing anything about them. I don't feel that you listen to me when I try to express myself. Living together requires a lot of communication, but we don't seem to be communicating. I just want to be fair and say that if we can't work these things out, you'll need to start looking for another place to live."

Omar was shocked. This was the first time he had heard there was a problem. He had no idea what Wes was talking about. He also didn't want to lose a great apartment at a super-low rent that was five minutes from his office. He said to Wes, "I'm so sorry but I clearly have missed something. Would you mind telling me again what some of the issues are? I should know, but I don't."

Wes said, "Do you remember when I told you that I had a standing date with my girlfriend who comes over on Thursday nights?"

"Sure," said Omar. "I like it when Julie comes over. You always cook something great on Thursdays."

The minute Omar saw the look on Wes's face, he got it. "Ohhh," said Omar. "You aren't cooking for me but for Julie. You want to be alone with her on Thursdays. We always did things in groups where I come from and didn't split off or even call it dating. I've got it now. Why didn't you bring it up before?"

Wes said, "Do you remember when I suggested you go get pizza with our neighbor last Thursday?"

Omar said, "Yes, but you didn't say you didn't want me to stay here. I guess you were trying to be subtle. It really won't hurt my feelings if you're just blunt."

Wes explained that he hadn't been brought up that way. When Omar asked what the other thing was that was bothering Wes, Wes told him, "Do you remember when I asked you to clean the bathroom thoroughly on the first and third Saturdays and I would do it the second and fourth?"

"Yes," said Omar. "I have cleaned the bathroom."

"Well, you've done some cleaning but it isn't thorough. Wiping the surfaces with a cloth is not getting the job done. Do you remember when I showed you last week the way I scrub the bowl with one brush and clean the tub with a different one?"

"Sure, but I thought we just had different methods," said Omar. Once again, a light bulb came on in his head. "I see. You were emphasizing how to be thorough in a nice way. I get it."

Wes said, "And you are pretty approximate about when you do the cleaning. Sometimes you let it slide for a few days and it gets pretty raunchy in there."

"I didn't realize it had to be so exact," said Omar.

"I was brought up to keep to a schedule and that was the schedule," said Wes. "I can see letting it slip a day, but not three or four. It defeats the purpose of having a schedule."

Once Omar understood, he immediately began to do the things the way Wes had asked. He also made himself scarce on Thursday evenings.

Omar almost lost an ideal place to live simply because he was treating Wes the way he treated people of his own generation. In this case, Omar's willingness to learn and adapt saved him from making a mistake. He called his mother and said, "You'll be happy to learn that California has taught me several things you always wanted me to learn. First, pick up on what people are trying to say and don't make them spell it out. Second, follow directions and do things thoroughly and not halfway. And finally, have a schedule and stick to it."

This was part of Omar's growing process and he became skilled at dealing with customers and others of all generations.

Guidelines for Building Cross-Generational Relationships

At the risk of generalizing, the following are some broad guidelines to generational tendencies and preferences and some ideas for building relationships with each group.

COMMUNICATION TIP

In most of our lifetimes, we will experience a new phenomenon. According to the U.S. Census Bureau, soon the number of people over 65 will outnumber people 18 years old or younger. The aging population could affect your career, your finances, and your community.

GI Generation and Silent Generation (a.k.a. "Matures"): Highly responsible about most everything from doing high-quality work to showing up on time or early. To build a relationship with them, mirror these same behaviors. These generations are risk-averse, so don't expect their support when you want to quit your job and do volunteer work for a while or try something that had nothing to do with your major. Managing your expectations of this generation is important, as their reactions may not feel as socially supportive as what you receive from your peers. Show them you are a hard worker and you will gain their respect. Brush up on your manners, as this generation still can be insulted if you don't follow "the rules," such as establishing strong eye contact.

Baby Boomer Generation: To a lesser degree, most of the information about the Matures relates to the Boomers as well. This generation highly values initiative, so don't wait to be asked to do something—offer. The Boomers are very concerned about stability and their future, and they will care about yours, including benefits and retirement plans. Show your awareness of the importance of these signs of stability, even if you make different decisions from your Boomer friends. The way this generation shows caring is to provide for their families, so be prepared to have some conversations about that. When you interact with them, show energy in your voice, body language, and behavior. This generation may text but not often, so if you want to connect with a Boomer, power off all electronics. Many Boomers did not use email until they were in their forties, so they generally prefer face-to-face communication or a phone call.

Generation X: This was such a transitional generation that they are hard to define. They may not have had a computer in their homes in elementary school, but probably did a bit later and embraced technology enthusiastically. They watched the older adults in their lives lose jobs and experience disillusionment during an era of downsizings and corporate greed, so they have earned a reputation for being a bit disenchanted with employers. They don't count on loyalty in the workplace, so they don't feel obligated to give it. Don't come on strong with extreme optimism, as they may be suspicious. They are the first generation to seek balance as enthusiastically as they seek monetary rewards, so don't try to incent them with money alone. This is the "show me" generation. Don't be insulted if you need to prove what you say; this generation will make you earn their trust, but with a little effort you can.

Millennial Generation (a.k.a. Generation Y): This large generation was brought up with helicopter parents who did much for them and believed in praising and rewarding them for every little thing. Don't blame the Millennials that you must acknowledge their routine contributions and praise anything they do well. Take the time because they are worth it. They are kind and generous with their time and resources—big sharers. They believe in giving and are more likely to buy products or cooperate if you can link your goal to a socially conscious cause. This generation loves to work on a team, so find a way to make routine tasks a team effort. They are optimistic, so leave gossip or criticism out when talking to them, if possible. Social media, especially Twitter, is their main communication mode and source of information, so be sure to connect with them in this way, even if you have to establish an account.

Generation Z: Everything we said about the Millennials can be said about Generation Z but to the extreme, except this is a smaller group. They are multitaskers to the point of distraction and may seem less focused. They may have owned a cell phone as a very young child and almost certainly were computer savvy in elementary school. Being online and communicating minute-to-minute with their friends makes them feel they are relational. They don't think of Boomers as relational because Boomers can go days without talking to a close friend. Don't be offended if the tweeting and texting does not stop when you talk to them; they think of this as normal and not insulting. Experts disagree about whether this multitasking has made the brain evolve or is leading to loss of memory and human connection. Try not to be judgmental, as they do not see the inability to connect with the person right in front of them as a big problem. Treat them as you would someone from another country whose ways of life are different from yours.

COMMUNICATION TIP

You can make personal connections with each generation if you have the patience to learn about them. The skills in Chapter 2 will serve you well, because if you listen, people will tell you their interests and preferences. Adapting to these multigenerational differences is similar to adapting to the various personality styles described in Chapter 20. Observe, listen, and adapt, and you will find good friends and colleagues in each generation.

How You Can Find Value in Each Generation

There is much good news about how the various generations are learning to live and work and create communities together. Great relationships are being formed across generational lines.

Management experts studied and prognosticated for years about what would happen when the Millennials met the Boomers in the job market. Almost all predictions were pessimistic. To everyone's amazement, the two generations are finding great value in one another. They are embracing and truly appreciating each other in unexpected ways.

A survey done for my book *Managing the Older Employee* asked young managers from Generations X and Y to state what their greatest challenge was in managing older employees. Here are the responses:

- Differences in use of technology
- Differences in our timing, such as the pace of work, speed, and slowness
- Differences in style, such as formality and judging what is appropriate
- Differences in collaboration and working in teams

Though the answer was overwhelmingly that there were definite differences in the way older employees embraced technology, a second question on the survey indicated that this difference was minor. In follow-up interviews, young managers said that although the learning curve for older workers was slightly longer, the difference was usually hours or days, and then the older worker was trained. In fact, younger managers showed a slight bias toward hiring an older employee over a younger employee!

Mirela's Story

Mirela is just such a young manager. She is 28 and has recently graduated with a degree in information technology. Because of her expertise in a certain software that helps call centers deal with customers, she was hired to be the team leader over a group of 10 employees of various ages. Her first job was to train the 10 employees in the new software. They had used the same software for five years, and no one was looking forward to the change. Mirela decided to set up appointments with each employee in her office in order to hold individualized training sessions. She anticipated that each employee would need three one-hour sessions to become proficient. Mirela also felt that the one-on-one time with each person would help her get to know her team and for them to get to know her.

The first employee she met with was Josh, a 25-year-old with two years of experience in his position. Josh arrived about 10 minutes late and did not seem to notice his tardiness, as he did not mention it. He brought a soft drink with him and behaved very casually with Mirela. She was not offended but wondered if this casual attitude would be a problem. Josh seemed to learn the software very quickly and the appointment ended on time despite the late start.

The second employee Mirela met with was Joan. Joan was a 60-year-old employee who had been in the department for 19 years. She arrived promptly and immediately began apologizing to Mirela for the fact that she always had difficulty learning new systems. Mirela assured her she was going to spend the time with her needed in order to help her learn the system. Despite their meeting starting on time, this meeting went over by about five minutes in order to be sure Joan had mastered the first lesson. Mirela did not feel the extra five minutes was a problem.

As the weeks went on, Mirela had completely different experiences with the two employees. Josh was often distracted and would stray to nonwork topics that Mirela did not always think were work-appropriate. He acted so familiar with her that it made her a bit uncomfortable at times. Still, Josh whizzed through the lessons and was prepared for the launch of the new software on May 1.

Joan, on the other hand, didn't learn the software as swiftly, but she did learn it. Mirela noticed that she was practicing with the software whenever she had a moment, and that she was very serious about being proficient by the deadline. Joan was almost too formal with Mirela and treated her with a great deal of deference. By May 1, Joan could perform the required tasks. An added bonus for Mirela was that she had learned that Joan had great insights into all the team members and also had a great memory. She could tell Mirela about various customer situations and what had worked and what had not. Mirela came to value Joan's opinions and went to her as a resource often.

During the month of May, Mirela noticed several things about the two employees' performance. Josh had made an above-average number of errors due to carelessness. Joan, on the other hand, had made almost no errors. Josh also did not push to make the same number of calls per hour that Joan did. At the end of the month, Joan had accomplished far more than Josh had.

This taught Mirela a valuable lesson. She learned that the extra patience it took to teach an older employee amounted to minutes or hours in the learning phase. Carelessness and a slack work ethic, on the other hand, would cost her department productivity permanently if not corrected. Mirela began to develop a bias toward hiring the older employee. When training these folks, Mirela saw the extra minutes as time well spent. She also liked the respect they showed for her position and their respect for her time. The next time Mirela was allowed to hire someone, she was very open to hiring an older employee.

COMMUNICATION TIP

Young managers, in general, have much to say about how the experience and insights of older employees have proven valuable to them and all the reasons they like them. Who knew?

What Do You Have to Gain?

You may be resistant to developing relationships with people older or younger than you, but you should at least try it. What do you have to lose? The better question is, "What do you have to gain?" The answer is, "A lot."

Each generation is colored and enhanced by the politics, history, fads, trends, and events of its time, giving each a unique point of view. Being a man or woman of the world means learning to look at your current happenings and circumstances from a variety of perspectives. Your outlook will broaden and you will make better decisions if you consider the various ways of viewing your circumstances, opportunities, and choices.

Try seeing your neighbors, your project, or your task through the eyes of someone of a different generation. What would they value that you may not? What would they criticize that you may have missed? What would they offer to do to improve a situation that does not come naturally to you? Trying to see things through the lens of someone from a different generation is a wonderful exercise. You will gain new insights you didn't have before.

In particular, ask yourself how the other person would prefer to receive information or prefer to send you information. Be more adaptable to their preferences. Spend some time thinking about areas of your own weaknesses and how the other person's strength might be used to complement your skills.

Our multigenerational society is a strength and an asset. As you view each unique person you meet, take into account his generation and all the ways that could influence him and your dealings with him. Make it work for both of you.

The Least You Need to Know

- With longer life expectancies, we now are adapting to coexist with at least four generations today.
- Understanding what most in a generation prefer is helpful, but each individual is different.
- Millennials think they are relational because they stay in constant touch with their friends through Twitter and text. Boomers think their own generation is more relational because they establish eye contact and take the time for extended conversations.
- Despite predictions, most Millennials and Boomers work together harmoniously.

PART

6

Speaking to Groups

Part 6 covers the wide range of skills needed for a wide variety of speaking situations. Learn to start with a dynamic opening, deliver information with credibility and interest, and leave a favorable impression. Whether you are asked to talk to a familiar small group of teammates or to 500 strangers at a conference, Part 6 gives you the way to prepare and execute any speaking situation.

Chapter 22 prepares you to communicate with people in small groups or to a team you work with regularly. From the minute someone says, "Will you say a few words?" you need to know exactly what to do. The chapter also covers the how-to's for holding productive meetings.

Chapter 23 builds on the speaking skills in the previous chapter and adds the skills needed to speak to large groups. You will learn everything from how to take charge of the room from the very beginning, to body language, to creating memorable conclusions. Learn tips for researching, crafting, and organizing speeches that are tailored to each unique audience.

CHAPTER

22

Speaking to a Team or Small Group

You may be asked to say a few words in a small group setting, to your team, or to a group of friends at a small social gathering. Even more of a thrill-ride is when you are not asked in advance and are put on the spot. Are you prepared to graciously accept the offer to speak and to leave people with a favorable view of you and your message? Will you be able to convey your message clearly and enhance your credibility?

This chapter equips you to speak with great appeal to a team or small group of people. Some of these ideas also provide a foundation for speaking to larger groups, which will be discussed in the next chapter.

In This Chapter

- Defining your role and the expectations of others
- Ways you can deal with nerves
- Engaging your team or small group
- Closing a meeting
- Giving a speech on the fly

What Is Your Role?

When you're asked to speak, your first question to yourself is, "What is my role?" You need to ask yourself why you were chosen. Are you the subject matter expert on a certain topic? Were you asked because your team or group sees you as a leader? Is this a sentimental invitation because you are popular or beloved? Or are you going to be asked to defend an action or viewpoint you have supported? Are you speaking just for yourself, or will people perceive you as speaking for the group or for your company?

Knowing in advance the audience's expectations of you is critical to your success. If you're a subject matter expert, they will expect you to bring more factual information, advice, and recommendations. If, however, you are a sentimental choice, you need to spend more time developing the relational part of your message and expressing your appreciation and acknowledgement of the audience.

Once you've identified your role, define your purpose. Is your goal to give information? To persuade others to take an action or support a viewpoint? To motivate the group to work together for a common goal? To comfort your audience or inspire confidence? To bring a diverse group of people together to collaborate?

COMMUNICATION TIP

Before you speak, be sure to 1) define your role, 2) establish your purpose, 3) analyze your audience, 4) choose your approach, and 5) choose how you will organize your remarks.

Next, take a few minutes to think about the unique makeup of the people you will address. Are they formal or informal? Do they like data, descriptions, humor, or stories? Is there some type of content they do not like? Is there some content they prefer more than other content? Are they liberal or conservative? What subjects are sore spots with them? Is there a topic they have a history with that you need to be aware of? What excites them? In short, create a profile of your audience.

Profiling your audience is actually very similar to the way you see FBI agents on television profile criminals. Even though you may have never met your audience, you can make educated guesses based on clues—their occupations, their social activities, their neighborhoods, their conversations, and the other details you observe.

The *demographics* of the group may affect what you plan to say. For example, if you're speaking to a room full of educators, you will probably want more descriptive information. If you're speaking to a group of accountants, try to pepper your content with numbers and data. If you're speaking to a group of college athletes, you may want to build in more interactivity or motivation. If you are addressing a group of young mothers, you may choose different examples and information than if you are addressing a men's hunting club. Though you should not stereotype, considering whether your audience is a group of young college students or a group of senior citizens is just considerate of the people you will be addressing. Even considerations such as urban versus suburban, northern versus southern, and global versus local may shape your message.

DEFINITION

Demographics include age, gender, educational level, ethnicity, urban or suburban orientation, and other factors. These are considerations of your audience that should be respected.

Next, think about the receptivity level of the group. Are they going to be delighted at what you have to say or will there be some resistance? What objections or questions might they have? Be sure to prepare content that will address those issues.

Try to determine whether your unique group will respond well to your telling a story or an example. What do you think is the best storytelling approach for these listeners? For their demographics, what kind of story would they respond to best? A heart-tugger? A shocker? An impressive but objective journalistic report?

Finally, is your information best told in chronological order? Or should you start with the most important fact to grab their attention and then slowly work toward the least important fact? Or will you arrange it according to three main points you will preview in your opening?

Even though you will be speaking and not reading, it's a good idea to write out what you plan to say for your own benefit. Writing out in complete sentences what you plan to say at the start is excellent for showing you what *not* to say. As you write your full sentences, you will see phrases that may sound awkward or even offensive. You can see where you may begin to get off the subject, and you can remind yourself not to go there.

Above all, be sincere. Speaking from notes or sounding memorized makes people feel you are not authentic. You diminish your credibility when you don't talk to your audience as if you're having a natural and honest conversation with them.

HOLD THAT THOUGHT

Try not to speak from notes to a small group. People want to feel you are speaking from the heart. They will forgive mistakes and bobbles. They often won't buy in if you're just giving what they think is a canned talk.

Dealing with Nerves

The best-performing racehorses get extremely nervous and high-spirited just before they run for a victory. Most of the best speakers also confess to a "case of nerves" just before speaking. Some famous actors and comedians actually get sick just before going on stage, even after years of success.

Believe it or not, people want to see you enjoying yourself when you speak to them. Does this surprise you? People like to see that you're connecting with them, smiling at them, feeling good about the message you have for them, and happy to be with them. You cannot convey all that if you look worried.

Some nervousness or apprehension is normal and actually good. The nerves will give you a slightly excited demeanor and perk up your voice and your body language. Some people who have no nervousness at all speak in a monotone and are very dull to listen to. Make your nerves work for you. Remind yourself that part of that nervousness will be perceived as excitement by your listeners. Try to think of what you're feeling as excitement and not nervousness.

You can also perform simple exercises before you speak that will diminish your nervousness. First, be sure to do some deep breathing for at least five minutes before you are to speak. Don't do this at a fast pace but very slowly. Exhale through your mouth, inhale through your nose. Exhale by pretending you're blowing the candles out on a birthday cake and you have to get that last one. You should actually feel your stomach muscles as you push all the air out of your lungs. Now breathe deeply in through your nose—you should feel the air deep in your lungs.

Next, do some muscle-tightening exercises. Tighten and release muscles like your thighs or your hands. Squeeze these muscles and hold them for five seconds, and then relax the muscles and shake them out. Move on and flex and hold your biceps like Popeye. After holding the flex for at least five seconds, relax and then move on to more muscles. Your body will begin to relax, which will help your mind function better as well.

How to Start: First Impressions

After you practice what you will say, polish your opening. The first words and the last words you say are the most important when you speak to any group, no matter the size. The opening is by far your greatest opportunity for impact and influence. It is the one time that you can be fairly sure that everyone is listening. People tend to drift throughout a spoken presentation or conversation, but they are usually focused for the opening. Is this a group that you trust will be comfortable enough for you to start with something humorous? Is the situation too serious for lighthearted treatment?

HOLD THAT THOUGHT

Humor is dangerous. Different people and groups have different views of what is funny, so use humor only if you are skilled at it and know that you will make no one uncomfortable.

If you are about to address a tense situation, start with a buffer as described in Chapter 8. A buffer is a sentence or two that postpones the direct statement about a controversial or unpleasant subject. When you don't want to start with a blunt statement of the actual topic, put in a buffer. Start with something that the group is comfortable with before you get to the more stressful part. A buffer may be a summary of the less controversial facts or some data that relates to the subject. You may start with a question to the group about their experience with this subject before you offer your information. That approach can sometimes help you identify your allies in the room. Or you may give an example or story that illustrates your point, perhaps building support before you begin.

If there is no need for a buffer, start with pleasantries and perhaps a welcome. Many people want to feel a connection with you before they connect with the information. Acknowledge guests and thank anyone who helped with the meeting. Above all, be cordial. The first two minutes set the tone for the entire meeting.

Though you do not need anything dramatic for a small meeting, try to say something interesting. State the primary purpose of the meeting and share the agenda, as described later in this chapter. If needed, summarize the past meeting or recent information everyone needs to know before the discussion starts.

So now you've planned a friendly and appropriate opening. Next, you need to deal with the most important part of the delivery system—you!

Strategies to Engage Your Team or Small Group

Involving others is usually a good idea in a small group setting. Adults don't like to be lectured to; instead, they like to discover things for themselves. Asking your group to help you brainstorm lists or to do small-group activities will contribute greatly to their enjoyment and your success. Try to convey a feeling of collaboration and interactivity. Unless you're speaking to an extremely large group, some type of partner or group exercise is usually possible.

Also, try to make sure that everyone has a voice or input into group discussions. You may need to ask easy, open questions to quieter teammates in order to draw them out and let their voices be heard. Involving everyone improves the experience for them but also reinforces their support for what you're presenting.

Some of the strategies for interactivity in addition to brainstorming might include one or more of the following:

- Partners interview each other.
- Each person presents one topic or definition on your agenda.
- Team members engage in role-play.
- Teams perform short exercises that require them to create something or find a solution.
- Partners compete in crosswords and games.
- Teammates are paired for scavenger hunts for physical objects or for online information to share later with the larger group.
- Each person tells what kind of car or animal best represents who she is. For example, "I am a panther because I move fast and am agile" or "I am a Land Rover because I am solid, dependable, and have long-term potential."
- Teams do ropes courses and other outside activities at national parks. (You may need an expert facilitator for this one.)

Most small-group presentations are interactive, so think of ways to engage the group. If you're about to assign parking spaces after years of allowing people to park anywhere, ask "How many of you have ever had difficulty finding a parking space?"

An important rule in asking questions, however, is never to ask a question you don't know the answer to. Be sure you know the majority wants assigned parking spaces before you ask a question like this. In presentations, never ask a question if you don't already know the answer. People will surprise you!

The main thing is not to lecture for long periods of time without some kind of break for interactivity or even just a break for refreshments. Today's attention spans are shorter than ever, so acclimate to today's audience.

Delivering Your Main Points

So now you have planned and organized what you will say and have some ideas for interactivity; you have done your relaxation exercises, and you have opened in a way that states your purpose and grabbed the interest of your audience. Now it's time to deliver your main points in a very organized way.

COMMUNICATION TIP

One way to keep on track is to have a written agenda and circulate it a few days before the meeting by email, if possible. Circulating the agenda gives people the chance to tell you ahead of time if key items are left off; that way, you are not blind-sided at the meeting. Agendas keep people on track and help avoid overly lengthy meetings. Giving attendees an opportunity for buy-in at the meeting increases their support of the meeting plan and of the leader. You should also hand out the agenda at the beginning of the meeting or project it. If you have made revisions based on the input of attendees, most will notice that and appreciate it. You can also ask someone to take notes or minutes at your meeting. You think you will remember things, but often, key names or numbers are forgotten. Notes do not have to be in paragraphs. A table with the agenda items in one column and bulleted discussion points in the next will work just fine. You may or may not choose to add the person's name who was responsible for each item.

Be sure you've written in an outline form or have a list of exactly what the main points are. If you aren't clear in your own mind about your two or three main points, how can your listeners be? Be sure you stress the main points as you bring them up. You may even use transitional words, such as *first, second, on the other hand, finally,* and so on to help listeners follow you.

Use descriptive words to tell great stories. Make sure you describe the colors, sights, and sounds so the listeners can see the word picture you're trying to create.

Keep sentences short. Long, wordy sentences tend to lose audiences. Describe exactly what is happening and tell it in the right sequence with no do-overs that make you appear unprepared. Tell the audience what you're willing to do for them and what your ideas, products, and services will do for them.

Ask for feedback by saying things like, "What are your thoughts?" or "Do you have any questions?"

The Big Finish

Always remember to thank everyone for participation, comments, refreshments, attention, or anything else you can think of. Leave the group with a promising or optimistic fact. Because the ending of a presentation is the second most influential part of it, make sure it is pleasant and encouraging, maybe even exciting and inspiring. You may also want to reiterate the main takeaways.

For teams who work together regularly, it is usually best to clarify the follow-up you are expecting each person to do after the meeting is over. Clearly state next steps, recommendations, and your summary of the decisions made in the meeting.

Be sure to be very clear if there is a call to action. A call to action contains two clear components:

- An action verb that tells the listener the precise action she is to take—email, call, vote, buy, lease, support, tell a friend, avoid, and so on
- A step to take that is clearly one the listener and not the speaker should do

The second component seems obvious, but speakers fail to do this all the time. If you haven't gotten the results you wanted when you've spoken to groups, consider that the problem may be that you haven't been clear that it's the listener who must now make the next step.

If you are in a position of authority, you may even state a deadline for the completion of the actions. Most of the time, the goals you set for people should be SMART goals: Specific, Measurable, Action-oriented/achievable, and Timed. Setting SMART goals increases the likelihood that the tasks will be completed. Working with teams requires you to set clear expectations. Team or group members need to communicate to make sure that every member has heard the expectations the same way.

Bridgett's Story

Bridgett was trying to convey to a group of volunteers that they would no longer be allowed to accompany elementary school children on field trips if they had not taken the school system's CPR class. Bridgett was speaking in April and there was only one more CPR class left in the school year, in May. No CPR classes are offered during the summer. The problem was that there were going to be two field trips in August and September.

Bridgett urged the volunteers to become certified, but she sensed that no one detected her urgency. She was right. That was because she stated her request that they be certified like this:

> "We would need to all be certified before the upcoming school year. The school system offers this certification in a class in May."

Nowhere in this request is a clear action verb telling the group directly what they must do. The request is implied but not directly stated. You need to be very direct and clear when you give a call to action.

Bridgett would have seen more people sign up for the class as she desired if she had made her request like this:

> "Please sign up for the May CPR class. We need twelve volunteers for the August field trip. If you do not take the May class, you will not be able to serve as a field trip volunteer on the first two trips. May 4 is the last date the certification class is offered, so please enroll after this meeting today. We want to keep our valued group of volunteers who have worked so well together with our students and with one another."

There is no doubt from these strong verbs and from this phrasing that the volunteers need to take action.

Effective Closers

You don't need a gimmicky closing, but your closing should be so emphatic that your group knows the meeting is over. After you summarize the meeting and communicate action steps and expectations, say a sentence that is the cue that people can leave. You may simply say "That concludes our meeting for today. Thank you for coming." Or you could say "If no one else has anything to discuss, we will close the meeting. Thank you." Some endings are more forward looking, such as "Great meeting, folks, and I look forward to hearing in two weeks what each of you found out about venues for our Client Appreciation Weekend."

Impromptu Speaking

What do you do if someone unexpectedly turns to you and asks you to say a few words? Consider just some of the ways people are sometimes caught off guard and asked to speak:

- At a retirement reception, someone turns to you and says, "Would you like to say a few words about Bob?" Bob is your friend, so you don't want to act as if you have nothing to say to him after his 20 years of service.
- Your boss is every excited about a new project that few people, except you, know much about. You have just begun work on the project. At a departmental meeting, your boss turns to you and says "Lena, tell the team about the hospital project you are working on."
- Five friends chip in to buy a luxury stroller for a good friend. You get together to present the gift and have a dinner. After dinner, your friend looks at you and says "Would you present the gift?" You don't want to say simply "Here it is," so you are floundering as you think of something appropriate to say.

When you are put into a situation such as this, there are a few things to remember. First, expectations are low, so take the pressure off yourself. No one expects you to make a formal speech that you had time to prepare for. Second, people really don't mind simple facts and sentiments. Don't feel bad if you come up with well wishes or comments you have heard before. Say them with a smile on your face and a bit of warmth, and they will be well received. Even if you say something quite obvious, the recipient will probably appreciate your effort. The key is to start with a warm and friendly comment that is extremely positive.

HOLD THAT THOUGHT

Don't panic—smile! A warm smile and positive first remarks make an audience embrace what you have to say, even if it is poorly prepared and simple. They will respond to the positive nonverbal and be less aware of the specifics of your comments.

Some of the obvious but positive comments that fit the preceding situations might include the following:

- For a retirement: "You have been an excellent manager and colleague. We appreciate all your years of service and will miss you."
- For a work project: "This project is exciting for a variety of reasons."
- For a baby shower: "We are so happy for you and know you are going to be a great mom."

The next step is to get descriptive. What mundane, easy details can you mention to fill out your speech? The following are examples for the previous situations:

- For a retirement: Summarize the parts of the career you know about—current responsibilities, where he started, number of years of service, major clients, and any awards or accomplishments.
- For a work project: What is the task? How did it start? Who is working on it? When or where will it be completed? What are the reasons for starting it, and what outcomes do you hope for?
- For a baby shower: Mention all you know about the baby—the gender, the due date, and the father's name, if appropriate.

Finally, end on a forward-looking note. Express your hopes and wishes for a great future of the retiree, the project, or the mother and child. As one wise speaker said, "Be brief and be gone."

In short, speaking to small groups or teams requires you to be thoughtful and positive, even when you have no warning that you will be asked to speak. One point might help you through this experience: the person who asked you to speak felt you could do it and are the best person to handle it. With practice, anyone can be a great speaker. Why not start now?

The Least You Need to Know

- Before you speak, define your role and assess the expectations of the audience.
- Clearly state your purpose in the opening.
- Adults like interactivity, so build in discussion and exercises.
- For impromptu speaking, start with a cordial, positive statement and then describe the traits or characteristics of the person or project.

CHAPTER

23

Speaking Formally to a Large Group

Although almost everything you learned in the previous chapter can be applied to speaking to larger groups, an entire set of additional skills are also needed. When you speak to groups of 20 or 200 or more, expectations are higher for preparation, delivery, and even entertainment value.

This chapter shows you how to deliver a speech with poise and professionalism, as well as how to make your material and yourself appealing to larger groups of people. These groups may start out as total strangers, but your winning presentation skills will help you end the day with some new friends.

In This Chapter

- Using confident body language for a great approach
- Making eye contact with your audience
- Researching and preparing your content
- Delivering high-impact openings and closings

The Approach: Body Language

Whether you are speaking while standing at the head of a table, on a platform, or at a podium, the walk to your starting point is a critical moment in your delivery of the speech. You should walk to your designated spot with as much enthusiasm and vigor as you can demonstrate, even if inside you are not feeling that way. If your gestures and gait are peppy and enthusiastic, you will build excitement in your audience before you even begin.

On the other hand, if you slowly drag to the front of the room, you might as well be wearing a sign that says "Boring." After all, if you don't look as if you have something wonderful to say, how can the audience feel any different? Some very prepared and earnest speakers have sent the wrong signals to audiences simply by slouching their way to the front of the room. A lackluster approach may send signals you don't actually mean, such as that you are condescending to the audience or even hostile. For an audience to like you, you have to appear to like them, and walking as if you are dreading to speak to them is not the way to start.

You show your credibility by also managing your nerves, as you learned in the previous chapter, and appearing self-confident. Take deep breaths and breathe slowly. Give yourself positive messages, such as "This is going to be great" or "You've got this." Do not do negative self-talk, such as "This is going to be bad" or "I am so nervous." You will learn to take any nervousness you feel and turn it into excitement and enthusiasm because you will know exactly how to communicate to a group.

Throughout your presentation, your energy and positive body language are far more important than your words. Throughout your presentation, remember that people are influenced positively or negatively far more by what they see than by what they hear. They won't buy your message if they don't buy you. Your face, hand gestures, eye contact, movement, and posture determine much more than your words whether the audience embraces what you have to say. Smile and remember to sustain positive facial expressions from start to finish.

HOLD THAT THOUGHT

Don't neglect one area of the room. We all have a tendency to favor one side of the room or table. Combat that by consciously making yourself look at each quadrant of the room.

If you're presenting while standing, be sure your hips and knees are level and that you are not slumping or throwing one hip out. People like speakers who are "on the level." Your relaxed but level posture says to the audience that you're respectful of them and care about your message.

Use gestures that hover around the center one third of your body. With wide reaching gestures, you can appear to be out of control. Moving a bit is okay unless your movements are random, such as pacing back and forth. Don't put your hands in your pockets, lean on anything, or jingle keys or change. And by all means, don't stiffen and lock your knees; this can possibly lead to you passing out.

If you show slides, try to use a remote control device. Never stand in front of your slides but to the side of them. Your focus should remain on the audience. Don't look at your slides except to occasionally be sure you have advanced to the correct slide. Slides are only for emphasizing content; your object is to get your audience to fasten their attention on you and not on your slides.

Using Eye Contact to Engage the Audience

When speaking to a large audience, try to create a personal connection by making eye contact with as many people as possible. You can use all kinds of tricks to help you maintain good eye contact with everyone in the audience. For example, you can have your main points written on a 5×7 card and set it on the desk or podium in front of you so you can glance at it only if needed. For short presentations, you should not need notes, but it is helpful to have the main points available on the card. Don't write down details or you will be tempted to read or look down instead of looking at our audience.

You can also have a laptop or electronic tablet in front of you showing any slides you are showing. It can be synched with the screen behind you. That way, you will be looking forward and never have to look back at the screen.

When you begin your presentation, find one friendly face toward the middle of the room. This can be someone you know supports you or just a really nice stranger. While you say your opening lines, look at this person alone. Tune out everyone else. Pretend you are having a relaxed conversation with this designated person, and that you are sharing what you know about your topic in a friendly manner.

After about 30 or 40 seconds, start to fan out and look at the right side of the room. Find another face to look at while you tell your story. Slowly go back to center for a while. Next, look at someone on the left side of the room. After you focus on this person for about 30 seconds, return your gaze to the center.

Use this technique to talk to the four corners of the room. If you have ever been to a presentation where every person felt he had been spoken to personally, the speaker may have been using this technique. Most of us have a tendency to neglect one side of the room; by using this fan-out technique, no one gets neglected.

Making Your Voice Appealing to the Audience

Your speaking voice can make your message even more appealing or it can be a distraction. The good news is that your voice and voice mannerisms can be improved and enhanced. Your goal is to have a tone that conveys enthusiasm for your subject, regard for your audience, and a proper amount of concern when a serious topic arises.

COMMUNICATION TIP

Think of your voice as a musical instrument. Be sure to have high notes for exciting points and low notes for more serious topics.

Avoiding Certain Mannerisms

When speaking, you want to avoid these distracting mannerisms:

Voice breaks and hoarseness: These are usually caused by one of two factors: not getting enough sleep or irritation from allergies or not resting your voice. Be sure to rest your voice as much as possible in the 24 hours prior to speaking. If you are prone to allergies, be sure to take your appropriate medications before speaking. Melting a lozenge in your mouth can soothe your voice, as can a cup of warm tea with honey and lemon.

Voice clicks: The clicking or smacking sounds made by some speakers are usually from "dry mouth." Drink plenty of water prior to speaking. Hydration will usually overcome dry mouth and make you feel and perform better. If you have a persistent problem with dry mouth, try chewing gum before you speak. Do this in private, however, perhaps as you drive to your presentation. Do not chew gum in public, as many people find the habit offensive.

Harsh or screechy tones: Nerves are usually the cause of screechy tones, or it could be just a bad habit. In either case, listening to recorded books read by people with melodious voices can relax you and give you good role models to follow.

Clearing throat or sounding thick: Be sure to clear your throat and blow your nose in private just prior to speaking. No audiences want to hear the sounds of you clearing your throat or sinuses. Have a handkerchief in your pocket in case you develop a runny nose.

To help you avoid these mannerisms, practice your presentation on one or more people. Only practice with a live audience can help you learn to play your voice to capture the right tone and quality, as well as help you with your timing.

HOLD THAT THOUGHT

Practicing your speech alone will not give you a true sense of how short or long it is. You must say the words aloud with the same pace and emphasis you plan to use with the audience in order to get a true sense of your timing.

Jeremy's Story

Jeremy's first experience speaking to a large group did not go well. His boss had asked him to have a part in the annual sales meeting. All Jeremy had to do was get up in front of 30 other sales representatives and share the report that showed that sales were increasing and that profit margins were higher than ever. This was good news and should have been exciting. Nothing could have been less exciting due to Jeremy's weak delivery.

The first mistake Jeremy made was to beat himself up with negative self-talk. He chided himself in his thoughts as he waited to be called up to the front of the room. To himself, he mentally thought "I am just not a public speaker. I don't feel prepared. What if I embarrass myself?"

When his boss called him up, Jeremy walked to the front with slightly stooped shoulders and a slow pace. People wondered if he might be mad about something or about to deliver bad news.

Jeremy had practiced his speech by himself several times the night before, reading the speech over and over again. His voice tone sounded exactly the same when he was reading the next day. His voice had no variety and was very monotonous. It sounded as if he were reading the ingredients off a box of crackers. When reading the part about the sales increases and high profit margins, his voice sounded as discouraged as it had when he started. People were not sure if they had heard the good news right because the nonverbal message was so negative.

When Jeremy finished, he didn't know what to say as a conclusion so he just walked off. He knew he had not done well. The next step he took, however, was a winning one.

Jeremy did not wait for his boss to tell him he had not measured up as a speaker. Jeremy went to his boss and asked for his help to become a better speaker in larger group settings. Jeremy had been very comfortable with three or four customers in a conference room; speaking at a podium was different. His boss told him he would work with him and asked Jeremy to shadow him at his next few presentations.

Jeremy also took the step of joining Toastmasters to improve. Over the next year, Jeremy perfected his speaking skills with a small, supportive group and got plenty of practice.

One year later, Jeremy was surprised when his boss once again offered him the opportunity to present the sales numbers at the annual sales meeting. This time, Jeremy planned a dynamic opening and a memorable conclusion. He practiced on his roommate and best friend and made sure his voice conveyed excitement. When he walked energetically to the podium on the day of his presentation, he knew he was far more prepared than had been last year. He had straight posture and a broad smile before he started, as he had seen his boss do. The positive facial expressions and voice energy rallied the crowd. In fact, they applauded the numbers when Jeremy announced them with excitement in his voice. The audience was really applauding Jeremy, and he deserved it. In one year, he had learned to become a speaker people looked forward to hearing.

Doing Your Homework

In addition to your delivery style, your content must also be developed. Preparing your content differs with each presentation. Sometimes you are asked to say a few words about something you know a great deal about. Even when you know your subject, you should spend time working on what content you will include and what you will leave out. Ask what your time limit is, and be sure to stick to it.

At other times, you will need to gather some information in order to inform, entertain, or persuade the audience. If you're taking five minutes or five hours of a group's time, make it worth their while. Online research and timely news articles are just a few of the ways you can prepare to be a credible speaker. Even if you feel you are knowledgeable on a subject, the audience will appreciate it if you go online and quote what an expert or two says on your topic. Be sure to give credit by simply saying "According to a *BusinessWeek* article …" or "A CNN report states …." Have the source written down in case someone wants to know more.

Doing simple surveys can also be a real crowd pleaser. For example, if you're speaking to your homeowners association and have everyone's email address, you can use a free service such as SurveyMonkey (surveymonkey.com) to do a very short survey asking everyone to click through to say which improvements they most want to invest money in—enlarging the pool, expanding the landscaped greenspace, or replacing the signage. Your neighbors will appreciate the timely information and your willingness to ask them for their input.

COMMUNICATION TIP

Almost every community has a Toastmasters (toastmasters.org) group where you can learn presentation techniques with people who will support and help train you. Many larger companies and civic clubs also have their own groups, and many top speakers have gotten their start this way.

Making Your Opening Line a "Grabber"

After deciding what you will say and developing your content, it is time to craft a powerful opening. A great opening "grabber" makes an audience sit up in their seats, pay close attention, and think "I can't wait to hear what comes next!"

Be sure your opening sentence grabs the attention of the audience. You can quote a startling statistic, such as "Facebook just purchased WhatsApp for $19 billion." This would be appropriate for an address to a room full of entrepreneurs or small business folks. Or you can start with a challenge: "You are about to hear how you can cut bullying in our local schools in half, if you will do three things that will take you less than fifteen minutes."

Another way to engage audiences in your opening is to ask an intriguing question: "When was the last time you were really scared?" This would be a great opening for a talk on security alarms. No matter what you choose, you should choose something that lets the audience know that you are not a boring speaker and that you paid them the courtesy of preparing your remarks.

Delivering the Main Body of Your Speech

After your grabber, you need to state exactly what the topic and purpose of your presentation is. The audience should not be wondering exactly what your point is. Right up front, let them know the topic.

As you look at your material, decide how it should be organized. Some of the most common ways to organize presentations are as follows:

- **Chronological:** Tell what happened in sequence, like a story or timeline.
- **Topical:** Choose three or four topics and address them one by one. Give the audience a preview of these topics so they know this plan in advance.
- **Comparison or contrast:** Take two options and show how they are similar, different, or both.
- **Spatial:** Take your audience on a virtual tour. You can take them from the front of your new state-of-the-art warehouse or you can take them from northern to southern Italy with your descriptions.

As you phrase your material, be sure you stress the main points as you bring them up (see Chapter 22 for transitional words you can use). Using analogies and metaphors also helps keep things interesting.

> **COMMUNICATION TIP**
>
> Toward the end of the presentation, you might ask for feedback if appropriate. You might say things like "What are your thoughts?" or "Do you have any questions?" This will keep the audience engaged and even give you some things to discuss the next time you speak.

Always keep the identity of the audience in mind and tailor your remarks to their motivators and stressors. If you are persuading the audience to do something, show how your idea can be the solution to one of their problems or be a reward of some kind. For example, if you were a leasing agent for a large apartment complex and you were addressing college students, you might show how living in your off-campus apartment complex is a convenient distance from the campus, which allows them more free time and to save on gas. For a family, you might stress the outdoor space and larger bedrooms of the apartment complex. Tell the audience what you're willing to do for them and what your ideas, products, and services will do for them.

Finishing Well

Toward the conclusion of a presentation, summarize briefly in one sentence the two or three points you most want the audience to remember. Often, people will be asked "What was covered in that meeting?" This is your chance to reiterate the main points that are most urgent in your mind.

Finally, deliver a last line that has a punch. All the ideas discussed previously for the opening can be used for the closing as well—startling statements, challenges, quotes, or other creative ideas you come up with. The main thing is to deliver this last line with emphasis and then stop. The audience should know that this is the end, finis, full stop. Often speakers "dribble" at the end. They keep saying side remarks and don't let the audience feel the full effect of their dramatic last words.

As you go into the ending, pause and slow down. This will increase the dramatic effect you're going for. Be sure not to rush your words as you deliver the last line. And when you end, really end. Don't say "That's it" or "That's all I have for today." Coming to a dramatic and definite end gives your presentation polish and makes you seem more professional.

If you have a strong opening and a strong closing, people will view you as a highly effective speaker. You can actually be less precise in the middle, but these two bookends must be planned, prepared, and have pizzazz.

If you follow the steps in this chapter, your presentation will be memorable—in a good way. Preparing for these opportunities is just common courtesy. Being able to communicate to larger groups elevates your people skills and connects you with more people.

COMMUNICATION TIP

I highly recommend that you ask a friend or colleague to video every presentation with a camera, laptop, tablet, or phone. Video is the best teacher any presenter ever had. By watching a video of yourself, you will learn from your mistakes and what worked that you want to try again. The first time you watch, listen with the sound off. You will see every distracting gesture and can concentrate on your body language. Next, listen only to the audio without the picture. You will hear any fillers, such as "uh." Watch it a third time with audio and video to get the complete picture.

The Least You Need to Know

- Make sure your first line is a "grabber," such as a startling statistic or a quote from a famous or locally respected person.
- Practice on real people to perfect your timing and your voice tone.
- Use online research, simple surveys, and other resources to make your content interesting and informative.
- End with a last line that has a punch so people know it's the end.

APPENDIX

A

Glossary

acquaintance A person you know but do not have close ties to. Someone you have met or may see occasionally, but with whom you have not built a bond of friendship.

aggressive Crossing the line from being assertive to pushing for a stance, need, or desire. Taken too far, can be a win-lose attitude wherein the aggressive partner wants to win the point at any cost.

apology An expression, either spoken or written, of regret for having made a mistake, hurt someone, or omitted something. An expression of concern for the feelings of someone you have let down, hurt, or caused difficulty for.

assertive Initiating ideas and opinions in an appropriate and considerate way when needed. Being able to voice and support stances and needs to others in a measured and effective way.

boundaries Limits you set with friends, family, and acquaintances to let them know when they may have gone too far in their expectations or behaviors. Defining what you will and won't do in given situations.

buffer A sentence or two of pleasant or neutral information that should be stated before you deliver bad news. It postpones the bad news briefly while you establish rapport with your listener or reader.

complementary friend A friend who completes you in some way. Your complementary friend will be different from you and may have strengths that you need to develop. Your friend will also be lacking in some areas where you can make a contribution.

conflict When two forces or people engage in a struggle with one another; a dispute or argument. When the experience or idea of one person is not in alignment with another person's, and they experience disharmony.

conflict resolution The solution to the differences between two or more people. This can involve steps toward mediating the differences between two people who desire competing outcomes or processes and coming to a win-win agreement.

consensus Coming to an agreement that is the best combination of a group's ideas and opinions. It's about building a blended solution from all factions and ideas in a group.

constructive criticism Giving a friend or colleague information that will make her better in some way. The information about her performance or habits can lead to more success and better outcomes for her. This type of criticism is not about blame or judgment, but about factual ways this person can improve. *See also* criticism.

criticism An evaluative view of what you see or hear; analyzing the information you receive in order to form or share an opinion. Often, people perceive criticism as negative, though correctly used, it can be constructive.

demographics Groupings by age, gender, educational level, ethnicity, urban or suburban orientation, and other factors. These are considerations of your audience that should be respected.

emotional intelligence Using your words and actions to create productive relationships with others through self-control, consideration, and insight into others. This kind of intelligence involves making the right choices and uses of your emotions and will.

empathy The ability to see an issue through another person's viewpoint. You identify with the feelings and opinions of others, even when they differ from your own.

extrovert One who performs best and derives pleasure from a high level of interaction with other people, gaining energy from human interaction. This is a person who works best in a team and excels in groups.

friend A person with whom you have a strong connection of feeling, shared experience, and/or mutual support. A friend is a sponsor or contributor to your life.

gestures Movement of hands and fingers to convey meaning nonverbally.

inflection Playing your voice like an instrument to emphasize words or emotions in your message. This involves stressing some syllables to convey additional meaning.

introvert A person who is most productive and content when alone or when not interacting at a demanding level socially. One who thinks more clearly and is more energetic with less conversation, an introvert may be drained by being in constant company of others. This person does not dislike people, but it taxes her to perform socially.

lilt Modulating your voice in a positive way to convey a positive feeling or to be more charming, with a sway and pace that is pleasing.

listening Going beyond just hearing words and discerning the meaning and feelings your partner is trying to convey. You skillfully and intentionally evaluate what is said so you do not miss any hidden messages.

mien A composition of personality, confidence level, presence, and posture.

mirror To imitate the actions or style of another person. You copy certain actions or wording of someone else and try to incorporate them into your style in order to be in alignment with that person.

mixed messages Hearing or receiving two different messages that seem to contradict each other. This conflicting situation may cause frustration because one set of directions or information seems to be in opposition to earlier information.

nonverbal assessment An evaluation of your ability and style when communicating nonverbally. This usually requires the sender of communication to ask four or five friends to describe certain facial expressions and gestures they often see you do and whether they are effective and positive. It may also include a video of you engaged in conversation so you can self-evaluate and identify nonverbals that could be improved or omitted.

nonverbals or **nonverbal communication** Any communication that takes place without words. This involves conveying meaning without speaking or writing and may include gestures, facial expressions, posture, body language, location, environment, and so on.

passive-aggressive A behavior that promotes the agenda of one person who desires to hide that agenda. In fairness, a passive-aggressive person may not even recognize he is pushing behind the scenes for his self-oriented agenda. He accomplishes his goals obliquely and subtly, and he may see more forthright styles as too aggressive. Make no mistake, however; this personality style still can achieve goals through wearing or waiting you out.

people group A group of people who have something in common, such as culture, ethnicity, a common physical trait, or other unique attribute. For example, Hispanics, people with disabilities, and homosexuals are different types of people groups.

personal space The distance between two people that is comfortable for each person. Different situations call for different measures of distance between two people. For example, a person may feel comfortable being very close to someone on a crowded bus but would feel uncomfortable with such a close distance during a one-on-one conversation in a job interview. Cultural backgrounds create different desires for space between people and must be considered for optimum communication.

pitch The highs and lows of your voice. This also refers to controlling the vibrations of your voice to show emotions, such as excitement with a high voice and concern with a lower voice.

presence The ability to make a positive impression by your bearing, poise, and personal authority. With this, you are making people aware of you in an admirable way by your demeanor and communication.

receiver In the flow of communication, the role of the person who receives the message by listening, reading, or deciphering nonverbal signals. The roles of sender and receiver switch back and forth during a conversation.

scriptwriting The habit of thinking of what you want to say next while your partner is still talking.

self-actualization To become fully and successfully integrated into your world through understanding and developing your assets and managing your developmental areas. You accept self-knowledge of your strengths and weaknesses and do what it takes to live up to your full potential.

sender In the flow of communication, the role of the person who sends the message by speaking, writing, or demonstrating nonverbal signals. The roles of sender and receiver switch back and forth during a conversation.

style flexing Adjusting your words and actions to connect with another's style.

subvocals Sounds you make that let the speaker know you're alert and engaged without your having to interrupt her to ask questions or interject your own comments.

tempo The pace, fast or slow, of the flow of your words. This is the speed of the way you talk and how you vary it depending on your emotions and meaning.

tone Expressing yourself through the sound of your voice, using pitch and inflection to convey underlying meanings and feelings.

touch Contact made between people. Touches include conversations, phone calls, texts, emails, and so on. Relationships are built on touches.

APPENDIX

B

Four-Week Plan for Improving Your People Skills

This four-week plan contains many options for improving the way you build and strengthen your relationships with friends and strangers. Each week, you have a list of suggestions that fall into three categories:

- **Read:** Articles and books to teach you new skills and give you insights from expert sources
- **Do:** Exercises and tasks to help you practice new skills and identify ways that are especially tailored to your needs to build your people skills
- **Go:** Events, meetings, and other places you can go to build your base of friends and your network, as well as learn from workshops and other mentors and coaches

Choose at least one item from each category every week to do. If you choose more from each category, you will see even faster improvement. Most of these sources can be obtained online or from your public library, so if you need some help, ask the librarian. Many of the activities are self-guided and can be done at home.

You are about to have one of the most exciting and challenging four weeks in your life. Get ready to see real growth and to make some noticeable advances in your people skills. Prepare to revolutionize your life by acquiring techniques and skills that will transform you into the gracious and engaging "people person" you want to be.

Week One: Prepare to Meet and Engage with People

Read

Carnegie, Dale. ***How to Win Friends & Influence People.*** **New York: Pocket Books, 1981.** Whether you read a few pages or the entire book, you will learn something valuable from this short book. Over 15 million people have bought this classic people skills book and recommended it to their friends.

Ask.com Before you go to this website, take a look at the table of contents and decide which topics you would like to know more about. Do you want to know more about meeting new people, introducing yourself, handling conflict with a friend, or keeping a friendship for the long term? Whatever interests you, this site probably has an article or a referral to an article for you. Read the content for at least three topics that interest you.

Sandberg, Sheryl. ***Lean In: Women, Work, and the Will to Lead.*** **New York: Knopf, 2013.** This is a book that even men find helpful. If you are trying to learn to be more engaged, confident, assertive, or noticed, this book can help you both professionally and personally.

Do

Review Chapter 3 to consider thoughtfully the three questions people have about you when they first meet you. Where do you think you need to improve? Are you likeable and do people warm to you on first meeting? Do people think you are knowledgeable because you have a strong conversation bank or can speak expertly (but not too much) about your field? Do people respect you and find you highly credible? Focus on improving just one of these areas.

For likeability, you may need to improve your listening skills by applying the techniques in Chapter 2. To be perceived as smarter, you may need to build up your conversation bank. And you may need to see if there is anything about your image or the way you are presenting yourself if trust and credibility are the issues.

For any of these, you may need to ask someone who knows you well for some honest feedback and suggestions for improvement.

With a friend, devote at least 30 minutes to practicing the empathy statements in Chapter 2. Ask your friend to tell you what has been going on with him for the last month and say that you will be responding with empathy statements. Are you able to guess at some of the underlying emotion words for the first part of the statement? Are you able to repeat what he told you for the second part? Keep practicing with others until you master this technique.

Review the five signs of a great conversationalist in Chapter 3. Do you have these qualities, or are you seeing signs you might be a weak conversationalist? Identify the areas where you need improvement and change. For example, are you talking too much? Remember to strive to let your partner talk 75 percent of the time by asking him questions and by responding. Be more intentional about this or any other weakness you identify. Practice great listening skills.

Work on your handshake. Men, in particular, judge other men by their handshake when first meeting them. Ask four friends to give you feedback on your handshake. Try role-playing that you're shaking hands with them in a receiving line at a wedding. Ask if your grip is too tight or loose. Are you engaging with your hands so that your webs (the flesh between thumb and forefinger) are touching? Do you give a couple of short, perfect shakes or are you shaking too long or too little? Now adjust your handshake based on the feedback the majority of people give you. If two out of four people tell you that you have a wimpy handshake, grip a little more firmly and shake twice energetically.

Ask a friend if you can use your phone or a video camera to record a video of yourself as you have a conversation. Tell your friend that you only want to see your face and mannerisms as you speak. Try to have at least a 10-minute conversation. Now watch the video with the sound off. Just look at your face and other nonverbals. Are you smiling in a friendly manner? Are you showing energy, interest, and enthusiasm? Do you show any distracting movements, such as touching your face or slouching? Work on correcting these. Then listen only to the audio of the recording and don't look at the picture. Do you talk too fast? Do you hear any distracting habits, such as too many "uhs" or a clicking noise? Are you using too many fillers, such as "you know," "like," or "listen"? Be intentional about improving these habits. Remind yourself before future conversations to avoid them. You won't change overnight, but gradually you will improve.

Review Chapter 5 on facial expressions. In a mirror, practice until you develop relaxed natural expressions for the following: the three kinds of smiles, the fascinated look, a look of interest, and a look of concern. Try these expressions out on a friend or family member.

Go

Consider working with a coach to develop your people skills. You can find coaches and mentors at a variety of places: local colleges in the communications or business communications departments; psychologists; churches and other religious organizations with staff counselors; and consulting firms. You can also contact the local chapter of your National Speakers Association. Many of these speakers also coach.

Tell a supportive friend or family member that you are embarking on this four-week plan to improve your people skills. Ask him to give you feedback on any improvements he sees and keep him posted once a week on the steps you're taking.

Week Two: Engage with People

Read

Read a biography of the early life of someone you think is a great "people person." This person may be in entertainment (like Oprah Winfrey), politics (such as Bill Clinton), or any other walk of life. What did this person need to overcome? What are some things this people person does to be skilled at dealing with people?

Lindgren, Amy. "If your communication skills need work, put in the effort," ***The Atlanta Journal-Constitution,*** **Nov. 5, 2013.** While this article is career-oriented, it has a global message on self-improvement that's interesting to know.

Goldman, Daniel. ***Emotional Intelligence: Why It Can Matter More Than IQ.*** **New York: Bantam, 1995.** This is the classic text on the topic of emotional intelligence. Many people cannot develop their people skills until they understand their emotional intelligence and how to develop it. Just as you have to have skills and smarts in technical fields, you have to have a different type of skills and smarts if you are to succeed with people. This book is a great start.

Note: Many chapters in *Idiot's Guides: People Skills* deal with opening yourself up to meeting more diverse people and would be a good review before engaging with people. You expand your opportunities to meet interesting people if you reach out to people who are not in your age group or are not similar to you in other ways. Chapters 19 and 21 are good for mental preparation.

Do

Make a list of at least three events you can go to in the next month where you could meet new people. Your local newspaper may have an online list of public events, such as races, fund-raisers, charitable events, tastings/cooking classes, lectures, and many other opportunities. Also consider neighborhood or community events, alumni events, discussions offered by your public library, parades, sporting events, and classes on anything from wine to Excel. For a more complete list, see Chapter 13.

Take a friend to lunch and ask for help making new connections. Tell him you're trying to engage with more people because you're in a rut. Tell him that because you like and value him, you feel that his friends would probably be great people to get to know. Ask him if he can arrange for you to have coffee or lunch, or to play golf or do something similar with him and one or two of his friends so you can meet new people.

Think about where you met the last two friends you made. Try to engage in similar activities that may lead to your meeting new friends.

Go

Look at the list of events you created under "Do." Now get out your calendar and plan to attend at least three events.

Ride a bus, take a walk, go to a park, sit in a waiting room, go to a museum, or do something that will encourage you to encounter strangers. Speak cordially to at least one person. If they are receptive, make conversation about your surroundings, the weather, the museum, or whatever you are experiencing.

Week Three: Polish Your People Skills

Read

emilypost.com What three social skills do you need to improve? It may be table manners, making introductions, introducing yourself, responding to invitations, knowing what topics are appropriate for conversation, or knowing what is appropriate for any other occasion. Look up your questions at emilypost.com. For decades, the Post family has been advising people on how to conduct themselves socially. This site will help you handle everything from a dinner party to an apology with graciousness and poise.

911dispatch.com/info/cust_serv.html Do you have a difficult person or situation to deal with? 911Dispatch.com is designed to help 911 dispatchers handle the many stressful calls they receive. The tips and advice given are extremely useful in handling difficult people and situations in everyday life as well. Disregard the portions that talk about procedures. Look at the parts that tell the dispatchers how to respond to irate or stressed-out people. Are there any phrases you could use to talk to the difficult people in your life?

Markiewicz, David. "Up close: Learn to be a better communicator," ***The Atlanta Journal-Constitution,*** **May 21, 2011.** This article can help you decide if attending a class by a professional speaking coach might help you.

Booher, Dianna. ***Creating Personal Presence: Look, Talk, Think, and Act Like a Leader.*** **San Francisco, CA: Berrett-Koehler Publishers, Inc., 2011.** This shows you how to look, walk, and act like a person with great confidence. She addresses everything from manners to how to enter a room with great presence. If you feel ignored or just want to polish your image, this is a helpful book.

Do

"51 Ways to Enhance Your Cultural Understanding," pharmacy.wisc.edu/diversity-office/cultural-competence/51-ways-enhance-your-cultural-awareness, University of Wisconsin at Madison School of Pharmacy, 2013. This article has some of the most specific and creative ideas available to help you broaden your base of acquaintances and friends by meeting diverse people. Choose three of the ways listed that you think you might enjoy doing in order to make new and interesting friends who can add variety to your friendship base. Try to do all three in four weeks.

Think back over the last two friendships you have had that either ended or are not as close as they once were and try to pinpoint what you might have done to strengthen those friendships. Review Chapter 14. Were there any hurdles you could have avoided or worked through more successfully? Was there anything you could have done to prevent or resolve any friendship fizzlers? If you think going to those friends and apologizing or asking for a do-over is a good idea, then do so. But if you think that the season for that friendship is over, consider all you have gained from the experience. You now know what you want to do differently with your new friends and know the pitfalls to avoid in the future.

Read Chapter 20 and make a list of the unique gifts you have as a friend, a colleague, or a communicator. Describe your personality style based on the information in this chapter. Now think of someone you would like to communicate better with. Make a list of three things you will need to do to adapt your style to this person so he will enjoy communicating with you even more.

Go

See if the American Management Association (amanet.org) or Development Dimensions International (ddiworld.com) has any events scheduled in your area. Are there any one-day courses on interpersonal skills or communication or personality that you might be interested in taking? If not, are there online courses you might attend? Not only will you learn from their excellent instructors, you will be attending with people who want to improve in the same areas you want to improve. You will automatically have something in common with the new people you meet.

Consider joining your local Toastmasters group. You can find a group at Toastmasters.org. If you want to polish your ability to speak to 2 or 200 people, Toastmasters is the best organization out there to help you perfect your skills. These small groups of people encourage each other and form strong bonds as they help one another learn to communicate better.

Check out American City Business Journals (acbj.com) for networking opportunities. ACBJ has premier networking events in various cities. You can meet different people working for non-profits or for-profits.

Call or go to the website of your local Chamber of Commerce. You can find a partial list at chamberofcommerce.com/chambers/. Most Chambers of Commerce sponsor many different seminars that provide a good way for meeting people who are interested in the community and self-improvement. Attend at least one event. If you are in the workplace, consider joining the Chamber.

Week Four: Strengthen Existing Relationships

Read

Psychologytoday.com While reading this book, were there some psychological terms you wanted to learn more about, such as *extroverts, passive-aggressive behavior,* or *assertiveness?* Would you like to learn more about personality types? Most importantly, would you like to learn about yourself? Go to Psychologytoday.com and search for more information on these terms to give you greater understanding of yourself and others.

Goleman, Daniel. *Emotional Intelligence: Why It Can Matter More Than IQ.* New York: Bantam Books, 1995. It may be surprising to learn that emotional intelligence is far more important to your people skills than typical book learning. This book will give you information on this type of intelligence and how to cultivate it.

Hawley, Casey. *100+ Tactics for Office Politics.* Hauppauge, New York: Barron's Educational Series, 2010. When dealing with others, especially in your daily office environment, you need to know how to communicate and act effectively. This book shows you how to do things such as avoid conflict and deal with difficult situations and people.

Do

Washingtonpost.com (Carolyn Hax, "Tell Me About It") Carolyn Hax writes a popular online column about all kinds of situations people get themselves into. Go to her site and search for information about any problems you have experienced in relationships. Better yet, write her and ask her for specific advice on your situation.

Hawley, Casey. *10 Make-or-Break Career Moments: Navigate, Negotiate, and Communicate for Success.* New York: Ten Speed Press, 2010. Study the M.I.S.S.I.O.N. model for meeting new people and starting conversations. Use this model the next time you attend a party or other function that allows you to meet strangers.

Hawley, Casey. *Effective Letters for Every Occasion.* New York: Barron's Educational Series, 2000. Think of two people who have invited you to something or been kind to you. Write each of them a thank-you note based on one of the templates in this book. Now think of one person you could apologize to. Even if the other person was also to blame, write an apology note according to the template in this book. These are steps to more deeply developing your people skills.

Hold a conversation according to your partner's preferences. Is there a conversation you need to prepare for? Before you have that conversation, use the techniques in Chapter 9 to prepare.

Call an old friend you haven't talked to in a long time. Discuss the four-week plan you're working through. Tell him you were asked to reach out to someone you valued as a friend and you thought of him. You can sometimes find old acquaintances through Facebook, LinkedIn, Whitepages.com, and other social networking sites.

Identify someone you think you have nothing in common with and try to find an item of common ground. This person can be a friend of a friend, a neighbor, or someone you knew in high school and have not seen in years. Make it your mission to learn enough about this person to pinpoint one thing you have in common, whether it's values, interests, pet peeves, or likes. This exercise will strengthen your ability to relate to all kinds of people and broaden your opportunities for friends who can make a contribution to your life.

Go

Use the information in Chapter 10 to help you deliver difficult information to a person. Whether it's announcing a death or disaster; resigning from something or leaving a location; offering constructive criticism; asking for time, money, or other resources; or apologizing, this information will give you an idea on how best to approach someone for a difficult conversation.

Learn how to deal with difficult people. First, study my advice on dealing with different types of difficult people in Chapter 12. Next, try to have a conversation with this person using the new techniques. The third step is to ask yourself if you have any of the tendencies of one of the difficult personality types. To do this, consider going to a mentor and asking; you may need to explain what they are or ask him to read the chapter first.

Improve your collaboration skills. Is there anyone you feel you are not collaborating with as well as you would like? Are you dissatisfied with something about the partnering, or does your partner ever feel disappointed? Go to your partner and tell him you are working on your collaboration skills. Ask him if he will read Chapter 17 and then give you suggestions on how you can be a better partner. After reading the chapter, he may even find some things he can do better!

Work on a close friendship. Do you have a close friend? Ask that you both read Chapter 20 and identify any hurdles or friendship fizzlers you need to avoid so that you strengthen your friendship for the future. Agree not to take offense as each person shares honestly about pet peeves and differences. Be very careful, diplomatic, and complimentary as you share.

APPENDIX

C

Resources

The following are some websites, articles, and books that provide further information on improving your people skills.

Websites

Acbj.com

American City Business Journals (ACBJ) owns 40 publications in various cities and advertises and sponsors some of the premier networking events in those cities. Whether you are interested in meeting leaders in the nonprofit or for-profit sector, you may meet them at one of the ACBJ events.

Amanet.org

American Management Association sponsors seminars and offers a wealth of resources to strengthen your interpersonal and career skills. Its materials are available in online or print format, and its events attract people from all professions. Great networking occurs at its public workshops, which are quite reasonably priced.

Ask.com

This general source of quick information on almost any topic is a goldmine of facts. If you need a quick summary or overview, just go to this website and type in the term or topic you want.

Chamberofcommerce.com/chambers/

Most cities have a Chamber of Commerce that sponsors everything from seminars on people skills, to food tastings, to career-related events. Chambers are a good tool for meeting people who are interested in the community and self-improvement. This site helps you find your local chamber.

Ddiworld.com

Development Dimensions International is one of the premier training companies delivering onsite and online courses in people skills. Though it markets to businesses, its materials are applicable to everyone.

Dispatch911.com

This website is designed to help 911 dispatchers handle the many stressful calls they receive. The tips and advice given are extremely useful in handling difficult people and situations in everyday life as well.

Emilypost.com

For decades, the Post family has been advising people on how to conduct themselves socially. This site will help you handle everything from a dinner party to an apology with graciousness and poise.

Grammarcoach.net

Expressing yourself correctly is part of your image. This site offers self-tests and self-study tutorials to improve your grammar over several weeks.

Grammargirl.com

If you sometimes are not sure of the correct way to write or say certain things, you can look the phrases up at this site.

Psychologytoday.com

A wealth of articles on various types of personalities is available at this site. You can learn about introverts, extroverts, passive-aggressive behavior, and—most importantly—yourself.

Toastmasters.org

If you want to polish your ability to speak to 2 or 200 people, Toastmasters is the best organization out there to help you perfect your skills. Your city will have many chapters, if you want to attend a group.

Washingtonpost.com (Carolyn Hax, "Tell Me About It")

Carolyn Hax writes this popular online column about all kinds of situations people get themselves into and don't know how to handle. Think of her as today's "Dear Abby."

Articles

Lindgren, Amy. "If your communication skills need work, put in the effort." ***The Atlanta Journal-Constitution,*** **Nov. 5, 2013.**

This article has more of a career focus, but the self-improvement advice applies to everyone.

Markiewicz, David. "Up close: Learn to be a better communicator." ***The Atlanta Journal-Constitution,*** **May 21, 2011.**

The article describes the experience of working with a company who specializes in developing speaking skills. The author's learning experience may also help you learn a bit about yourself.

Books

Carnegie, Dale. ***How to Win Friends & Influence People.*** **New York: Pocket Books, 1981.**

This classic book has changed the lives of millions of people. Dale Carnegie's advice for engaging people and building cordial and productive relationships with them is as relevant today as when it was written.

Goleman, Daniel. ***Emotional Intelligence: Why It Can Matter More Than IQ.*** **New York: Bantam Books, 1995.**

Emotional intelligence is far more important to your people skills than your intellectual abilities. This book is the definitive work on emotional intelligence and will tell you what it is and how to develop it.

Hawley, Casey. ***10 Make-or-Break Career Moments: Navigate, Negotiate, and Communicate for Success.*** **New York: Ten Speed Press, 2010.**

If you've ever feared you might get that deer-in-headlights look in a social or career situation, this book is the solution. It tells you how to network, meet people of all levels of intelligence and power, and develop other necessary social skills.

Hawley, Casey. ***Effective Letters for Every Occasion.*** **New York: Barron's Educational Series, 2000.**

Not only does this book show you how to write killer thank-you notes, apology letters, and requests, it actually gives you the templates to do most of the writing for you. The same skills it teaches you in written form you can also apply to the conversations you have throughout life.

Hawley, Casey. ***100+ Tactics for Office Politics.*** **New York: Barron's Educational Series, 2010.**

Touchy situations can occur whenever you deal with others. This book shows you how to avoid conflict, how to deal with difficult situations and people, and how to meet people effectively. Whether you need help dealing with your neighbors or your boss, this book has unique approaches and great ideas for you.

Roebuck, Deborah Britt. ***Improving Business Communication Skills, 4th Edition.*** **Upper Saddle River, NJ: Pearson/Prentice Hall, 2006.**

This textbook is written by one of the most respected professors teaching business communication. Her approaches to interpersonal skills work equally well outside of the business arena.

Index

D

E

D

E

F

G

H

I-J-K

Q

R

S

T-U

V

W-X-Y-Z